Carol Marchant Gibbs cares deeply about justice, believing that God loves all people and desires everyone to live in freedom and safety in this world.

An educator by schooling and experience, Carol taught middle and elementary school, then devoted herself fully to raising her two young sons.

Family is one of Carol's greatest sources of joy. She treasures every moment with her two married sons, daughter-in-law, son-in-law, and four wonderful grandchildren and longs for them to live in a world that is reflective of God's heart.

Carol has a Bachelor of Arts degree from Goucher College and a Master of Arts degree from Towson University, both in Towson, Maryland.

In 2018, she published *Who Do You Say I Am? Personal Life Stories Told by the LGBTQ Community* in response to their family's experience of belonging to an Evangelical church and loving their gay son.

In memory of Jim Gibbs.
For 43 years, you taught me the greatest
expressions of love and compassion.
This book is for you, my love. I only wish you were here to read it.
I will love you forever.

Carol Marchant Gibbs

Radical Resilience

When Lives Are Changed by Extraordinary Compassion

Austin Macauley Publishers™
London • Cambridge • New York • Sharjah

Ordering Information
Quantity sales: Special discounts are available on quantity purchases by corporations, associations, and others. For details, contact the publisher at the address below.

Publisher's Cataloging-in-Publication data
Gibbs, Carol Marchant
Radical Resilience

ISBN 9781685626174 (Paperback)
ISBN 9781685626181 (Hardback)
ISBN 9781685626198 (ePub e-book)

Library of Congress Control Number: 2023912710

www.austinmacauley.com/us

First Published 2024
Austin Macauley Publishers LLC
40 Wall Street, 33rd Floor, Suite 3302
New York, NY 10005
USA

mail-usa@austinmacauley.com
+1 (646) 5125767

I am so thankful for the many people who willingly shared their stories with me. Each story was a special gift. It has been a privilege to be invited into the depths of their lives.

I am also thankful for the organizations and the individuals that have recognized the value of all mankind and have made it their life's work to love and serve others so that they are positioned to thrive.

To my dear family and friends, your constant love and support has encouraged me to press on through this very difficult year. I don't know what I would have done without you. I love you with all my heart.

To my husband, you are missed more than you will ever know. Your consistent love throughout our lives continues to inspire me to go forward for the greater good. You have been my greatest champion. I will always love you.

To God, my heavenly father, you have met me every step of the way, even when I was unaware of your presence. Thank you for providing me with the creativity and courage to complete this project. May it bring you all the honor and glory.

Table of Contents

Prologue
Be Bothered

I am constantly amazed at the wisdom young children often voice. We, as adults, have so much to learn from them.

It was a beautiful day, and my eight-year-old grandson, Fletcher, and I were sitting by the pool waiting for his younger brother to finish his part of swim team practice, when our conversation gravitated to justice. I was moved by his certainty about justice and the depth of his love for people. He was so young but the wisdom of his words has continued to capture my heart.

It all started with a discussion about the upcoming swim meet and the races that he would be swimming. Though he was too young to swim in it, he shared about the coed relay race. For those of you who are not swimmers, most races are men or women but not both. He was excited about that race because he knew about how women had been treated unfairly throughout history, and this was a way to show equality. We talked for a while about what women endured, how they were not permitted to vote, etc.

Then, he turned to me and said, "Mimi, I am not a woman, but it really bothers me that they were treated unfairly like that."

He thought for a minute then continued with, "You know, Mimi, black people have been treated unfairly, too."

We talked about the injustice toward African Americans throughout history, much of which he already knew. He mentioned Martin Luther King and what an amazing man he was and I could feel my heart swell.

Then, he responded with, "You know, Mimi, I am not a black person but it really bothers me when they are treated unfairly."

It made me think about my younger son who is married to my wonderful son-in-law and how deeply my grandchildren love their uncles. It gave me hope for our world.

Oh, that we, as adults, would love people in such a way that we are "bothered" by the injustice and teach our children to be the same.

Since that conversation with my grandson, I can't stop thinking about the very courageous people who saw the injustice and have worked to change our society so that it reflects love for all people… "and justice for all."

Be bothered by the injustice and strive to bring change.

Everyone Is Someone

By Erich Becker

Rayshard Brooks...Elijah McClain...Amy Cooper...David McAtee
Breonna Taylor...Ariana McCree...George Floyd...Ahmaud Arbery

Incidents of injustice...betrayals of confidence
externalized prejudice...and senseless violence
As we witness new outbreaks of racial unrest,
we march our moral outrage in anguished protest,
and we rally in community with tears of lament.
An alarm bell is ringing...will we wake and repent?

Change is only conceived now in these moments we share,
but it will be miscarried unless an impassioned few dare
to turn moments into momentum, to keep speaking out,
risking danger and censure, pushing through every doubt,
sounding long enough, loud enough in every context
to ensure that this moment's not silenced by the next.

True change begins in a person's heart and soul—
in worldviews and prejudices now centuries old.
Only then can lasting change be nurtured, given birth
in every system everywhere which ignores the inherent worth
of each person, every color, not just the white one,
and those in power acknowledge: Everyone is Someone.

Only power can affect any change that will last—
just ask the numberless unheard voices from our past.
Whites with courageous conviction need to speak from inside,

to become allies, to reach out from their side of the divide
and on behalf of the powerless-many set all things right:
justice and righteousness for every color, not just white.

Today's awakenings are hopeful, but we've a long way to go,
and our sisters of every color will tell us what they know:
culture-shaking change takes ongoing noise and protest,
so let's delay our rejoicing and continue a full-on press.
The next moment is coming. We can't celebrate yet.
Today we keep fighting so tomorrow's we won't forget.

Racism and discrimination, and privilege and fear,
and ignorance and prejudice…they have no place here.
The profiling and reviling and defiling must cease,
until all know equality and dignity and peace.
Justice must be the experience of each and every one
because Everyone is Someone…Everyone…Someone.

Chapter 1
Introduction: Radical Resilience

If you are a human being living on the face of the earth, you will at some time experience adversity. Difficult life circumstances occur every day and attempt to prevent us from embracing life to the fullest.

However, built into mankind is a superpower, a unique ability to withstand adversity, adapt and recover quickly from difficult life experiences; *Resilience.* Much of the time, man is able to engage with this superpower and can recover on his own, but what happens when that is not enough? Sometimes societal forces and personal limitations can make it impossible for some people to thrive.

In this incredible world of diversity, there is a darkness that blinds us from recognizing the beauty and value of all humanity. We can be held hostage by our misconceptions, prejudices and fears. Entire communities are misunderstood and targeted based on their race, international background, disability, sexual orientation, homelessness, those living with HIV-AIDS and people who have been sex trafficked. These circumstances necessitate greater support and the education of our society. They require a *radical resilience.*

Radical resilience occurs when courageous people are moved by the situations of those before them. They see into the human heart and respond with a radical compassion that inspires hope and rebuilds the human spirit. They recognize the value of all people, rising up against the injustices, offering community and providing opportunities for people to fully embrace their best life.

May these compelling stories illustrate how investing in the lives of others, removing the obstacles and helping them to recognize their potential, empowers and creates a legacy of hope.

It is my heart that this book will encourage a new vision for *others* that challenges our thinking and inspires us to recognize our part in bringing radical change to the world.

***

Jim's Story of Radical Resilience

This book would be incomplete without the story of my husband, Jim, and the courage and strength he exhibited over a four-and-a-half-year period as he fought appendiceal cancer.

Jim was always an extraordinary man. I first met him when we were in high school so it's hard to remember my life without him. He had been dating a close friend of mine so we became casual friends for years.

He was a scholar athlete; president of the senior class and on the football team. We would never have dated back then. I was more artsy and in every dramatic production I could possibly be in. We were different as night and day.

What I remember most about Jim initially was his kindness. He drove a very old Volkswagen van to school and whenever he saw me walking, he would stop to offer me a ride.

He was the one that every parent wanted their child to befriend because he was a straight arrow and kept everyone else from getting into trouble. He was a really great friend.

Jim was a few years older than me so when he graduated and went off to the Naval Academy, I saw very little of him. We attended the same church, so whenever he was home, we would catch up there.

Then, one day, we had an encounter one Sunday that was the beginning of our deeper relationship. I remember seeing him and thinking that he looked especially handsome that day. The first thing we talked about was his girlfriend. I was pleased to find out that they had broken up. He immediately showed me his adorable new red car, a 240Z and asked if I would like to go out to the reservoir with him while he waxed it because it was shady there, so I did.

This began a few months of dating. He would drive up from the Naval Academy, pick me up, we would dine in a wonderful restaurant in Washington DC then go to the theatre. He really wined and dined me and was quite fun to spend time with but when it became apparent that he was far more serious about me than I him, I ended it. Years later, he would laugh when I told this story denying the validity of it but it was absolutely true. He was crazy about me.

One year later, I started thinking about this dear man that I so foolishly stopped seeing and decided to get in touch with him. Jim had graduated from the Academy by then. I knew his family well and reached out to his mother to get his address in San Francisco. The day after I mailed the letter to him, I received a huge package in the mail. He had written a note on the back of a photo of the Golden Gate Bridge inviting me to accompany him to a wedding while he was home over Christmas. We got together over the holiday…and the rest is history. We were engaged four months later.

We married and I moved to Charleston, SC, where Jim was stationed on a submarine. After being away from each other during his sea duty, we decided that being a career naval officer was not for us. He resigned from the navy after six years and went to law school.

One of the wonderful things about Jim was he really knew how to love. For our entire marriage, he always put me first. He was my confidante, my greatest cheerleader, lover and best friend. He lifted me out of despair and talked me off the ledge regularly. He allowed me to verbally process just about everything. He helped me to filtered my responses to others, and loved everything about my passionate nature. I thrived when I was with him. He believed that he was married to the most wonderful woman in the world. I felt loved and cherished and I loved him right back.

Jim was a wonderful father to our two sons. He walked the floors with them at night when they were sick, sometimes sleeping on the floor beside their cribs. He listened to their hopes and dreams and encouraged them to seek their very best. He inspired them to greatness. But, more than anything, he taught them to love people and gave them a strong sense of justice. He helped raise two extraordinary men.

But it wasn't just our immediate family whose lives were changed by my husband. Everyone who knew him felt loved by him. He had a deep compassion for all people, especially those who were marginalized by our society and he served with his entire heart.

So, when he became ill, it was very difficult for many people. People depended on him to show them how to live and how to choose the best path forward and he did, even as he battled cancer.

We were first alerted to Jim's illness in February of 2016 when he began to experience abdominal pain. He had had kidney stones several times before and the symptoms were very similar to prior times so we really weren't concerned. But, upon examination, his general practitioner believed that a deeper investigation was necessary. He tried to schedule a colonoscopy, at the doctor's request, but available appointments were slim so I gave him the one I had scheduled for myself.

The coloscopy showed what the gastroenterologist believed might be some minor inflammation but thankfully did biopsy anyway. The biopsy indicated that Jim had a very rare and aggressive form of appendiceal cancer. This type of cancer travels on the surface of organs and the first step of the treatment was surgery. We were shocked and overwhelmed with fear but trusted that everything was going to be okay.

Surgery was scheduled for May 16th. Jim went into the hospital the day before for preliminary testing. Several people came into the hospital to pray that evening. The next morning, surgery was bright and early.

God was so very present every step of the way. While waiting in pre-op for surgery, we saw a dear friend of ours walk by who was a nurse at that hospital. We had no idea he worked there. He came into the room, gave us much needed hugs, bringing the peace of God into the room. Our anxious hearts were immediately calmed. And later, our dear nurse friend was Jim's recovery room nurse. We were so thankful.

I went into the waiting room and was met by many family members and friends who wanted to wait with me and pray for Jim during the surgery. It was fun to watch community build between people who had never even met previously. Perfect strangers became fast friends and at lunchtime, they went out together. Again, God showed up.

What was supposed to be a five-hour surgery became a ten-hour surgery. The mission was to surgically remove the disease and then perform HIPEC; a chemotherapy that gets poured into the abdominal cavity while the organs are still disconnected. The operating room table is moved so to coat the organs for about forty minutes. It is drained out, the organs are reconnected and the body is closed up. The operating room nurse checked in with me periodically to keep me apprised of the progress. When we came to the seventh hour, I really started to get worried. I had the waiting room clerk call the operating room and asked to talk to the doctor but he was unable to take my call. We discovered later that the disease was far more advanced than any test had indicated.

My sons and I met with the doctor after surgery. Once again, a friend from our church, who just happened to be a surgeon at that hospital, walked by and asked if he could be in the room when we spoke to the doctor to help if we needed him. I was very thankful for his presence. Where the surgical oncologist believed he got all the cancer, he gave Jim a life expectancy of five years. We were distraught.

Through this entire process, I had to believe that God would heal him. That was the only way I could handle what I did. My adult children though had a different experience. They told me just recently, after their dad died, that they started to grieve his loss when they heard the original news. They talked often with each other because my inability to deal with his loss kept me from being able to engage with such a conversation. I know that was difficult for them. I just couldn't let myself go there.

Jim spent his first night in the ICU after surgery then was moved to the oncology floor. He was a superstar, working very hard to do whatever he needed to leave the hospital a week later. That was just the way he was. He met every challenge head on.

Chemotherapy was a necessary option but it couldn't start until after his body healed from the surgery so he elected to begin after our annual trip to the Jersey shore in July. He was a little slower than usual but was able to engage in every activity. We had a wonderful time together as a family.

When chemo started every two weeks, we were very much controlled by his schedule. There were times when we could stretch it to three weeks but that was rare.

Every September the oncology practice involved with HIPEC have a walk, *Heat It to Beat It,* to raise funds for their research. Jim created a support team and participated in the race, walking three miles that day, less than four months after his surgery.

In October, he was much stronger and not only traveled to our son's wedding in Palm Springs, but performed the ceremony. He was amazing!

As Jim became stronger, he began to train for a race that he had always wanted to do. *Walk Across Maryland* was a forty-mile hike sponsored by the

Maryland Hiking Club. He trained with friends for months and participated in the race two years but was never fast enough to finish. He did hike twenty plus miles at a time which was a real win in my book.

He did many amazing things over his remaining four and a half years. In addition to walking part of the Appalachian Trail, he preached at our church, built a fence around our large yard, landscaped, wrestled with his grandchildren, accumulated new gadgets, discovered new recipes and traveled with me. He tried to live every day to its fullest and encouraged us to do the same.

Then, in January 2020, the year of the pandemic, Jim once again experienced abdominal pain and had surgery to correct a bowel blockage. It was during that surgery the surgical oncologist found a reoccurrence of the cancer. After the surgery, when I asked the doctor how the surgery went, he told me that he probably gave him a few more months to live.

I came unglued at that point and told him, "No, that does not work for me. You do whatever it takes to save him."

I did not tell anyone about my conversation with the doctor, not even our children, until November, eleven months later, when we talked with them about their dad's life coming to an end.

The COVID pandemic made life extremely complicated over that year. Jim's battle with cancer was difficult enough but being isolated from other people during that time made it even more so. We were left to fend for ourselves.

In some ways, it was a beautiful way to end our life together. It was just us and we depended on each other completely but as his health began to deteriorate it became increasingly more difficult for me to manage. We spent most of 2020, running back and forth to the hospital for chemo and then for fluids. When the pandemic hit, I was no longer allowed to stay with him during chemo so I had to drop him off at the door. That was one of the hardest things I had to do.

For most of the Pandemic, our children and grandchildren were kept at a physical distance so there was not the possibility of their infecting us. It was painful to not be able to hug our family. Fortunately, our older son and his family lived locally so they were able to come over and sit out in the yard at a distance. We tried to find creative ways to connect with them; laser tag, bubbles, Red Light, anything we could do to bring fun to our lives.

Our younger son and son-in-law were a different story. They were college professors at a university out of state that had very little restrictions to protect the students and professors from the Pandemic. Coming to visit was out of the question. Into the Fall, the boys entered a COVID vaccine trial and were able to come visit in November for Thanksgiving. By then, Jim's health had plummeted and it was clear that he was not going to make it.

As time went on, he began to have serious complications due to the chemo. He experienced a great deal of pain and had to go to the hospital to have the pain managed for days at a time. He would be required to go through the Emergency room each time and I was forced to drop him at the door. That was heartbreaking. He was in so much pain and I couldn't even go to support him.

In September, a fistula developed in his abdomen that required him to start wearing an ostomy bag. This was devastating for him. The changing of the bag occurred every other day unless he had a leak. I remember one day changing it four times.

Jim began to get weaker and weaker, requiring more and more fluids. For a while, he was getting them three times a week at the hospital. When he started needing them more, a nurse trained me how to give him fluids through his port every day at home. I'm pretty squeamish when it comes to medical procedures, so the fact I was able to do this is a miracle in itself.

As the months went on, it became more obvious that Jim was not going to win this battle but as a last resort, in November we started TPN, intravenous feeding. The home nurse started to come twice a week and taught me how to inject vitamins into the TPN solution, flush his port, get the air bubbles out of the line and repeat every day. It was grueling but I loved this dear man and was not ready to let him go.

Because our younger son and son-in-law had entered a COVID vaccination trial, we were able to be together over the Thanksgiving holiday. We spent the holiday talking about the reality that was before us. Jim had asked me to gather our adult children together to talk about his impending death. He talked about finances and how they could best support me. Then, he shared about how much he was going to miss us and we sobbed with grief. Our situation suddenly became real. It was at that moment that I realized, we were going to lose him. I had done everything I could to keep him alive. I really believed it was in my power to do so. I was wrong.

That weekend, our daughter-in-law had made arrangements for us to have family photos in our yard. It was very tearful time. Jim could barely stand but I am so thankful that we could memorialize our family in such a way.

Our younger son and his husband had to return to their university after that weekend to complete their semester and submit grades. We really hated to see them go. It was so nice to have our family together.

Jim's illness began to progress quickly, making nights increasingly difficult for us to sleep. Our older son, started spending nights with me to ensure that I would get some sleep. We took turns caring for his dad throughout the night, capturing sleep in another room. I watched as our son slept beside his dad, holding his dad's hand so sweetly, just like when he was young.

As Jim's health continued to plummet, our daughter-in-law contacted our younger son to return home to us. He and his husband were back within a week. Our older son was able to go home to be with his family and our younger son took over. Though we started to have a healthcare professional at night, they were not permitted to give medication. Our younger son kindly offered to take over the responsibility of medications so I could sleep. This required constant monitoring and connection by phone with the on-call nurse throughout the day and the night as the pain increased. Our younger son set his alarm and every four hours, rose from his sleep to administer his dad's medication. I watched as our son lovingly whispered into his dad's ear as he cared for him. Sometimes my husband would respond with a smile bringing my son and I to tears.

It was an amazing gift to have our sons be there to support us. As they took over much of Jim's care taking, I was free to be his wife, to sit beside him and hold his hand, to sing songs into his ear. I needed to grieve that I was losing this man that I dearly loved him and that had not been possible until then.

Our dear son-in-law was really amazing during this time as well. He was always nearby to give me a hug and cry with me. He did many dishes and walked both our dog and theirs often, among many others things.

Our daughter-in-law was a constant source of support throughout the year. She brought the kids over often and we were able to be with them even at a distance. We just needed some sense of normalcy despite the challenge before us. We ate meals together and played games…all at a distance. Nothing was too much for her to handle. She was always there for us and still is for me.

On December 13, at 2:10 pm, Jim took his last breath and was finally at peace. No more cancer, no more pain.

We miss him terribly and go forward forever changed by his presence on this earth and will love him forever.

Overcoming Racism

by Carol Marchant Gibbs

Uniquely created was mankind
A masterpiece of beauty and created out of love.
All were valued without question.
And deemed precious from the start.

But a darkness came upon the earth, blinding people from all goodness
Injustice filled the land and, like a virus, hatred spread.
People suffered persecution, pleading "mercy." No one listened
Oppression overtook the land and hardened people's hearts

Then one day, a light shone in the darkness.
People recognized the plague.
Together, they rose up to overcome their greatest fears.
Courageously, they battled, there was power in their fight.
Then the mighty beast was conquered, because all did their part.

A cry of celebration could be heard across the land
They remembered their creation and were thankful once again.

Uniquely created was mankind.
Beautiful in diversity, a masterpiece of love.
Value was unquestioned.
All deemed precious from the start.

Together we can end racism…forever.

Chapter 2
Overcoming Racism

The Story of Byron

For most of his life, Byron trod the well-worn path of assimilation into a white dominant culture. Outwardly he embraced it fully and accepted its tainted fruit, but inwardly, he felt a deep void that couldn't be satisfied. He tried to fill it with education, sports, the military and finally religion. In recent years, he discovered that experiential connection with the divine is what he had been seeking. Soon, he began to find this connection everywhere as he journeyed within and became true to himself.

In the mid-sixties, my mom and dad met at North Carolina Agricultural and Technical State University, in Greensboro, NC, during the civil rights movement. Dad was the oldest of four children and coming from a poor family one generation out of slavery, he was the first to go to college. Driven with a strong sense of right and wrong, he was a journalist for the school paper and soon became part of the student uprising on campus, protesting against inequality.

When Dad graduated in 1965, my mom left school as a sophomore and they married. Nine months later, I arrived on the scene.

During that same time, there continued to be a great migration of black families from the south moving to the north. Beginning in 1915, blacks began leaving the oppressive, caste system of the south to seek better lives in the north. This continued until 1970, and in 1967, our family became one of them.

When I asked my dad recently, "Why Michigan?" he explained that he had seen an advertisement in Ebony or Jet magazine for a job as an accountant. He applied for the job, they flew him up for an interview and hired him.

I was a year old when we headed north and never questioned why we moved into an all-white suburban neighborhood until I became an adult. Three years ago, I was watching a documentary about black families being rejected from moving into white neighborhoods and asked my parents about their experience. That was not at all what they encountered. Their budget helped to dictate where they would locate. They really weren't strategic about their move. Mom and Dad knew what they wanted and found a house. It just happened to be in an all-white neighborhood. I grew up feeling very accepted by the white community and never really questioned race until nine years later.

During the next few years, my brother and sister entered my world. My brother was born three years after me then our sister, three years later.

All things considered, we experienced an almost idyllic childhood, seemingly sheltered from any prejudice or racial disparity that was occurring in much of the country.

My heroes were Martin Luther King, Abraham Lincoln, John F Kennedy and Bobby Kennedy. I was encouraged by what I heard about their accomplishments. They were about justice for all people. I remember seeing their pictures plastered on the hand-held fans from funeral homes and on the walls in those hot black churches on surly summer days.

Though it did not seem to affect me directly, I was aware of the tension between black and white people. It was in the air but it didn't really seem to impact our family. When Martin Luther King and Bobby Kennedy got shot for their stand for equality, I remember being shaken but again did not realize the full implications of these acts of violence. We seemed to be protected, isolated from it all.

I grew up in a religious household but I do remember a time when my dad's life was completely changed by his faith. As a child, it had been my job to bring him his cigarettes and beer. There came a point when that stopped and we were going to church all the time. When my dad dedicated himself to our faith, there just became a lot more rules for me to follow. God gave us a bible that we *had* to follow and now my parents, especially my dad, were the chief enforcers of that. Mom was the grace side of things.

We were always at church and I hated it. I didn't want anything to do with it. All I could think about was getting out and watching football and playing baseball. My siblings and I worked very hard to resist falling asleep there. If we did sleep, our Sundays were gone. My dad made sure that we caught up on our sleep when we arrived home. That meant no football, no baseball, no fun.

So, I tried my best to follow the rules to keep my freedom. That was my religious experience early on.

We attended a black church in the center of town. I would leave my suburban, on the edge of a farm white world, and go into the city. I remember passing the streams and rivers of the suburbs on the way to church, then seeing the broken glass, tires, and bicycle parts of the city.

Playing in the city environment was an amazing experience. It reminded me of the show we loved to watch, *Fat Albert and the Cosby Kids.* Going into the abandoned buildings of the city was a cool adventure. It wasn't until years later that I realized that much of what I experienced there was poverty and many of the people were trapped in their situation.

I didn't understand the black-white divide. I had black friends that I played with in the city and white friends at home. I viewed the differences through a country-city lens rather than a white-black lens. My mom would take me into the city to play with my friends there and sometimes they would come out to the country. When they came to my house, we would play together with my country friends, just like we usually did. There seemed to be no division.

My parents did their best to instill deep life values in us.

My dad was the disciplinarian. We lived by the law. Perhaps because my paternal grandfather died when my dad was young, my dad had to step up and help care for his younger siblings. As a result, and because of his personality as the first-born child, he was a strict disciplinarian which my siblings and I experienced firsthand. He did not spare the rod so we obeyed to him. We would be disciplined severely if we stepped out of line. We got "whoopings." He was a compelling force in my life. That was all I knew.

Where my dad was the law, my mom was grace. She was always trying to soften the punishment. I remember getting into trouble at school and the teacher would call home and share with Mom what had happened, who in turn shared it with Dad. When I got home, I had to wait in my room for my dad to come home to dole out the punishment. I would lie there anxious as all get out waiting. After 5pm, every car that drove by the house made me wince. Is that Dad pulling in?

When he finally got home, I'd hear that door shut and my mom would immediately start pleading with him, "Now Troy, please don't be so hard...please don't break his little spirit," or something like that.

We had a large extended family. Some lived in North Carolina and others in Florida and we would visit them on occasion. I was closer to my mom's family than to my dad's.

I was especially close to my maternal grandmother who lived in Florida. She was a teacher and the first single-parent I ever knew. Because her husband died young, my grandmother had to raise my mom, her brother and two sisters all alone. She was a formidable force of a woman and took no crap from anyone.

Grandma was a teacher by profession and in her everyday life. She taught by the way she lived and learning how to listen was a lesson she taught regularly.

One day, I learned the "listening" lesson the hard way. I remembered my grandmother telling me that bumblebees couldn't sting you. You can imagine my surprise when I caught one in my bare hands and felt the pain of its stinger entering my flesh.

"Grandma, you told me bumblebees didn't sting!" I said through the searing pain in my hand and tearing eyes.

"I said bumblebees won't go after you to try to sting you like yellow jackets will." From then on, I became a better listener. I learned to ask more questions and be a little more inquisitive. I will always remember how Grandma taught me how to listen.

Grandma, who was the first and hardest working single-parent I ever knew, also reinforced my father's lesson of how hard work would pay off. She never remarried, worked hard and encouraged others to do the same. If you wanted something, you had to work for it. She gave me my first tree cutting job. I used a hacksaw to cut down a super sappy tree in her front yard. For payment, I received enough money to buy some white corduroy Levi pants that I had been admiring.

My maternal grandfather died when I was three weeks old so I never knew him. He was a free-spirit who rode motorcycles, flew airplanes and was an expert car mechanic. Oh, how I wish I knew that man. As a WWII veteran, he was part of the first group of African Americans to hold a rank in the U.S. Navy, other than a cook or a janitor. He was recruited to play in the Navy band that was the result of Eleanor Roosevelt's encouragement to her husband to integrate the U. S. Navy. The Navy searched throughout North Carolina to find

African Americans that would represent America well. This is how my grandfather and his brother became part of the B-1 Navy band.

There are many family stories about my grandfather being a rebel, and a trickster of sorts. When the B-1 Navy Band was stationed in Hawaii, he would steal off in the middle of the night and take an airplane for a little spin. He stayed under the radar so as not to be detected. His brother, a rule follower, would never join him. Both of them knew how to fly planes. We suspect that they learned when they were at the Tuskegee Institute, around the time they were learning to play the trumpet in New Orleans. I loved my grandfather's spirit. Sometimes, I feel his rebellious spirit rising up in me.

When we were old enough, my parents would send my brother, sister and I to Florida to stay with our grandparents. We thought we were getting a break from our parents, when they were the ones actually getting off from parental duties for a while. My grandmother would take us to the beach after church on Sundays. She had a strict "no swimming for an hour" rule after we chowed down on Kentucky Fried Chicken. I mean, she was not playing either. We would sit there on the beach, our stuff neat and orderly on the sand, waiting for a whole hour. The beautiful aqua water was so tempting but our grandmother would not budge. We did not enter the water until the clock struck one hour past whenever we had eaten.

My uncle John taught me how to play tennis after Grandma tried unsuccessfully. One day during a game of doubles, she whacked me in the back of the head with a steel framed Jimmy Connor tennis racket after I had disrespected my sister somehow. She always had a way of getting her point across.

Both my maternal grandparents were very light skinned and this often worked to their advantage. It wasn't until recently that I learned about colorism being a real thing. It is prejudice or discrimination against individuals with a dark skin tone, typically among people of the same ethnic or racial group. I am not sure how this impacted my grandparents, but I know that it helped me to assimilate into white culture easier. As a lighter skinned black man, I was afforded a measure of privilege more than my darker skinned brother and sisters. There is a good deal of research out there about this sinister phenomenon. I don't know how it all works, but I know that I have been treated differently my whole life because of my lighter skin.

My mom had a debutant air about her but there was a fire inside that made her tougher than she looked. She had entrepreneurial spirit and wanted to start a daycare when she was younger so she studied Home Economics in college. She abandoned the idea of a daycare after raising my brother, sister and I. She'd seen enough!

Being in Home Economics introduced my mom to sewing, which became a life-long passion for her. She offered sewing classes during her time in college, and to this day, she sews all the costumes for the performing arts youth ministry that she founded over twenty-five years ago.

Did I mention the entrepreneurial spirit and fire about her? She was also an adventurous and tough cookie. In the late 70s, women were not allowed to take on jobs that were considered physically demanding and for men only. Pole climbing for the telephone companies was one of these occupations. My mom became a pole climber for AT&T for a short period of time. Her career got cut short however when she had a few tense conversations with Dad and it was decided that she would stay home and make sure we kids were raised properly, by a stay-at-home mom.

Dad was a force of nature, as well. Maybe it was because he was the first born in his family and was forced to take care of his brothers and sisters, that he developed a very firm belief in right and wrong. When he made his mind up to do something and he believed he had a right to do it, nothing could deter him.

When *Carolina Power and Light* downsized in the mid-eighties, Dad went on to start his own business, a lawn maintenance and landscaping company named *The McMillan Group, Inc*. I'll never forget the day we went down to the lawyer's office in a high rise building in downtown Raleigh to sign the *articles of incorporation*, together. I'm pretty sure that moment galvanized my brother's and my own entrepreneurial spirit. I have never felt at home in my own skin working for anyone else.

For over thirty years, my dad has worked and grown that little business into one that has provided jobs for many people, including jobs for me a couple of times. It has afforded desperately needed resources for my mom's youth ministry to survive, as well. Each year, Mom's ministry, *Make a Joyful Noise (MAJN)* would take a nine-day performing arts tour somewhere across America. Mom would rent two, sometimes three fifty-five passenger coach buses for over one hundred and twenty-five youth, chaperones and all associated equipment for a three-hour performance. The costs were astounding and no matter how much they fund raised during the year, they would come up woefully short on funds to take the trip. Every year, at the last minute, the money for the show would mysteriously appear. I know that money came from *The McMillan Group.* I didn't realize it early on how my parents were modeling how the world can change through hard work and following your dreams.

My extraordinary parents made sure that my brother, sister and I had a typical all-American childhood.

Life was an amazing adventure. The area where we lived was a perfect place to raise children. I loved the outdoors and across the street from our home was a large field that bordered a farm. In the field was a big swamp. My friends and I would go to the swamp, dam up creeks, play with crawdads and climb trees, fish, hunt and play with bee-bee guns. We were always out in the woods, never indoors. There were no video games. During the summer, we would stay outside until the street lights came on. At night, we would play kickball and *Jailbreak* in the neighbor's yard, then, we would catch fireflies. It was an awesome experience.

My parents made sure that we wanted for nothing. We had everything we needed, and more. Christmases were a big deal. My dad loved to go all out decorating the house. Christmas Eve, we would get into the car and drive around to see all the Christmas lights. Then, we would come home to put on our new Christmas pajamas and wait for Santa Clause to come. My parents did it up right; gifts that family gave you and gifts that Santa brought in the middle of the night. My most memorable gift was a cardboard spaceship, an astronaut's spacesuit and space helmet. I sat in that cardboard box peering through the clear lens of that helmet many days, dreaming of space, dreaming of being someone big, important, and giving to this world.

Though my dad was very generous, he was also very frugal. Being an accountant, he counted every penny. We thought he was cheap, but he made sure that we were well cared for. I always felt a little less than the other kids at school because we wore off brands not designer clothes. I compared myself to those higher on the social scale by their clothes. But we always had what we needed.

Our family vacations created some of my happiest memories. It was time away from everyday life, together as a family. We traveled often, going to Lake

Michigan, Cedar Point Amusement Park, and several trips to Disney World The trips to Disney were incredible. I remember vacationing in pop-up trailers at Lake Michigan. Being in the beautiful mountains was an amazing experience. When I became a parent myself, I began to really appreciate everything my parents did to make moments such as these.

I never even thought about race growing up. It just wasn't talked about in our family, though we saw it all around us. The divisions were especially obvious in the church but we never discussed it.

When we lived in Michigan, I was the only black child in the school and never thought a thing about it. I walked to the white local school with my white neighborhood friends. My siblings joined me a few years later.

I was not a great student so I didn't like school very much. I just wasn't good at it. I always felt like I was in the middle of the pack; not the worst but not the best either. I believed that I wasn't very smart. Math was a real challenge, as was writing. I could grasp concepts pretty easily but people couldn't understand what I was trying to convey. It was a burden for me and because my dad was a driving force, I did just enough to get by with him. I used my charisma to carry me through the rest of the way.

I loved sports and was really good at baseball and football. All of my friends played, as well. It was like the movie *Sandlot.* There was always a pick-up game going on. I played basketball, too, but I wasn't as good at it as I was at other sports.

Some of my fondest memories were made playing baseball. I loved baseball more than anything. I remember when I learned about the position of the catcher. Not being the most attentive person, I heard the coach say who wants to catch. I thought he was asking who wanted to start playing a game of catch and I immediately raised my hand.

"Well get over there, put on the gear and get behind home plate," he said.

Say what? I had no idea what I was getting myself into. After I put on all the catcher's gear and tried to squat down behind the plate and catch the balls he began throwing me, I'd had enough. This was the only position I never played again. I loved the roaming, wide-open nature of shortstop and centerfield, so these were the positions I played for the rest of my competitive days.

I played football but I never really enjoyed it apart from the radical camaraderie that it elicited. There was something about the brotherhood, the struggle, pain and suffering of the sport that I'll never forget. It drew me closer to my friends more than any other activity, outside of war, and I will always look back on those times fondly. I hated the constant pain of it all though. I always had a headache and I'm pretty sure the ever-present ringing in my ears started from my time playing football.

Because of our age differences, I never really felt close to my siblings growing-up. Being the oldest, my younger brother was somewhat of a nuisance. My sister was fun to play with for short periods of time. I was interested in making my own way in life without them. But we always did family activities well together.

My siblings and I, also, worked together to keep our dad from disciplining us. We learned to craft stories to stay out of trouble. Overall, my dad seemed to know the truth. He had this "Spidey sense" so we could never get away with anything…but we continued to try.

Dad's work ethic was *law*. He taught us how to work really hard. We all had chores around the house, inside and out. The air-conditioning or heat was only used when absolutely necessary. We would go into the woods to get firewood together. We'd down trees, load up the truck, take it home and dump it on the ground. I learned how to use a chainsaw and ax.

Dad would say, "By the end of the week, this needs to be split," and we made sure it was. If it wasn't split, we had to spend the weekend doing it.

Firewood would be seasoned and ready for the wood stoves every year. All summer long, we would prepare for the winter. To stay cool, we depended on the ceiling fans in each of the rooms.

Even when we went on family vacations, we never used the dishwasher. My dad would say, "I have three dishwashers in the house and their names are Byron, Tyron and Tronita."

All of this drew my siblings and I closer together. We had a common sense way of seeing the world; what was right and what was wrong. Our father was the chief enforcer of this way. He took his queues from the Bible. It was the be all and end all of every issue and life occurrence.

We always did our homework because making good grades was part of the equation. I was not a great student, but I always did enough to get by. We knew that abiding by the rules would keep our dad off our case. Abiding by the rules was our main road to freedom out into the social world.

I really didn't like my dad much growing up and couldn't wait to move away when I was old enough. Today, many kids love to hang around at their parent's house as long as possible. That was something I never experienced. Getting out from under the controlling eye and hand of my father was of paramount importance. Looking back, I can see that he was preparing me for a world that was far harsher than he was. He was teaching me to follow the rules for my own self-preservation.

In the summer of 1976, when I was ten years old, my mom got tired of the cold in the north and wanted to move south, so we moved back to North Carolina. My dad got a great job with *Carolina Power and Light.* I remember sitting in the back of the car while we were leaving Michigan crying because I thought we were moving to a plantation or farm or something. The only thing I knew about the South was from the Andy Griffith show. I cried the entire trip. I was actually shocked when we pulled into our suburban neighborhood. The houses were brand new and construction was still going on there.

Our neighborhood was a magical place. There were plenty of wood piles and woods where we could build forts.

Very similar to our last community, this one was mostly white, having a few additional black families. It was great to have a little more diversity in the neighborhood.

We attended a black church out in the country not far from our home. Church in the south was very different than in the north. You could feel faith in the air. God was real and was watching you. It wasn't just your parents.

It was also then that I really started to feel the black-white divide. I began to see racism in the church. I heard teachings about the black struggle, and the difference in socioeconomics, how blacks needed to work harder in school and their careers to get ahead. Our church was all-black and the most segregated of anything I had experienced. None of my white friends were there. They would often invite me to their churches every once in a while when I would spend the night. Their churches were very different from mine. My church put more emphasis on singing and sermons that got you all riled up. Theirs seemed to be more rational and intellectual. In my mind, they seemed smarter and not as emotional and entertainment oriented. I'm sure my bias toward the superiority of white culture tainted my view of the black church.

When I was eleven, I went to a revival meeting with my family during the summer. The music was loud and stirring. It was hot and I had an overwhelming desire to do the right thing. I needed to accept Christ as my Savior. I wanted to show my parents I was growing up and get them off my case. So, when the pastor did the altar call, I went forward. I spoke to the pastor and made arrangements to be baptized. I thought that when I got baptized that a dove was literally going to come out of heaven, land on my shoulder, and I wasn't going to want to sin anymore.

After I was baptized, we had a nice chicken dinner and I got a bible with my name and a five-dollar bill in it. I thought, "Well, I'm all grown up. I am a Christian now. I have to live right and hopefully not sin."

As I grew, my hormones started to rage and I began to desire to do the things my friends were doing. They were having a good time partying, and they were not going to church. That is when a divide between my parents and me started. Their goal was to get me to walk in faith and I rejected it.

A few years ago, I began to recognize, during meditation, after I had listened to a podcast about the difference between guilt and shame, that there was much more to my revival experience than I realized. The podcast mentioned that "Guilt is what you have done" and "Shame is who you are."

This prompted a painful memory of a time not long after we moved back to North Carolina when I was eleven years old. We had gone to visit a family friend's house and there were other kids there. They were older, a lot bigger and stronger than me. I respected them but I was also afraid of them. During our time there, they took *advantage* of me in a sexual manner. I knew that what they were doing to me was wrong. It was traumatizing and I believed it to be my fault. As I reflect on the incident now, I think that this incident is what drove me to the altar that summer night at the revival. I remember feeling shame after that and that I needed Jesus to take it away. I was told Jesus would take away my pain and let me know how much I was loved by Him but I continued to carry the burden.

When I think back to that time, I realize that those older friends were living in a broken world of systemic injustice. The deck was really stacked against them. They grew up in tough poverty without so many of the privileges that I grew up taking for granted. Single-parent, multi-generational poverty, everyone being under stress just to survive, was normal for them. They lacked many of the resources that I had growing up. As a result, they have gone on to live very tragic lives; caught up in America's industrial prison complex fueled by the so-called war on drugs and the mass incarceration of black men. Their health, especially their mental health, also suffered greatly as they experienced disparities so prevalent in communities of color.

I never told my parents about the incident and successfully distracted myself from thinking about it for years. It remained buried deep inside of me as I busied myself with sports, a modicum of education, the military and then finally, religion. Subconsciously, I think I was trying to prove that what I had done to me, was not really who I was. So, I let it drive me to a life of achievement.

It was at this same time that I began to experience injustice in the school system. The school system was attempting a very progressive experiment to transform what had been a segregated society. The inner city consisted primarily of poor black families and the suburbs contained more affluent white families. The new school I attended was very modern and not far from my neighborhood. Every day, I walked to school with my friends, most of whom were white. This particular year, the school system started bussing black children from the inner city to suburban schools, trying to equal out the inequities that had arisen.

This scenario encouraged a very challenging encounter for me with the black children from the inner city. They had been on buses for forty-five minutes to an hour each day.

The children were rough and tough and criticized me vehemently for being who I was, asking, "Who do you think you are? Uncle Tom, Mr. Whitey-Black? Listen to the way you talk."

This was the first time that I really started to see race. I was intimidated by the guys from the inner city. I was nothing like them and never wanted to be.

Sports helped somewhat to be the great equalizer for me. I was able to relate to them on the fields but it was at that critical moment that I decided I needed to get my act together and I made the decision to assimilate into the white dominant culture. I wanted to be accepted into the white world and I spent decades of my life trying to make that happen, and to some degree, I was successful. I was ten years old when I made that conscious decision to assimilate.

I recently read a 1965 Jet magazine article about a speech that President Lyndon B. Johnson gave at Howard University about the assimilation. In his address, he called for the assimilation of black people into mainstream American society as one of the highest priorities of his administration.

This happened the year before I was born. I entered a world calling for assimilation of blacks into white American culture. This was assumed to be the acceptable norm at the time. Ten years later, I absorbed the message about white culture and sought to fit into it as best I could for my own survival and flourishing.

School was always academically challenging for me, especially math. It was not until eighth grade when a teacher took an interest in me that set me on a new trajectory. My Geometry teacher took extra time for three of his struggling students, to reinforce geometric concepts using a very creative approach. We were encouraged to meet him on the football field after school twice a week for three weeks. He greeted us there with three sets of golf clubs that he had purchased from *Goodwill*. Each bag had a three iron, a five iron, a nine iron and a putter.

He said, "I am going to teach you guys about Geometry through golf."

For three weeks, he taught us geometry out on the football field. We learned how to swing a golf club and about all of the rules of golf. We learned about the properties of space related to distance, shape, size, and relative position of figures. At the end of the three weeks, on a Saturday morning, he took us to a public golf course and bought us our first round of golf. I fell in love with the game and made a B+ in Geometry. This was the only Math class that I excelled in in school but it made me realize that I was smart and could learn when I applied myself.

In high school, I applied myself just enough to get by academically so that I could go to college, even though my parents were pushing me for much more. I didn't aspire to go to the big-name colleges or the Ivy League or anything like that. I was far more interested in excelling in football, baseball and making an impression with the ladies.

I did alright for myself in those areas. I made all-conference teams in both sports over the four years, though I was no superstar. I ran for student council and won some minor roles to which I didn't really contribute much.

I often relied on my charm and so-called dashing good looks to get by. As a result, I was voted "Mod Bod" for having the model body for our Senior Superlatives. I believed people liked me and being recognized for having a model body was good enough. Deep down, I really wanted to be known for my mind and clever wit, not just how I looked. In the end, I was happy just to be recognized for something.

After graduation, I went to a college that my dad didn't really approve of because it had a reputation of being a party school. I was more interested in playing baseball, but my sports career was finished when I didn't make the team. I had never been cut from anything before in my life and I immediately took up a life of partying. I almost failed out my second year because of it.

I was directionless and one day made the decision to join the Army. The Army recruiter told me I was smart and could go in as a *specialist*. He made it sound very appealing. At the end of the school year, I drove home and told my dad I had joined the Army. He went ballistic.

He said, "You are never going to go back to college. You just wasted two years of schooling. This is a big mistake."

I said, "Well, it's too late. I have enlisted in the Army already and I report at the end of the summer." Instead of getting into a big argument over it, my dad uncharacteristically went into silent mode. Looking back on it, I realized he took a new tact and went into *trickster mode* instead of the authoritarian enforcer that he'd always been.

A few weeks later, a gentleman, fully dressed in uniform came to my house to take me out for lunch to discuss my enlistment. He was an officer and had been in the ROTC at St. Augustine College in Raleigh, an Historical Black College. He asked me why I went into the Army and I gave him a litany of reasons.

Then he asked, "Do you know the difference between an officer and an enlisted man?"

I did not and he explained, "An officer is a leader and makes more money. Do you like to lead or do you like to take orders?"

"Well, I would rather lead," I said.

"Would you rather stay in nice housing or poor housing?" He asked.

He painted this whole case for me to strive to be an officer but I thought I had already been sworn in and I could not change.

"You aren't sworn in until you report to your duty station at the end of the summer," he responded.

"If you tell me you would like to go to the ROTC program at the college, I'll tell you how to get out of your commitment," he continued.

"Sign me up! Tell me what to do," I said.

The officer explained the whole process. I did what he told me to do and I got out of my commitment. But I did not want to go to a historic black college so I checked to see if they had ROTC at the college I had been attending. They did and I continued my studies there.

Life turned around for me at that point. I had direction, studied hard and I made the dean's list for the next two years. I completed school with a degree in History, raising my grade point average to a respectable level. I'm pretty sure my parents were much happier about my decision and it literally altered the course of my life.

I was commissioned as a second lieutenant and went into the Army. My parents were at my commissioning. I remember thinking, my dad was right. Hard work does pay off.

In 1988, I went to Fort Knox, Kentucky to begin my time in the Army. The Army was nothing compared to the strictness of my dad, so I was able to excel there.

I had to grow up very quickly, however. I was away from my dad, took over my expenses entirely and bought a new car. During that time, I met a young woman at the Officer's Club and we fell in love. She became pregnant and I had a crisis on my hand. I was not ready to be married nor did I want to but I felt God was calling me to grow up. I needed to become a man and do the right thing. I felt like I was living the movie, *An Officer and a Gentleman,* where women around military bases would entice young officers into marriage. We married and life became a whirlwind.

Many changes soon occurred in rapid succession. I was sent to my first duty assignment in Germany in the summer of 1989. It was an accompanied tour so my wife was able to join me. The Wall in Germany came down in November, shortly after our arrival. The Cold War was over and America had proven victorious. My daughter was born a month later and I became a father.

In the August of 1990, Saddam Hussein invaded Iraq, and a week later, American troops were sent over. Everything began to escalate, and in December 1990, our unit in Germany got deployed to Saudi Arabia and became part of Desert Storm. I went to war with the 1st Armor Division, Old Ironsides, and led my tank platoon of sixteen young men into combat. I was a twenty-two-year-old kid. It was hard and glorious at the same time. I was doing what I had been trained to do. I was a patriot for America. I bought into American exceptionalism and our role of saving the world from evil.

This experience brought me back to my faith. I was getting on that plane, going to war and vividly remember leaving my young wife and one-year-old daughter in Germany. The thought of possibly never seeing them again brought me to my knees. It was at that moment, I began to pray and trust that God would watch over me. I carried a small Gideon's Bible in my chest pocket and read it every day memorizing its words, just as my father had forced my brother, sister and I to do when growing up.

After three years in Germany, we moved back to Fort Knox, Kentucky and I attended the Armor Officer Advanced course to prepare me for command in the military. This was home for my wife. I never met or spoke to any member of my wife's family in Kentucky because of the color of my skin. She was white. Our marriage was unacceptable to her family. It was as if I did not exist.

During our time there, my wife became pregnant with our second child.

I began thinking about our future and put in a request to go to Korea. This was an unaccompanied tour. If I chose to do a tour such as this, afterwards we would be able to go anywhere we desired.

At the same time, I began thinking about getting out of the Army. I realized after Desert Storm that the Army was not what I wanted to do with the rest of my life. I did not enjoy being a *hunter* or being *hunted.* When my wife began to have serious medical issues associated with the second pregnancy, we decided it was time to get out of the Army. I was able to get a medical hardship discharge and we bought a house near my home in Raleigh, North Carolina.

I started working with my dad when we returned to North Carolina. He had added a lawn maintenance and landscaping division to our family's entrepreneurial endeavor, *The McMillan Group.* What started out as a small vending machine operation, and then grew through a parking space business he created in Downtown Raleigh, turned into a viable corporation with the addition of lawn maintenance and landscaping.

The lawn maintenance and landscaping part of the company grew out of a few accounts my brother had created cutting the grass of neighbors and banks in our community. When my dad was laid off from *Carolina Power and Light Company,* he took over those few accounts and began to develop them.

Today, *The McMillan Group Lawn Maintenance and Landscaping* division has three crews servicing over three hundred accounts in the Triangle area of North Carolina. *The McMillan Group* put my brother and sister and me through school and helped fund the dreams and aspirations of hundreds of youth in the community through *Make a Joyful Noise.*

Now, I was living in Raleigh, raising my family in the same area where I grew up. Church, once again, became a major influence in my life.

The church growth movement was in full swing with the gaining influence of Bill Hybels and his rapidly expanding megachurch, Willow Creek in Chicago. Conservative, evangelical megachurches began sprouting up all over the country by emulating the example of the Willow Creek model. I was completely captivated by it all and I felt the strong desire to become one of those big-time pastors who spoke to thousands in a packed football stadium or who led congregations over a thousand in a megachurch.

It was also the time of the Promise Keepers movement, where millions of men were filling football stadiums across the country and vowing to be men of promise, just as Jesus had been. I was enamored with it all.

Even though I had the best job I had ever had in my life with Cisco Systems, a company driving the growth of the Internet, I wanted to be a Christian leader more than anything else. I wanted to be a warrior for Christ in the growing culture war that was taking place in America. I began sensing that God was calling me into the ministry to preach the Gospel.

I belonged to the first mega church in Raleigh modeling itself after Willow Creek. My wife was not all that enthusiastic about going so I mostly went alone. My faith deepened as I sensed the country was moving away from its Christian heritage and I joined the crusade to bring us back to our foundations as a nation.

As my vigor for the faith grew, my marriage began to fall apart and I held off on plans to go to a Southern Baptist seminary nearby that was becoming renowned for its faithful teaching of the Bible as the inerrant Word of God.

I had become a radical Christian man. I was super committed to my family and I wanted to be like Jesus but I had become obnoxious, and perhaps a little overbearing.

It was really difficult to reconcile my deepening faith with my disintegrating marriage.

But I thought, “Well, this is just the price you pay for being different in the world. You follow God and things can fall apart.”

It was the *Promise Keeper* movement that drove me. I told my wife things I had done early on in our marriage that I wasn’t really proud of but now, I was completely committed to she and our family. I was going to do everything I could do to be a great husband and father.

But my wife wanted the old Byron back. She didn't want this new and improved version.

I told her that "Byron is dead and gone."

All of this was occurring while I was learning that my wife struggled with bipolar disorder and depression. This explained a tumultuous seven years of marriage up to that point. I was elated that there was a reason for all the turmoil. I remember being hopeful that we could move past all the difficulty and settle into being a good Christian family, serving the Lord and our neighbors for the good of the world.

All of these hopes came crashing down when soon after learning of her condition, she informed me that she was joining the Mormon church and would be moving out to Idaho. I was shocked when friends told me she had met a Mormon man and was moving away to be married. I did not have much time to process it because she was in a hurry to start her new life. She wanted to split the kids up and take our daughter out to Idaho with her. I would keep our son in North Carolina. I was warned by many in my cadre of Christian friends not to let my daughter go out there. You will never see her again, they warned. I went to the courts and petitioned for an emergency restraining order to keep my daughter in North Carolina and it was granted. Overnight, I became a single dad raising two young children, one seven years old and the other two years old.

I remember hearing God speak to me during that difficult time.
He said, "Stay around my people and stay in my word and you'll be okay."

It was also during this time that I began to understand what it meant to be *the least of these*. Being unmarried in Christendom was something to get out of. It was as if something was wrong with you. If you were divorced, it seemed the unforgivable sin. God might let you off the hook for eternity, but churches here on earth held it against you and you were damaged goods. Many churches would not let you work for them. It was as if you had a Scarlet D on your chest, a modern-day Hester Prin, untouchable.

Through it all, I continued to go to the mega church that had many resources. There were great programs for the kids. It was like Christian Nickelodeon or Disney World. They also had great coffee and tremendous learning programs for adults. Small groups were the key to everything and you learned about God in groups of people with whom you had some affinity.

My main affinity groups were the youth group and the singles ministry. I enjoyed working with teens because they were like mini adults without all the judgement. For the first time, religious faith felt cool and hip. Christian music gave me an alternative to the old Christian hymns I'd grown up with and teachers were retelling the ancient stories in refreshing and compelling new ways.

I spent a great deal of time in the singles ministry. Many of the singles there were also single parents and we helped to support each other. We took trips to the mountains and to the beach and participated in all types of activities together. It was like a big old extended family and I made a lot of friends there.

It was here that I met my second wife. She had three kids all the same age as my two. We fell in love and sensed that God was calling us together to raise these five kids in power, love and self-control in a broken and wounded world. After three years of single fatherhood, I now was part of a blended family of seven. It was a very challenging and rewarding time.

It was during this time of being in the singles ministry and beginning the process of formal religious training, that I recall my first inkling that something was wrong with the *religion* I had been growing into. It occurred when I finally enrolled in that Southern Baptist Seminary as a single father.

A representative from the seminary said to me one day, "Look, we are glad you are here. You are going to learn a lot. We have a place for you and your family while you are here but we just want you to know that you are never going to be able to pastor a church because you are divorced."

I remember saying, "Well that's okay, I really wasn't planning on being a pastor, maybe a youth pastor."

I just wanted to be a preacher of the Word in a church or some parachurch organization. I didn't understand the hierarchy or leadership structure in the church. It was like having that conversation about the difference between an officer and enlisted all over again. It all just flew over my head.

As the duties and responsibilities of being married again increased, especially with five young children, my ability to stay in seminary was strained and I had to make a decision. I was working three jobs to make ends meet and something had to give. I decided to leave seminary.

Perhaps, it was because I had taken most of the general courses of a Master of Divinity degree and I started to lose interest in the more specific Baptist education. More likely however, was the realization that Baptist faith was too restrictive for my way of thinking.

I remember in a Systematic Theology class when we were asked to share our views on *freewill* versus *predestination.* Everyone shared which view with which they most identified. Being a Baptist institution, most agreed with some form of *predestination.* At the time, the movie *Forrest Gump,* was my greatest teacher on the subject.

I said before the class when it was my turn to explain my view, "I think it is like Forrest said at the end of the movie when he was at Jenny's grave, 'I don't know if we each have a destiny, or if we're all just floatin' around accidental-like on a breeze, but I, I think maybe it's both. Maybe both are happenin' at the same time."

The professor then replied, "Forrest also said, 'Stupid is as stupid does,' and the whole class laughed."

I think it was right then and there that I decided to leave seminary. It seemed that the whole institution was unable to hold two seemingly opposing views at the same time, even though very thoughtful people were making sense of what they believed on both sides. It was my first brush with the duality of religion and I realized that I had begun to think non-dualistically. The world was not full of black and white, right and wrong, up or down. The truth was somewhere in between the poles and it is where I wanted to live.

Raising a blended family in this world reinforced this thinking. I began to learn more from my kids than I realized I could ever teach them. Their views on relationships, religion, drugs, politics began to break down my set categories. Nothing was as it seemed and I needed to learn to listen and consider other viewpoints. For the most part, all of our children got along fine with each other and fell in line with our laissez faire parenting style. All except one, that is.

My son was the *wild card* in the mix. He was only two when I separated from his mom. He often didn't want to *just* go along with the program. He had his own way of seeing the world and he tried to exert that view every chance he got. He is a contrarian by nature, and no matter what everyone else agreed on, he would disagree. Oftentimes he was right, but the way he went about proving it set everyone else on edge.

Our kids were active across the broad spectrum of activities available to kids these days. From sports such as football, basketball, baseball, lacrosse, and cross country, to band, color guard, trumpet, guitar and even the trombone. As a family, we camped and hiked in the mountains and at the ocean. My wife had a thriving jewelry making business and the kids joined in the making and selling of her incredible creations. Setting up her tent and spending the day at art fairs was a favorite endeavor for us all to participate in, and it provided much needed revenue for our family. It taught us all valuable entrepreneurial lessons that we all carry with us today. We lived in a mostly white suburban neighborhood, but the kids all attended the most diversely populated high school in the city. It gave them a broad perspective on how to live, work and play with across race and cultures.

It is important to note that both of my wives were white. I had assimilated completely into white dominant culture. My children from my first marriage are biracial and my second wife's children are white. This made for an interesting family. We were a blended family on many levels and this created great challenges and great rewards. I believe our family was an example of where the world is heading as we mature as human beings. We are all connected and intrinsically the same, and we all need each other. On the surface, America appears to be a land of equal opportunity for all, a melting pot of cultures and people groups working together for a greater cause. But this is *fake news*.

The ideology of race is a uniquely American construct used to create a caste system that is older than our nation itself. From 1619, when the first Africans came to this continent as slaves, up through 1776, when our nation declared its independence from Britain, on through a Civil War and the Civil Rights movement of the 1960s, America has had legal, economic, educational, and medical systems that oppressed and explicitly reinforced the idea that one race of people is superior to all others.

Some of my toughest moments were when I visited my son or daughter's school for the first time. I knew that I had to mind my p's and q's and prove something. As soon as the students and teachers in their class saw that I was a black man, I knew that they would be judged differently.

"Oh, that's your dad?" I would hear them say.

Or, "Oh, you're Zack's dad?" a teacher would innocently say when meeting me for the first time.

Though their words didn't come right out and say it, I knew what they were talking about.

Over the years, I held many different corporate jobs to help provide resources for our family. I worked for Electronic Data Systems, Cisco Systems, Underwriter's Laboratories and Cisco again. I even sold Honda cars for a spell. In between, I tried to start my own companies, a lawn maintenance company, a tree service, and many network marketing opportunities. I did whatever it took to keep some cash flow to keep the bills paid. My dream of being a pastor in a church, any church, not to mention a megachurch, faded and I grudgingly accepted the reality that I would never work in a church. I did have a Scarlet D on me that I could not get rid of.

It was during this time that I began to grow disillusioned with American capitalism and the commodification of everything. All of our individual talents and gifts are commodified to generate a profit. Nothing else matters except our ability to make a profit. It is a soul suppressing system that devalues humans who don't measure up to what people are willing to purchase.

At this point of my growing disillusionment, the megachurch I attended offered, what I thought would be, my dream job or vocation, the Director of Local Missions. I was to help 1ten thousand upwardly mobile, mostly suburban folks, mostly white, work with "those" people down in the urban parts of town. We would provide food, money and other resources to help those in need. We would also get to share the "good news" of Jesus Christ with them as we served.

It became my responsibility to set up hundreds of service opportunities, what I came to call the "Disneyfication" of service. These were to be authentic, safe, convenient, and fun teaching moments for the people of our church. We did these in conjunction with other churches, nonprofits and parachurch organizations in our city.

The goal was to bring people to Christ, to have them accept him as Lord and Savior. This would bring about transformation in our church and our city. I soon came to realize that this transactional form of ministry actually did more harm than good. A book that really helped me see this phenomenon was *When Helping Hurts: How to Alleviate Poverty Without Hurting the Poor and Yourself.*

An organization called the *Christian Community Development Association (CCDA)* really shaped my thinking during this phase of my life. This organization looked at the gospel of Christ in a very different way than I was used to. They believed that God had a preference for the poor that Jesus was sent to earth to live among the poor and teach us from their vantage point. Rather than trying to "fix" them and help them become successful like us, we should learn how to live with them, learn from them, love them, and together we will all be better because of it. They proposed a relational form of ministry over a transactional one.

I soon found out that transactional ministry is far easier to measure and manage. We provided services like giving away free food, clothing and tutoring. In return, we expected to be given the opportunity to share the good news of Jesus Christ. How many people did we serve last month? How many coats or bookbags did we give away? How many pounds of food or turkeys did we provide for the community? How many people prayed to receive Christ? These became the measurements of success.

Relational ministry is hard to measure. When you begin building friendships and falling in love with people, it often gets messy. How many people did you drive to doctor's appointments? How many late-night phone calls did you engage in? How many tears did you shed or wipe away? How many stories of heartbreak and travail did you share and listen to? These are very hard to count and manage.

Soon I found myself at odds with the leadership of the church.

"You need to check your job description," I kept getting told on a regular basis.

I was exposed to thousands of service opportunities available in our local urban areas. Building relationships and empowering people was not what I was brought into the church to do. Despite all this, I felt that I was exactly where God wanted me to be. Then one day, my son came to me to address the hypocrisy he was seeing in the church and was seeing in me.

"Christians are full of crap," he said. "When you are in the room and everybody is patting you on the head and telling you how much they love you and are glad you are here, everything is great. But, when you leave the room, and they don't know what team I am on because of the color of my skin, hair and eyes, and don't realize that you are my father, the way they talk about you and other people of color is just hypocritical." Remember, my bi-racial son has blond hair and green eyes. "Christians are full of crap and you are full of crap for working at a church like that. I can't believe you would pastor that kind of church. You are all just hypocrites."

I was shocked by his words and wanted to defend myself and the church but as I looked around, I knew he was right. I had learned to listen to what he has to say rather than try and get him to see my point of view. Khalil Gibran's words came to mind at this moment:

"Your children are not your children.

They are the sons and daughters of Life's longing for itself.

They come through you but not from you,

And though they are with you yet they belong not to you.

You may give them your love but not your thoughts,

For they have their own thoughts.

You may house their bodies but not their souls,

For their souls dwell in the house of tomorrow, which you cannot visit, not even in your dreams.

You may strive to be like them, but seek not to make them like you."

This conversation happened around the time that Donald Trump began ascending in power on the political scene.

I remember hearing my Christian friends saying, "Look, I don't like Donald Trump because of his character but I can't vote for Hillary so I guess I'll have to vote for him."

I slowly saw them progress to, "Donald Trump is a man of God. Donald Trump is the most Christian person running for President."

Then when he won, conservatives said that "This man is the most Christian president we have ever had."

I realized at that point that something was wrong with my theology. At the same time, I had begun reading the teachings of Richard Rohr, a Franciscan priest who espoused an alternative orthodoxy focusing on what is called *perennial wisdom*.

Perennial wisdom is a perspective in philosophy and spirituality that views all of the world's religious traditions as sharing a single, metaphysical truth or origin from which all esoteric and exoteric knowledge and doctrine has grown. In short, all the faith traditions are saying the same thing but using different metaphors, words and word pictures that point to a thing but are not the thing.

I began to read and learn from other teachers and spiritual authorities who have stood the test of time. My definition of authority changed to *anyone or any body of knowledge that authored life into me.* The most astounding revelation that I began to receive from all of these new teachers was that I could trust myself and the experiences I was having. Rohr's definition of *mysticism, "experiential knowledge of spiritual things,"* really resonated with me.

During my seminary days I was told not to trust my own experience. I was supposed to trust the authorities, the experts over me who were "rightly dividing the word of truth." My heart "is deceitfully wicked and cannot be trusted," they said. I "was born into sin and am a sinner who is only saved through grace."

Bonaventure, a theologian who wrote about the spiritual truths lived out by St. Francis of Assisi, really helped me. He taught that St. Francis believed that *we came from goodness, are sustained by goodness and we are going back to goodness.* The universe is ruled and guided by love and a loving the Godhead who is not out to eternally punish most of the universe's inhabitants for missing the mark during their short sojourn on this planet.

As a part of this perennial wisdom, I began to embrace indigenous cosmologies, especially from our Native American brothers and sisters. Robin Wall Kimmerer, author of the book, *Braiding with Sweetgrass: Indigenous Wisdom, Scientific Knowledge and the Teachings of Plants*, helped me to see how our different creation stories have shaped our human development and how we engage the rest of the world.

The dominant Christian view of Eve and Adam sinning and getting kicked out of the Garden to dominate and subdue the earth has led to violence and oppression the world over. The Indigenous view is of *Skywoman* falling to earth bearing seeds and other gifts and working with the inhabitants already here, to co-create Turtle Island. This has led to people who are generative, collaborative and trying to live in harmony with the ecosystems of the earth rather than working to make the earth do what we think it should.

I also had an amazing encounter with the spirit of Harriet Tubman during a ritual that took place as part of a *Male Rite of Passage* time spent in the wilderness of Colorado. Out of the clear blue, her essence appeared to me and told me that t*he earth would provide everything I needed to survive in this world. Trust it and walk boldly and courageously without fear and love will guide you home.* I know that many folks may be freaked out by such an occurrence and will surely chalk it up to the demonic but that is okay. I've learned to trust my experience and the lessons I am learning, especially when they occur out in nature, as Richard Rohr pointed out to me.

These are just a few instances of beliefs that began to change me and lead me to a transformation that was beyond anything I could hope for or imagine.

The catalyst for my transformation began when my son called out the issue of hypocrisy and covert racism in the church. I had a blind spot for this hypocrisy.

At the same time, the rise of Donald Trump and the way he was accepted into the Christian community revealed that something was very wrong with the way I was seeing God.

As I began to look at the church, our country and the life I had been living, I realized I couldn't continue to coast along, business as usual. I quit my job at the church and stopped attending altogether.

The last church that I attended was a beautiful Nazorean church in the inner city. A group of white Nazarenes had moved in years ago and began working with young black single moms. Their whole ministry way of life was to become friends with the single moms, ask them what they needed and allow them to help lead and be a part of what they were doing. This was a beautiful expression of the sacrificial life of Jesus and humans serving one another in their physical, emotional, and spiritual need. I went to that church for a year until my wife started having emotional problems.

I have been married to my wife for twenty years but her depression and my spiritual awakenings caused some serious issues between us. This led to all kinds of upheaval in our lives and we are in the midst of the fallout. It is very hard to write about this because much of it has not resolved itself. I know I am responsible for hurting a lot of people. This was never my intention but one of the main lessons I am learning is that above all, I have to be true to myself. Where this leads, I have no idea. I am learning to be okay with the uncertainty.

During this time, I began working for a global non-profit as a Director of Content and Training, *Jobs for Life.* When I came onboard, there were about ten people on staff and we were really starting to grow. The ministry was based on relational ministry, but what I found was that much of its funding was coming from the same conservative evangelical transactional churches that I had chosen to leave.

I realized that I could never go to any of the churches where we were associated, the ones we were training to use our ministry tools, especially our curriculum. As a way to alleviate poverty, we developed an eight-week course where we trained churches and other nonprofits to work with impoverished under-resourced communities to help them get and keep good employment. We were to enter into relationships with the people to prepare them to go to work. It was all about the theology of work and God's design for us.

After working for the organization for a while, I began to realize that they were supported by large evangelical churches and the overarching agenda was to get people saved. I found it hard to continue working there. The churches inadvertently were using the curriculum as a "bait and switch," not simply to help the poor.

"We'll get you trained for jobs but we want to share Jesus with you," they said.

Business leaders were using it as a way to get people who were ready to work. Relationships were not the emphasis of what was being built because relationships were messy and hard to measure. This was especially true when you began bumping up against issues of poverty catalyzed by systemic injustice; mass incarceration, multigenerational poverty, health and educational disparities, all with racism at the root. Systemic inequity sets people up for failure. It is an American system that needs to be addressed.

This was when I started recognizing some of the white privilege I had experienced as an assimilated black man. I could now see clearly all the issues that are dividing the country. We aren't a country of exceptionalism, better than all the other countries on the face of the earth. We are responsible for causing much damage in the name of Christ. Our society is a white male, dominated culture that is enforced by violence and aggression.

I began seeing and confronting the effects of the racial divide in my own family. Because my children are biracial, they have encountered much prejudice. Over the last four years, they have been willing to talk about their experiences with me and are attempting, in their own way, to help make a difference in society.

My daughter works for *Googl*e in a department that locates people in under-represented communities who are able to engage in *Google's* engineering practicum. Currently, eighty percent of engineers that work for *Google* are white males. The purpose of the program is to enhance the scope of their platform by going into communities to seek out people of color and women for the practicum. They recognize the value of diversity in creating products that are effective for the whole world.

My son deeply identifies with his blackness but does not look like it having blond hair and green eyes. He knows he has his privilege because of the color of his skin, but he still has to deal with prejudice. When people get to know who his father is, it can be a challenge. It is something my children have always had to deal with.

I know that my three step-children have had to address race head on as well. They always accepted me for who I am, their *bonus dad* and the color of my skin did not impact how they interacted with and treated me. They loved and trusted me as a human being.

All of our children grew up very aware of racial issues, being in a mixed-race family. They have learned to stand up for themselves. They empathize with the underdog and have fought for the rights of others less fortunate in our community.

My family is diverse and my kids have had to deal with that their entire lives. People stare and their comments can be quite offensive. I hope that they will use their experiences to make the world a better place, one that is just and right for all people.

I have learned that God is much bigger than the boxes in which religion has placed Him. When I was a conservative evangelical, I bought into the story that *we were created, we sinned, were separated from God, then Jesus died on the cross for our sin and restored that relationship*. I believed that we were separated from God and it was up to Christians to make that right. As I began to listen to other faith traditions, I noticed that there were so many beautiful people out there. They just had different views. I began to despise the term "believers" being applied to Christians alone.

Everybody believes in something. Why are our beliefs superior to everyone who disagrees with us? I now believe that we are connected to God and to each other. This revolutionized my thinking and opened me up to the beliefs and ways of living that gave me compassion for everyone. I see how polarizing religion can be. It doesn't need to be that way. We are all connected and trying to find our way home.

Conservative Christian friends have expressed that they are concerned for my eternal soul. That I have "gone down the slippery slope," but because I have accepted Christ, "I am okay. I am going to Heaven but shouldn't be teaching anymore." My beliefs "are dangerous."

After hearing that, I started rereading the words Jesus actually said. Jesus wasn't revealing a duality of Spirit and flesh, of Heaven or hell, right or wrong, black or white. He revealed that Spirit and flesh are one. Love and acceptance of individuals on their journey, no matter who they are or what they've done, will get you hung on a cross. The cross is where love takes you every time. And this is okay, because when you die to self, when you go to the cross, God resurrects you.

"*Unless a seed falls to the ground and dies, it cannot really live,*" he told us. I have been processing this for over four years.

When I share my story, I now share about the abuse that I have experienced whenever speaking to people about race, poverty, mass incarceration and health inequities. I have been able to overcome it all because of the transformative power afforded me by family, friends and the whole earth around me collaborating for the good. There are so many things that can hold us in bondage, some are external but many are internal. It is possible to break free from all that oppresses us and prevents us from being our authentic selves but we have to learn how.

I believe that our life's goal should be to find out who we are and live fully into it. Our soul is a blueprint revealing who we really are and what gifts we have to offer to the world. We must learn to trust what our soul is calling us to be. Then, we must go out and live courageously and in conjunction with others who are discovering the same and are willing to work in collaboration with us to co-create life sustaining and enhancing systems on the earth. We all need each other in this work, and we all need to be free to be ourselves. If you cannot be fully you, I cannot be fully me. If you are not free, I am not free.

Byron is currently co-developing an eight-month course for men on confronting and overcoming the shadow of white supremacy in our country, "Liberty and Justice for All: Confronting White Supremacy and Becoming We in America," for "Illuman," an international non-profit organization focused on men and based on the work and teachings of Richard Rohr.

The Story of Kathy

Kathy grew up in Baltimore city during the civil rights movement (1954-1968). Her experience as a young African American child during this time formed her to recognize the great need for racial reconciliation and the promotion of racial unity today.

As a child, I never sensed there was a "movement" of any kind going on. My life was filled with family. I was the oldest of five children born to teenage parents. My parents married a few months before I was born in 1957. I remember growing up with lots of love, laughter, and legacy building moments. These wonderful memories continue to carry me through to this day.

I spent a great deal of time with my extended family – my great grandmother, grandparents, aunts, uncles and cousins. My parents would load my siblings and I in the car on Saturdays with packed lunches and blankets and we would head to the beach. There, we would meet up with extended family to grill food and dance to the latest hit songs. At the time, I was unaware that the beaches we enjoyed were segregated.

At home, I spent many hours playing outside with my siblings and friends. We played hopscotch and tag, skated, rode bikes and played baseball in the street. On hot summer days, we would sit on the front steps of our house eating popsicles. Cherry and chocolate were my favorite.

My two youngest brothers were born in 1963 and 1968, the years President John F. Kennedy was assassinated and the Rev. Dr. Martin Luther King, Jr. was assassinated. Those were significant times in American History. I revisited these historical moments much later as an adult.

I vividly remember the night that Dr. King was assassinated. My sister and I were spending the night with my grandmother. I would usually take great delight in watching the shadows from the headlights of the cars making funny shapes through the blinds on the walls of her house. My grandmother lived on a very busy street, but that night, there were no dancing lights streaming through the closed venetian blinds as I played. I wondered why this night was different from others. What was going on? I remember peering through the blinds out into the darkness and being horrified by the commotion. There were army tanks and soldiers with long rifles riding up and down the middle of the streets patrolling and monitoring the behavior of the residents. No cars were coming or going. My grandmother said there was a curfew in place because people were rioting after learning of Dr. King's death. Rioting? I didn't know what that meant. I suddenly became fearful and wanted to go home to my parents but there was no way out. We had planned to go home the following morning but were forbidden to leave my grandmother's house because of the curfew. People were being arrested for breaking it. We stayed put for several days. I was ten years old.

When I grew-up and had children of my own, my husband and I realized the necessity to teach them about racial disparities in order to protect them. We openly discussed with our children about how the world had perceived African Americans and how there would be preconceived notions about them because of our race. We weren't alarmists. We were realists that had experienced racism personally. It was important that they not be blindsided by racism. Making them aware of racial perceptions armed them with the tools they needed to survive; "Watch your back. Don't trust everyone. Don't believe everything you hear or see. Be wise." Our children never questioned what we told them. They just trusted us.

Having your body, soul and spirit encased in black skin automatically sets misconceptions and stereotypes into motion. Our children experienced racism in both overt and covert ways. I remember an experience of taking one of our sons to the neighborhood barbershop when he was about four or five years old. It was white-owned shop, operated by three white barbers. They silently refused to cut my son's hair but they never told me that. I waited for hours as they kept "passing over" us. Finally, I had an "aha" moment! They didn't want to touch his hair let alone have the clippers touch it, so we left.

Prejudice also reared its ugly head in my kids' extracurricular sports activities. I felt they were often spoken to and "coached" with snide anger, disgust even. I tried very hard to overlook it, hoping I was imagining it but I knew deep within that I was not.

Nothing was more painful than what we experienced in our church. Prejudice in a white church was the most challenging to endure and understand. There were cliques in the church. Leaders shunned my family. Many of the children there were taught to hate a darker skin tone. I thank God for every bit of true brotherhood-sisterhood our family did experience. Their kindness was our saving grace.

The interesting thing is, I don't remember our children ever discussing their personal encounters with racism with my husband and me. We knew they had them. Their schools were filled with white people as was their church. I could see when they were being marginalized. I would pray about it and speak out about it but the response I received was out right denial.

The rules were never the same for black people as it was for the white so we taught our children how to live in that environment. When they were adults, they became fully aware.

Experiencing prejudice is almost an everyday happening for us. If you are not black, you would probably miss the subtleties of it. Sadly, there are far too many experiences I could mention. One in particular really stands out for me. About thirty years ago, my husband and I started searching for a home to rent for our family. A member of our church told us about a very nice house in a beautiful neighborhood, so we used her as a reference. When the landlord called to get a reference, our white friend mentioned that we were black. The landlord decided not to rent to us. She was asked to relay the message. He never even called us back. I'm not sure why our friend mentioned our race and she didn't know either but she did apologize for it. I was speechless, angry and very disappointed. We were rejected because of the color of our skin! We definitely felt the sting of it, picked up our hurt and moved on.

As a young child, I was pretty protected from racial injustice, making me oblivious to it and its effects. Though I had heard a myriad of stories about how that tragic night of Martin Luther King's assassination, April 4, 1968, came to be, I didn't understand how that directly impacted me.

By the time I was an adult, I had experienced first-hand the sting of racism. I had been spat upon and called a ni**er by a young white man yelling at me from his passing car. I had been overlooked, dissed and dismissed in a country that I proudly sang patriotic songs about in elementary school, just because of the color of my skin.

Even now, going on vacation as a family, it is necessary to use precautions that many people do not even think about. With something as simple as picking up carry-out food, I warn my sons to be sure to smile, get their food and get out. I do not want their presence to be misinterpreted. It's sad to even have to think about that.

I have found it healing to spend time researching about my family of origin. I always felt a strong connection to my ancestral roots, my earthly beginnings.

I was in my forties when my paternal cousin traced our family's American ancestral roots to a town in South Carolina. I was thrilled.

It was fascinating to read the names of my ancestors on the census' that were taken after they were brought to this country against their will. The historical documents revealed that our family could be traced back to the 1800s. They were brought to a plantation in South Carolina that still stands today. A few years ago, I was able to visit that plantation with my husband and granddaughter to pay homage to those whose shoulders I proudly stand upon. I literally touched the dirt that absorbed their blood, sweat and tears. My mom's and my husband's American ancestral roots began there.

Armed with this historical reference helped to shape me and my world view. I never quite saw the land that I loved through the naïve eyes of a child. I could see my father, a Sergeant in the U.S. Army, returning from active duty by bus being ushered to the back of the building to get a drink of water from the 'colored only' fountain while the whites entered through the front door. I heard about so many injustices to people of color that it made me cry and call out to the God I love. He continues to redeem that pain for me in ways I could have never dreamed.

Fifty years after seeing the National Guard tanks roll down the street, I am keenly aware that the fight for civil rights is still as prevalent today as it was then. As a sixty-year-old woman, I am reminded that the movement was and still is, in my lifetime…not that long ago.

It is my hope that the events of late will bring reconciliation to the past and usher in a new future. I long to see this country repent of the original sin of enslaving a people and building its wealth off of their backs and begin to respond differently. The recent murder of George Floyd and the uprising because of it has ushered in an awareness of racial oppression throughout the entire world. I have never experienced anything like this in my lifetime. I view this era as the Great Awakening. The walls of division are being torn down. Courageous conversations are being had between the races about racism in this country. Churches are leading in bold and declarative new ways. There's a holy boldness to confront racism at its core that is refreshing and long past due. It's a beautiful thing. I'm hopeful for the future. I continue to pray that the dream of Dr. Martin Luther King and my ancestors become a reality on earth as it is in Heaven, especially for my grandchildren and great-grandchildren.

I'm claiming this banner over my life, *I Am the Dream and the Hope of the Slave*. And so I am.

I am a self-proclaimed *Bridge-Builder*, standing on the shoulders of those who have gone before me. I want to do my part to call attention to the injustices that still exist today. My life is devoted to tearing down walls of separation through conversations. I am called to have conversations with others about what's going on in our neighborhoods, churches, cities, states, country and the world. I am called to be a bridge-builder by exposing those 'hidden' things that undermine the dignity of God's image bearers and call attention to it for those who don't understand.

I am a voice for those who are marginalized. I speak out in ways that my ancestors would never have dreamed possible. I can carry myself with the dignity and respect that they were not afforded. I am the dream and the hope of the slave.

I dream of a world that truly embraces the vision of unity, trusting in *John 3:16* "For God so loved the world." I do my part in my sphere of influence.

In the words of Dr. Martin Luther King, "Injustice anywhere is a threat to justice everywhere."

Kathy is a leader in her church and the community, and strives to build bridges to racial unity through conversations on her Facebook Blog Page – "Kitchen Table Conversations with Kathy."

She and her husband of 40 years, live in the northeast. Together, they have four children, seven grandchildren and will be welcoming a great-granddaughter soon.

The Story of Nikki

Nikki devotes her life to empowering others to move toward racial reconciliation. Using music, love and conversation, her work takes on many different forms to accomplish one goal; unity. Through her speaking engagements, consulting, concerts, workshops, and by the development of a curriculum, she strives to train people to engage in conversation around race.

Nikki's audience is primarily people of faith; churches, faith-based organizations and communities, but she also shares her passion with secular organizations, helping them to strive for unity. Adults, young adults of high school age, faculty and staff teams have benefitted immensely from her teaching on culturally competence.

I was so young when my father died that I don't remember anything about him. My mom and dad were married a few years before I was born. I was one year old when he died in a car accident. He was twenty-six. It was just my mom and I for the next three years until she met the man who became my step-father. They married and he raised me as his own. He was the only father I have ever known. I called him "Dad."

Though we were all African-American, my mom's side of the family and my step-father's side of the family couldn't have been more different. This created an interesting tension in our home and we often found ourselves at odds with one another. I didn't understand it until I got older. It was then that I could clearly see it for what it was. We were a bi-cultural family.

My mother's side of the family was very open and welcoming, so there was always a diverse group of people in our home. A white woman was my mom's best friend. I have known her my entire life. We always had friends from the deaf community and people living with other disabilities around. There was a family from India in our close community. We would go to dinner and even vacation with many of our friends. It was just a beautiful multi-cultural world on my mom's side of the family. I felt like I "fit" there. I belonged.

Most of my step-dad's side of the family grew up in the city in a different kind of neighborhood than I did. I soon learned that their experience in the city was totally different than what my mom's side of the family experienced in the suburbs.

The strong cultural tension between the two families had a huge impact on me personally. I never felt like I was "black enough" on my dad's side of the family. It created a little bit of a complex for me growing up. I remember my step-dad talking to me about his desire for me to concentrate on having more black friends when I was in middle school. I thought that was the strangest thing I had ever heard. I wasn't thinking of my friends as being White, Asian or Black. They were just my friends.

Apparently, for some people in my family, I wasn't measuring up to what it meant to be a black person. According to them, I spent so much time with my white friends that I even "talked white." I was completely confused about what that even meant. I was just being myself.

My extended family even questioned the kindness of my teachers at school. I was told that my teachers were only nice to me because my friends were white but I didn't believe that to be true.

If I would date a white boy every now and then, my biological father's side of the family would freak-out. They would strongly suggest that I was "losing myself." But I found that I identified and felt more comfortable around the white culture. It was familiar to me, and became a safe place where I didn't get judged.

Though I was aware that there was a Black-White issue for many people, it never really felt like it applied to me. I understood what it meant to be black in America but on my mom's side of the family, we never talked about our differences. We just enjoyed having a diverse group of people in our lives.

My mom was the most significant influence in my formation. She is an incredible person in every way. She has deeply loved and encouraged me, and has always appreciated me for who I am. Her joy has been a constant source.

The person I am today is really a result of my mom and her side of the family. My drive for education, my accent, dialect, everything comes from them. I am so very grateful for their consistent love for me growing up.

An early exposure to the arts contributed greatly to my love of music. I remember always loving music and have been singing my entire life. Dance was highly included in my interests. I expressed my talents in plays and other musical performances in school. In middle school, I also played an instrument.

Throughout life, my happiest memories have been of the creative collaborative processes I have engaged in with other people. Creativity breeds and forms community. Most of the environments I have been in, because I am a performer, have been racially diverse and inclusive. I am grateful for that because I am very comfortable around all races, ethnicities, and gender orientations. Music and community are life giving to me.

I was not raised in a church-going home. There wasn't any animosity toward the things of God, it was just absent in my life. I remember visiting a church once or twice on a holiday, with my grandmother but this didn't become part of my life until much later. I became the first Christian in my family when in high school.

When I started playing on the volleyball team in high school, I met a girl named Laurie who changed my life forever. I had never met anyone like her before. There was much joy emanating from her presence. I didn't know what was going on with her but I knew that I wanted what she had. We developed a close friendship, and she introduced me to Young Life. I started going to meetings, bible studies, and retreats. It was there that I heard the Gospel for the first time. It made sense to me, so it was then that I started following Jesus. When I returned home from that first life-changing retreat, my mom was concerned because she believed that I joined a cult.

Her response was, "You did what while you were away?"

After that retreat, I started attending a church and between that and the Young Life meetings. I was really discipled. I had never even read the bible before, but my Young Life leaders took me under their wings and helped me to grow.

My days in high school were very full, filled with basketball, volleyball, music, dance and Young Life.

There were a few other sports that I attempted to play in high school without much success. I was so terrible at tennis that I didn't last more than one semester. I was so bad, that when it came time to have a match with someone, I would go across the net and say to my opponent, "Can't we just say that you won?" I also made an attempt at softball, thinking I was going to pitch. I failed at that as well.

When I went to college, I started attending a church on my own, and it was there that I was able to see how music and faith were connected. I didn't have any faith background so I didn't know that Christian music even existed. I had never heard any hymns. There were no hymns in my house. It was a whole new world for me.

I went to Towson University for college, enrolling in the Music Education program. I was really more interested in performance but was told that I might want to consider education…to secure a job. It was supposedly impossible to get a job as a creative person. My father was the one most concerned about my future employment so I honored his wishes. I went into school as an education major knowing that I did not want to teach in the public school. The first semester of college, I was miserable.

The trajectory of my college career took a dramatic turn when Mr. Parker came into my life. Mr. Parker was a professor who taught one of my education courses. He was a wonderful man and boldly spoke truth into my life, one day, during one of his lectures.

He said to the class, "I have something to tell you. If you don't want to be a public-school teacher, you need to do something else. It is too hard out there to do otherwise. If any of you want to talk to me afterwards, let me know."

I immediately raised my hand to speak with him. That day, he told me that if I wanted to sing and be a musician, I needed to be a Music Performance major.

"You can get a job. There are many possibilities for work. You just can't teach in the public-school system," he said.

I really didn't want to teach in public school so after that semester, I changed my major to Music Performance. It was the best thing that I ever did. Thank you, Mr. Parker.

I anticipated this was going to be a problem with my step dad. So when I told him I was changing my major, I explained that I was miserable. I needed to do this and I knew exactly what I wanted to do with my life. I didn't ask him how he felt about my change and I didn't stay around for any response, either.

I started playing instruments, as well as singing professionally. Voice was my primary instrument then but I also played piano and guitar. Recently, I just started to learn to play the bass guitar.

Since I grew up in a bi-cultural family, I was very aware of not only diversity, but how people think differently about diversity. When my husband, David, and I decided to get married, we expected that *most* people in our families would be fine with our interracial marriage. He is white. I did anticipate an objection from my step-dad, knowing his desires for my life growing up.

"Have more black friends," he would say.

We were also worried about David's grandfather's reaction. He was from the country in the Midwest. Both men were from a different generation so we expected our marriage to be a challenge for them. We were very surprised by their reactions.

David and my story is not a *normal* one. He actually asked my step-dad for my hand in marriage. I remember the day so vividly. David came to my house and went down stairs to speak to my step-dad alone. After they had spoken, David returned upstairs where I was waiting for him.

He was in tears and I was thinking, "Oh, no! What did my step-dad say?"

That's when David told me the news. My step-dad's response was a total surprise.

"Absolutely, I would love to have you as my son-in-law," he said.

We were overjoyed.

When I met David's grandfather in the Midwest, we connected on such a deep level that I became one of his favorite people, and he reminded me of that the remainder of his life.

We were very thankful for the reaction of our families. for the most part. There were a few members of my family that didn't understand my choice but it did not affect our decision.

It's interesting how most of the problems inter-racial couples have are other people trying to speak into their lives. Not each other.

I never really experienced much persecution in my life. I did have a good friend in high school who I suspected her mom of having a race problem. I felt like the mom was just waiting for me to do something that gave her an excuse to tell me that I couldn't hang out with her daughter anymore but that never happened. But I never experienced much direct persecution around my race, other than in my family. Honestly, there might have been things going on that I missed because my personality tends to look for the good in life. I may have been oblivious to it all.

When my husband and I were dating, we noticed that people stared but there was no outward animosity toward us. David would get the evil eye from black men and I would get the *you sold out* look from black women. Older black and white people would look at us and shake their heads. Then, there were young white people in their 20s and 30s that would look at us and give us the look like, *Well, that's interesting*. They were curious.

For the most part, my husband's experience has been of acceptance. It helps that he is a musician. The circles that we run in are very diverse. But I actually believe that my husband is more comfortable around black people than he is around white. He's just more comfortable around different cultures in general. I think that has helped with his not having much persecution.

So, most of what my husband and I have experienced has been minor, a small comment here, or a misunderstanding there. By God's grace, we really haven't experienced intense persecution.

It wasn't until I was married, and my husband and I started attending church together that I felt the full impact of my formation. Finding a church became a real challenge. We were an inter-racial couple and it was difficult to find a church where people didn't stare at us. I wasn't black enough for the black church. He wasn't white enough for the white church. We felt like we couldn't attend the Asian churches because we would really stand out. We couldn't go to the Latin church because we didn't speak the language. As an inter-racial couple in 1997, we felt like we didn't belong in any church…even in the house of God. It was blindingly obvious that churches were segregated and we didn't feel welcome as a couple. Trying to find a church home was much more difficult than we anticipated.

We made the decision to not have children because of this experience. We thought about the fact that if we would have children, could our little "caramel" kids even go into a church to hear about Jesus? Would the other kids be kind and welcome them? Would they be asked the question, "What are you ?" These are the things that inter-racial couples think about when they go to church. Whose culture has to be checked at the door?

When we started attending our current church, it was the first church we had ever seen that was racially integrated. The longer we stayed at the church, the more we realized how intentional the church was around issues of race and culture. Everything we saw from staging to video to preaching to music was all intentionally crafted to welcome inter-racial couples. This experience helped me to begin to understand and put words around my unique upbringing. I understood the great need for racial reconciliation.

In our world today, I believe that most people can understand the pain of marginalization, being misunderstood, or "pigeon holed" based on how they were created. Being in touch with that should drive us to compassion, but the problem I see currently is that many people have amnesia. They have chosen to forget about the pain experienced with exclusion and marginalization.

As far as the church world is concerned, I am amazed at how homogeneous the Body of Christ is. The obvious nature of the way that people are siloed is what drives me to do reconciliation. I spent twenty-two years attending a multi-cultural church that was intentional about diversity. Seventeen of those years was as a worship leader/pastor. It was a privilege working in such an environment.

Every decision that I made as a leader was seen through the Jesus of the bible asking the question, "Does this make people feel seen culturally?" Seeing the impact that this has on a human heart is what drives me. It doesn't take much to make people feel seen.

I believe the church is starting to wake up and be more aware, asking the right questions about diversity. In this season of my life, with the work I am doing, I feel like God has called me, "for such a time as this," to step out of ministry and share what I have learned about building multi-cultural leaders, ministries, and organizations. This has become a stewardship issue for me, as well as a compassion issue. I am compelled to bring it forth.

The problem with many churches is that they don't know how to begin to become a diverse church. Churches don't have all the answers to dealing with pressing issues and that prevents them from moving forward. Fear of change is a huge factor. It's really difficult for white American churches that have been historically white to become diverse. It's hard for dominant culture churches to believe that they need to learn something. The first step is realizing you don't know how to move forward and the second is to ask for help. That is the hardest part.

One of the challenges to change is when a church is mostly one culture and they are saying that they want to be a diverse body but the people making the decisions on how to do that are from one culture and one ethnic group. This makes change impossible.

In my line of work, I help organizations learn to empower people and diversify the voices. Strategy is not the only solution. There must be strategy and philosophy behind the climate change. Its takes people working together every single day to make positive change happen.

The most important lessons I have learned are many. One that I am really embracing right now is to be myself, particularly in my work. The tricky thing about doing racial reconciliation is pressing up against the narrative that is told to my people group now.

I hear, "You don't have to help anybody. You don't have to tell anybody any stories. You don't have to teach anybody anything. You are tired. Let them figure it out for themselves or 'google' it."

For me, I can't do that. That's not what I have been taught. I don't carry around a lot of racial baggage. I am sure there are some deep-seeded things that come up once in a while but for the most part I am unburdened. Because of the way I grew up, the neighborhood I grew up in, I haven't had the oppressive experiences that many of my people group have had. I believe that

I have been designed by God to be able to facilitate dialogue and learning between others because of my upbringing, the way I was formed. If I was to lean into the narrative that permeates my people group, I would probably not be doing the work of reconciliation. I need to be true to the calling on my life. I need to be who God created me to be.

When I was thirteen years old and committed myself to follow Jesus, all bets were off. There is a way that He asks us to do everything; in love, in sacrifice, and with peace. I've tried to follow that life. I am compelled, no matter how bad my pain is. He has asked me to share my life and be generous with it. We are called to offer our lives to God. That may mean we experience challenges, suffering, for the benefit of others. If I believe my life is His, then I will keep forgiving, and I will keep believing the best in others, and I will keep trying to support and educate people. I'll deal with my own stuff with safe people.

The second lesson is, as a leader of anything, you have to learn to love people before you try to lead them anywhere. If you don't love them, you cannot earn their trust. I cannot accomplish my work if I don't love, operating in a state of frustration, anger and impatience is unproductive. This can happen with issues of injustice and in some arenas, it is appropriate to express it. In the area of reconciliation, you must care about all parties involved having a deeper understanding of one another so that they can live, walk, work and worship together.

Nikki believes that our work, our worship, and our dreams, flow out of who we are as people. We need to focus on becoming. Wisdom comes with knowing ourselves so it is critical to work on ourselves first. If we know who we are, all of our actions and decisions in life will be determined by our purpose. There are tools available to help each of us become the best version of ourselves through every season of life. Society will try to dictate our purpose if we let it, but we were designed for so much more. Find out what that is and run after it.

The Story of George

For the last six years, George has been pastoring a diverse church that he planted in the inner city. People from all backgrounds gather together, crossing the invisible boundaries that have been set by society. As he has served his church and community, he has seen firsthand how God can breakdown the divisions that plague our country.

I believe that when we open ourselves up to people who are different than we are, we get a broader vision of God. No one person can reflect all of God. It requires a combination of different backgrounds, socioeconomic levels, races and ethnicities to accomplish that goal. Having a church in an urban setting, which is often neglected and marginalized, has helped to broaden the thinking of the church and give a visible reality of the kingdom of God. It has been an encouragement to me to see this happen in significant ways.

There have been a number of moments, *fault lines* underneath our society, where a clashing of beliefs has caused *earthquakes*, unrest within our city. We had that happen in 2015 with the death of Freddie Gray, and again in 2020 with the death of George Floyd. We learn so much during times such as these. Our understanding is deepened, which makes us better equipped to speak into those moments, rather than about ideas. Knowing people and walking through their lives also reveals the things about us that need to be transformed.

My experience of growing up in the city as a black person has helped to build a special compassion for the people there. My family lived in the southern part of the city, a neighborhood defined by poverty and violence.

My mom raised four children on her own. I was the oldest, with two younger sisters and a younger brother. Mom always did an amazing job communicating love to us. Though I was named after my dad, he was never around. That was a weird dynamic for me growing up. I longed to have a dad in my life but really didn't know what I was missing.

My mom's commitment to her children early on helped to give me what I needed to communicate love to my family today. I believe that she is the reason I have a beautiful family of my own. I am so very thankful for my wife and three children. Raising three children with two parents can be a challenge at times. I don't know how my mom did it herself. I often call her to ask that question.

Being a single parent, my mom worked hard to support our family. She was employed with Social Security Services for a long time. Before that, she worked for ATT.

Life was not easy for us. We had some difficult seasons when my mom was in between jobs but she always persevered through. The food stamps helped somewhat but when she would get a raise at work, the amount of the food stamps would be decreased. It was difficult to get ahead. We always felt stuck.

We even spent three months in a homeless shelter. I was six years old at the time. Following that, we were able to get *Section 8* housing which is where I spent most of my upbringing.

My mom was a very good student and encouraged the same in us. She went to college but was unable to finish. This gave her a high expectation for her children to be successful in school. A few times a week, we would walk two and a half miles to the library. She taught us to value education and each of us went on to some type of higher education.

When I was nine years old, my mom's boyfriend moved in with us for the next ten years, most of my upbringing. He was an alcoholic and a gambler and was physically and verbally abusive. When he lost his job, he never got one again. He would occasionally do side jobs but never had consistent work.

Our home was wrought with many challenges with him there. It was difficult to come home from school to the abuse that he dealt out. He would belittle us about what we couldn't do and why we couldn't do it. Over and over, he would spew his negative comments about us, every single day. We had no safe place.

Mom's boyfriend would also tease us unmercifully. He would sneak into our bedroom on a school night after we had fallen asleep and tickle our feet, waking us up. Then, he would hide. He did this over and over throughout the night. We would wake in the morning exhausted from our sleep being interrupted. He would be sound asleep when we went to school.

This caused a barrier in my siblings and my relationship with our mom. Why wasn't she protecting us? If we did say anything to her about it and he found out, he would tease us about that. It was so dysfunctional.

We were not the main focus of my mom's boyfriend's abuse. Though he never hit my sisters, my mom was often a target of his anger. There was a tension for me to know whether to intervene when this happened. I was afraid it was going to escalate into a situation from which we could not return. Mom did not want us to come to her defense. She did not want us to get into trouble with him.

One night, however, I did intervene. I remember being awaken by my siblings because my mom and her boyfriend were fighting.

“Wake up, wake up! Tony is yelling at Mom,” they said, afraid of what was to follow.

My first thought was, “Why are they waking me, this happens every day of our lives. This is not any different.”

I got up, half asleep, and walked into the room where they were arguing.

As I entered, Tony said, “What are you going to do?”

He slaps me and I fall to the ground.

I remember thinking to myself, *Why did I even come in here?*

That moment sticks with me because I remember my siblings being so frightened and I wondering why I walked into the room. But I realized that my presence there made the fighting stop. I was thirteen when this happened.

This emotional turmoil continued in our home the entire time that Tony lived with us.

My siblings and I responded to the turmoil by drawing closer together. We were the only ones that we could depend on for many years.

As we got older. it was difficult for my mom to be as present with us as she was when we were younger. Work prohibited that for the most part, but the volatile relationship with her boyfriend made it easier for her to be away. She couldn’t just come home from work and talk about school with us because other *issues* demanded her attention.

The physical abuse finally stopped when I was fifteen. My brother and I were athletes and had gotten much bigger and stronger and could defend ourselves. But though the physical abuse had stopped, the verbal abuse continued. I never believed that verbal abuse was real until it happened to us. This took a toll on us and it continued until I went away to college.

My siblings and I have had lasting effects from the abuse-filled life we lived. We responded to it differently. I probably lean to the side of forgiving too easily. I learned at an early age to be a peacemaker, whenever possible. It was my way of coping. My brother was more of a fiery prophet. When things were not right, he would use all that he was to stop it. Though we were completely opposite, my brother and I worked together to accomplish the same goal, to stop the abuse.

Years later, as I reflected on my mom’s choice to stay in such an abusive relationship for so long, I began to understand her humanity. I realized that she must have had so much disappointment and heartbreak in her life to live in such a way. Though she rarely talks about it, I believe that she is disappointed in herself for allowing so much chaos in not just her life but in ours.

The irony of it all is that, many years later, I unknowingly planted a church in the same neighborhood that Tony lives. One day, our paths crossed as I was going to a bible study. I was walking down the street and saw this man in a wheelchair. We walked right past each other and I thought to myself, *This man looks so familiar.* Later, I realized who he was.

I have seen Tony a few times since then and we have had several conversations. I forgive him.

One day he said to me, "You have grown up to be a great man, a husband and a great dad."

I thought to myself, *No thanks to you.*

My brother would probably not even talk to Tony if he ever saw him again. He would prefer to fight him and rightly so, a response of righteous anger. He is not afraid to push back when he feels he is unjustly treated.

Despite all I had been through, I believe that I have become the person God intended me to be. As a child, I struggled with my faith. How could such a good God exist amidst such a difficult reality?

Church was foundational to my upbringing. My mom had us in church every Sunday. She was the youngest of nine children and her family attended the same Presbyterian church we did. My grandmother was the matriarch of the church, as well as of our family. We participated in everything possible; choirs, youth groups, ushers, acolytes. Our family had a great presence there.

When I was sixteen, I started preaching at the church. A year later, I began to question the inconsistencies that I was experiencing. I remember having this conflict of faith within me as I heard and preached about the good news on Sunday, then going home, I experienced a different life from Monday to Saturday.

My life was mixed with a deep love for my mom and siblings, with questions of why my mom's boyfriend was allowed to continue to abuse us, to great hope and joy connected with the church. It was confusing. Why was the work at church not changing our experience in the rest of our world?

After a time, I began to have no hope, and could not envision a future for myself. When there are so many obstacles around, you don't dream about ever reaching forty years old. You just hope that you make it to eighteen. When I finally passed eighteen, I thought, "Well, let's see how far I can go."

I attended the public elementary school. This was a time of life filled with much growth. Academics were a real challenge for me. I remember thinking so little of myself. I tried to improve but continued to lag behind. But I also experienced a season of hope there. I believed that life would get better.

I hated middle school. The school was filled with kids that had never been promoted to high school and that were older than me. They were much bigger than everyone else and let us know that. Middle school felt very unsafe because of these bullies. My daily goal was to avoid any fight with them. When that would happen, it was a very good day for me.

I really can't say that I learned much in middle school. I remember thinking that my toughest class was Health. We would go to class and the teacher would tell us the chapter in our textbook we were working on that day. We would proceed to rewrite the entire chapter. That was the class. We thought the teacher was so tough because we would leave class with hands that were tired and cramped. It took me years later to realize that we really weren't learning anything.

I loved sports but only played football for one year in middle school. I loved everything that came with playing sports; the discipline, the team comradery and the encouragement to excel. It was a place where I could shine.

At a certain point in middle school, we had to decide where we would go to high school. We had a choice and were told to provide a list of three possible schools. My top school was the one that my cousin attended. He was a little older and I knew he would keep me safe there. After I had filled out the paperwork, a counselor came to me to discuss my choices. She told me that I had the grades to go to any high school I desired, suggesting the most elite high school in the city. I applied and was accepted. If it wasn't for her, I would have never taken that chance.

Growing up in the environment that I did made me choose my friends according to safety. I had friends who I knew could keep me safe. If you are alone, you are not safe. I chose friends that I could get along with but safety was the primary concern.

Going to high school distanced me from the dangers of the community. I have many friends who are no longer with us anymore. That saddens me and makes me wonder how I am the one still alive.

The transition to high school took me from knowing all that was going on in the streets and how to stay safe, to having an hour commute to school and back. I left early in the morning and played sports at night. Time alone kept me off the streets. Though I still kept the friendships, I was no longer attached to what was happening there.

High school was a different world for me. Everyone was expected to go to college after graduation and lived their lives accordingly. They were focused, worked hard and studied. They didn't rewrite chapters from a book. As a result, my thinking about my future changed and I started to think about college, too.

I began to have hope for a different future that I never expected to have. I didn't know what my future would be but I knew what it would be if I didn't *swim*. I was afraid of that life so I worked as hard as I could to rise above it. I thought, well, even if I end up back in the streets, at least I will have tried to succeed.

I played football in high school. A month before school started, I practiced with some friends that were going to the same school. They helped me with technique and when school started, I had made friends with some of my teammates. There were many students that were much better than me but I didn't know what else to do. I had never been afraid to take a risk, so I went for it and made the team. The challenge of playing football was the unfamiliar. I was afraid. Most of my teammates knew one another because they were from the same communities and had played football together for years. I was the new kid. They were also from the wealthier communities. Very few were from poorer areas like I was. There were only two or three of us in the entire high school from the southern part of the city. This was a different world for me.

I have always been a quiet person by nature and that continued as a high school student. I worked diligently at academics and played hard at football, giving everything I had. What did I have to lose? People took notice of my determination and focus and they began to respect me.

I had a conversation with a one of my teammates with whom I have remained friends years later, and he reminded me of the first time he saw me in high school. The school colors were blue and orange and all of the football players wore blue helmets and orange facemasks, except for me. I had a blue helmet and a green facemask. That was all they had left. I really stood out but I loved the game and made some close friendships as a result. My friend also told me that I really was cheesy and he wasn't sure of the kind of player I was going to be. He began to respect me when he saw that I was an aggressive player. He said with laughter.

It was humorous that the students at my high school thought I was tough because of where I grew up. "Why don't you teach us how to steal a car?" They would say.

"I don't know how to steal a car!" I'd respond with a laugh.

Where I came from did carry some. They thought I was tougher than I really was. It was a rough neighborhood but that was not who I was.

I got into one fight my freshman year and no one bothered me the remainder of my time there.

Academically, I struggled my freshman year and into the beginning of my sophomore year. So much so that I thought I was going to be asked to leave the school. It was the first time in my life that I had to do school work at home. I didn't have to work in middle school. I use to get easy grades without any effort. High school was a culture shock and I needed to learn how to study. I worked hard to adjust to the new academic culture. It was then that I began to realize that if I did school work at home, the school day would go much smoother. School became much easier.

I didn't share my struggles with my mom. She had enough to deal with.

I was deeply insecure in high school and shy by nature so I didn't date very much. I had "no game." I didn't have good clothes and the ones I did have had holes in them as did my shoes. There was not much confidence in me. I did have my first girlfriend when I was a sophomore. She was the only girl that gave me attention. Our relationship lasted about a year. That was it!

My junior year, I began to understand for the first time that I was smart. Studying at home paid off and I started getting all A s. I began to thrive in the classroom and in athletics and my last two years of high school were a complete success.

I entered college the fall after graduation from high school, playing football and majoring in Nutrition. My goal was to become a professional football player, make millions of dollars and get out of poverty.

Most of my schooling had been in a black community. High school was somewhat diverse but when I got to college, I experienced serious culture shock because the school was predominantly white.

While there, I remember being amazed at the money that most people had. Several of the freshman had cars and only went to college because their parents promised to buy them one if they would go.

It was a small school so they did not give athletic scholarships and I attended there wondering how I was going to be able to stay. I went to this particular college specifically to play football. I knew that I couldn't afford it. My concern for my financial situation brought me into a conversation with my coach.

His advice was, "Take out as many loans as you need. You can pay it back later. You'll get a good job afterwards."

After my first semester, I went back to my coach to tell him I wasn't going to be able to come back the following year because of the cost.

He said, "Come back, and we'll work something out."

He sent me to the Bursar's office, two weeks after school had started second semester. A teammate told me that whatever they ask of me in that meeting to just say "Yes."

I went to this meeting expecting my coach to help me out, and the Bursar said, "Okay, you still owe this amount of money and this is the payment plan. Can your family do five hundred dollars a month?"

I knew my family couldn't afford that but I said yes because my teammate told me to just say yes. I was really disappointed because my coach misrepresented himself and really didn't help me, nor did he have the authority to. I agreed to the terms and got a credit card to pay for my books.

I was able to get some financial aid but it just wasn't enough to keep me there. I left the school after the first year but it took me years to pay off the debt from that one year of college. I would have been in deeper debt if I would have listened to my coach.

I left school frustrated because my wellbeing had not been taken into consideration. I was an eighteen-year-old kid. I returned home and enrolled in the community college.

Shortly thereafter, I transferred to a university nearby to study religion. The school was originally founded in 1867 to train men to become ministers. Overtime, religion became a very small part of what they did. Because the religion classes were only in the evening, and I had football in the evening, I could not pursue that major. My goal continued to be getting into the NFL, so I needed to choose a major that would support that goal. Because I cared about health, I chose to get a degree in nutrition.

My sister had taken a different path then the rest of my siblings, getting involved in Intervarsity on her college campus and her life was changed. She reached out to my brother and I to tell us about it. I was finished with the church and with God by that point. I had been in leadership roles in the church and found that it did nothing to help my situation at home. Church was all about numbers; the amount of people and the amount of money. But when my sister informed me that she had signed me up for a conference, completing the paper work and payment, I said I would go.

So, in my early twenties, I boarded a bus for what I believed was just another conference. What I found was a significant encounter with Jesus that changed my life. The conference took place in Atlanta and was primarily black college students. All week, I remember hearing about Jesus. I knew there must be a hidden agenda, waiting for them to ask me to join some organization and ask me for money but they never did either. The message was about the love of Jesus. They were just regular people. I hadn't seen people have a genuine relationship with Jesus like that before without any requirements; shirt and tie, sit in this box, and behave a certain way. This week was about a relationship. The pivotal moment for me was realizing the longing in my heart. All I ever wanted was this Jesus, to know God in a personal way. As a young man in the depths of grief, frustration, and despair, I didn't need to be attached to an organization. I just needed to know that God was real and near. That transforming moment summed up to one thing; *If Jesus is real than Jesus is all I need.* I didn't need a denomination. I didn't need to pay church dues. I just needed Jesus. That moment is what shaped my faith.

When I returned to college after that transforming week, I wanted to begin to work out my faith on campus. Many of my friends believed that they were on campus for a reason, so we started bible studies and doing events, allowing our influence as athletes to have an impact on campus. Those were some of my best years of ministry. We just loved students. Every athlete on every team was our ministry focus. I developed an identity as a student athlete there and everyone knew about my faith. Our group developed respect from the faculty and our peers, as they saw the work we were trying to accomplish on campus.

I felt compelled to go tell others about the love of Jesus. I was drawn to people in hard places because that's where I had been. If Jesus is who we say He is, we should be able to go to those hard places and He goes with us.

I was twenty-one years old at the time and it took a number of years for it to evolve, for me to develop a bigger perspective of God's heart toward society. I thought I understood about individual transformation but I wondered what it looked like for a society. I wondered, *What does it look like to have societal transformation for justice to occur?*

It took ten more years of personal transformation before I realized my part in societal transformation; walking with Jesus, feeling like my personal life was transforming, loving, serving with purpose.

When I graduated from college, I worked for *The Fellowship of Christian Athletes*. I started in leadership there while I was still a student in college. It was not a financially lucrative position, but I felt a call to give myself fully to ministry. I worked for FCA for three years.

I spent most of my life in the African American community so I never really encountered many issues with class and race. Our all-black community only had one grocery store where everyone shopped. There was very little investment in our community. I never experienced persecution because I stayed in my place, never stepping outside of my community.

My mom would sometimes talk to us about what the world was like outside of our community but we really didn't talk about racism. Most of our lives we were only around black people so it wasn't necessary. It wasn't until I got older that I would get more feedback from family members about areas where I might encounter challenges.

Once I began to go into other environments, I saw firsthand the marginalization that occurs in our society. I remember walking three miles with my family to a better grocery store than the one in our neighborhood and being shocked by the treatment we received. One very rainy day, we were walking back with our groceries and a car deliberately drove into a puddle of water along long the street to splash our family. As it happened, I thought, *Who would intentionally do that?* We were already wet from the rain but now we were drenched. It was so degrading. We knew we were in the area of the community, *across the train tracks,* where we needed to be more cautious but we had never experienced anything. I realized that this was only happening because we were in the white part of town.

This began a process of reconciling my faith with what I was experiencing in the world. This deeper understanding took about ten more years.

I have remained very close to my extended family. We got together every other weekend just to celebrate life and still do today. Our family crosses different socioeconomic levels and classes; some people are very financially successful and others are not. Then, I have some cousins that were poorer than we were and more in the streets. Life has been more difficult for them. There is every level in between, as well.

There were many ways that our family supported us during the early years. Without their help I may have missed some of life's special moments. In high school, I would never have been able to afford to go to the prom but some of my cousins and aunts pitched in to help me get attire and money so I could.

I still wonder if our extended family knew about the other challenges in our life. Did they know about the abuse going on in my family? If they knew, why didn't they do anything to help us? We needed their help. I wish that someone would have stood with us in some way. We were all alone.

Despite some of the challenges in life, there were many things that helped to build compassion in me. I remember when I was nine years old waiting outside a building while my mom went in to get free food for our family because we didn't have any at home.

As I sat outside waiting, an older woman approached me to say, "You have beautiful eyes. Has anyone ever told you that?"

I responded to her kind compliment with "No."

This moment really stuck with me because it was the first time someone saw past my "lack of" and acknowledged something in me that was positive. I don't know who that woman was to this day but she profoundly changed my life. It was so encouraging for someone to stop to affirm me.

There have been a number of experiences in my life where someone saw in me something that had never been called out before. Whether it was my teacher who encouraged me to go to the best high school or a stranger complimenting my eyes, it all helped to affirm who I was and it put me on a journey that I may never have traveled otherwise. It is like receiving a cold cup of water in a desert. It comes with little cost to the people who offer it but it can have a profound effect on someone's life. These life experiences have helped me to thrive. When people meet you in those moments and respond with love, it changes you forever.

I met my wife my last year of college. I was attending a very diverse contemporary church at the time and she was as well. This was my first exposure to a community of people from different backgrounds. I got to know my wife there and she also volunteered with FCA. We both had a heart for our city.

My wife and I are from entirely different back grounds. She was born and raised on the west coast in a very affluent family and I, on the east coast and poor. My wife is very fare skinned and I am African American. The Lord had been working in her heart to care about people in the city and appreciate diversity. As we began to work together, we had many conversations about how we could minister to the people in the city. That shared purpose created a bond between us and we fell in love.

I knew she was the one for me, but I still lived in a pretty rough neighborhood and I wasn't certain she could handle that. But she wanted me to read this book by Henry Nouwen, who I had never heard of at the time, and she brought it to my house at night. I thought to myself, *This white woman came to my house at night. She is serious!* Her willingness to be present in the neighborhood and with people who the world was saying she shouldn't be around, attracted me to her.

We had an interesting response to our becoming a couple. I wasn't sure how my family was going to respond when I first brought her home. When I told my mom and one of my sisters about our growing relationship, they were fine with it and loved her from the beginning. All of my family attended our wedding with joy.

Her family was a different story and more of a challenge. It was anticipated that they would not like that fact that I was black. This was my first exposure to wealthy white people and I wanted to understand them. Some of the conversations with her father, early on, were not the easiest of conversations. My response to conflict and desiring to be one who understands, was challenged. They had some preconceived ideas about me as a black man that we talked through. They grew to really love me. Though they believe that I am an exception rather than a part of the black community.

My journey took me on staff at an evangelical church in the suburbs, though we had always lived in the city.

We felt called to the city and wondered for a while why we were called to a church in the suburbs for so long. When the time was right, we made the decision to plant a church in the city that we loved. There was a tension between my having *made it out* of the poverty of the city, and now I was choosing to go back. Is that what life is all about? But, when I would watch the news, I would feel like whatever was happening in the city was happening to me. I just couldn't disassociate myself from the city. If people were hurting there, I wanted to be there to help them heal.

We, also, had our family to think about. The move would be difficult enough but our children were biracial and that in itself had some challenges. But we trusted in the Lord to care for our family and went forward with our dream.

My life was pretty crazy growing-up and mother always said to me, "You are not mine. I have given you to the Lord."

That has been so deeply embedded in me that I trusted that the Lord would care for our children. They had two great parents raising them, and He would help us navigate through life.

I don't want my children to, when they come up against the realities of the world, have to redefine who God is. I want them to live in community with people who are from all different backgrounds. There are issues in the world that they don't know about yet, but there are people in their lives that have been touched by those issues. When they begin to understand them, my hope is that it will be through a lens of love.

There have been many moments that my children have come to me to discuss something they have heard about an issue. I remind them that the issue does not define them. It is part of their story. I want love to shape their vision for someone, not the issue itself. That is my hope.

My children's life is unique. Where our church is very diverse, my children are often in all white and all black environments. As they are growing older, we are beginning to discuss racial and socioeconomic challenges that people live. They have experienced all of these spaces. The most misunderstood my children feel is when they are in some predominantly white spaces where they, at times, feel looked down upon. That is heartbreaking.

Our church planting efforts have had mixed responses. For the most part, the people from our former church could understand God's call for us and many did follow us there. In our current church community, whenever I am encountering teenagers and young adults, they can't understand why I have chosen to be there. Why would I come back to the city?

"Why are you here? You have a college degree. You have a family," they would say.

For those who have grown-up in the city, the goal is to get out. Others question the safety of my family there.

"Why raise your kids in a place like the city?" People would ask.

That often leads to good conversations. Even with people who question our motives, they see the work we are doing and begin to understand and appreciate why it is important to us.

I have learned that when you are part of a group of people that are marginalized, not seen or heard, you tend to have a perspective that views people differently. You know what it feels like to be left out. This helps you to be sensitive to those who are being excluded and you have the opportunity to bring them into community.

People look at life from several different perspectives. There is the *entitlement mentality*; I should have this or that. I should live this long. I should be able to see my kids graduate. Then, there is the opposite view. Anything that we receive in life, we are not entitled to having. But I believe that life is to be treasured. When you live your life not knowing how long you will be here, you receive everything as a gift; getting married, having children and watching them grow. When you see life as a gift, it leads to a heart of gratitude and thankfulness. That is the mindset that I want to hold onto and communicate to others.

I do have hope. My greatest hope is that I will get to see my family and our community live out their full potential in God.

I believe that our commitment to people will bring change in our world. For those who feel silenced and invaluable, I hope that they can see their potential and become the change in this world. People who are in position and power can help with support, but it is in giving voice to those who are voiceless that the greatest power is displayed. I want my life to be poured out in a way that empowers the *unseen*.

George became a minister because of the heart God gave him for the marginalized. He longs to convey God's love to those who are struggling. It meant a lot to him when people took time to extend lovingkindness to him growing-up. He wants to be present with others just like people were for him. The negative messages that people hear can be reversed regardless of what the world is saying. He wants to let people know how he sees God in them so they can have hope for a better future.

Forum about Racism

Every week, associates from all over the world *gather* to discuss the state of the 172-year-old multi-million-dollar company for which they are employed. The topic of discussion is usually the financial position but this particular week was different. In response to the latest social justice issues, the forum was about *racism*. The purpose of the discussion was not a political one but was cast as an opportunity to grow and understand more fully humanity itself. It was a time to understand how they, as a company, could create positive change in the society by reflecting an environment that is all-inclusive; embracing every race, ethnicity, gender and sexual identity.

It is not surprising that the CEO and President led the discussion. His leadership has not only created incredible financial growth in the company but has consistently encouraged a deep value for all human beings. He understands about how social attitudes can directly affect a person's life. He is an immigrant from the middle east that believes that, despite some of the imperfections, the United States is the greatest nation in the world.

The President and CEO explained at the commencement of the forum:

"In order to create positive change, we all have much to learn about each other. We need to become change agents in our society, promoting liberty and justice for all."

The panel included four African American leaders from their company, their colleagues, because they were known and had credibility. They each had been part of the company family for quite some time, one as long as seventeen years.

The discussion began with the CEO and President asking the larger group to take a minute to think about what was occurring in the country as of late in regard to racism.

"We all have a responsibility to be part of the solution," he explained.

The members on the panel were then asked to share about their experience with being Black in America.

Dana Started the Discussion

I would like to thank the CEO and President for allowing this platform and inviting me to speak.

When first asked to share about what it was like to be black in America, I really had to stop and reflect. What I realized was that being black in America is a full-time job. Blacks face discrimination and inequalities daily; discrimination in the church, in the grocery store, the library, taking children to school and in the workplace. We face discrimination more often than not. As a black woman in America, I live in fear every day, for myself and my family. If I speak up, I'm afraid I will lose my job, or the board position I hold. If I speak out, will I be judged by my words? If I stay silent, I could be ignoring the needs of black America? How will all this affect my family? Life can be overwhelming as a black female.

We talk about being "authentically you" in our country. But, when you look at it from the perspective of being a black leader in corporate America, being authentic is impossible. There are boundaries that were established many years ago by this country. These boundaries have been imposed based on past experiences people have had, biases that have been created over the years, and their upbringing.

I heard an NFL player call discrimination "contagious allergies." We develop attitudes according to how we are raised. We are shaped by those who raised us and develop the same attitudes about people and philosophy about life.

Corporate America has been very slow to change. They have not cared to understand the black community nor respected the journey they have traveled, and that makes it difficult. As a black female, I am constantly having people second guess my decisions and I am often challenged about my qualifications. If I speak up, I am an "angry black female." People often judge me before they even know that I have two college degrees. I am one of six children and was the first in my family to graduate with an undergrad and graduate degree and was at the top of my class. I worked hard while going to college and completely paid for my education. I hold those same standards for my children.

As a black woman, not only do I have to fight for my position in the home, I am forced to fight for my position in my community and the workplace.

Society has been designed to reduce black men in America since the days of slavery. If you listen carefully to some of the things that our past presidents and leaders have said through the years, you will begin to understand. J. Edgar Hoover suggested that the greatest threat to America was the unity of black men. He said that the Black Panther Party is "the greatest threat to internal security of the country," in an official memo in 1969. Because of that, black women feel like the world is against them, specifically because men are absent from our communities and our homes. They are feared in America, as leaders, and in corporate America. Black men are targeted in a system that is designed for them to fail, from a very young age.

The Criminal Justice System profiles black men unfairly so that a simple misdemeanor scars them for life and they are prevented from getting good jobs.

I fear for my son's safety every time he leaves the house. Will he be safe? Will he come back home to me on his own or in a body bag.

Educational injustices occur when the system directs many of our black children to become athletes instead of academically. I have a daughter who decided to become an engineer but because she was going to college on an athletic scholarship, she was forced to change her major so she could complete the program in four years and help them to get to the NCAA Championship. These are the things that we face in the Black community.

For me personally, I have had to become a "super woman" with an unseen cape. I fight to have the right position and posture in my work, my community and in my home. I fight to be qualified, to be understood, and to keep my family safe.

I strive daily to be authentically me, a black woman in America. I am a human being with feelings and I am a mother and a mentor to many people. I am a virtuous woman, educated and qualified. I am a single parent to black children and I take pride in building them up daily as the world tries to tear them down because of the color of their skin.

I am a black female American and I belong.

Michael was the Next Speaker

Opportunity helped to shape who I am today. I was not born in America but in the Caribbean, and became a citizen in 1992. My mom decided that she desired for her five children to have greater opportunities than what we were offered on a small Caribbean island so she packed up our family and moved us to America. I was ten years old. My mom had some role models that she could follow in her sisters who had made the move prior to the United States. My mother had hope, ambition and aspiration for her children. It has been a powerful experience for me growing up, a sense of pride and a sense that I live up to that risk that she took bringing us here. You may have wondered what motivates me. My mother has been a very large part of it.

I had boundless dreams at ten years of age and needed to learn how to be a proud American. Not only did I need to learn how to be an American but I needed to learn how to be a black America. There were rules there that I did not have the benefit of learning from a dad, uncles or my grandfathers. I had to learn it on my own.

I began to discover the nuances of life in America early on. Every opportunity that I went after, even if I got it, could be taken away from me in an instant, so, I became fearful. Of the natural instincts of "fight or flight," I chose flight, avoidance. I began to second guess myself and doubt my dreams and passions. I questioned if the system was too big for me to succeed. It was difficult being an exception. I felt like I was the only different one in the room.

When I was thirteen years old, I began to realize that I was not as free as I had thought. One afternoon, I was in my yard watering plants and I heard some kids next to the playground behind our property. They were talking about how they had just stolen someone's bicycle. I remember thinking that that was so wrong so I went inside and called the police. I told them to come right away. I didn't want to look like the guy who "ratted out" the kids so I went back outside and continued watering the yard. The police came and asked me what I was doing in my yard. I told them that I lived there and they said I needed to go with them. I told them I was sorry but I was just watering the plants. They insisted and took me down to the police station. After repeatedly explaining that I was the one who made the call, they called my mother into the station. I had to apologize to the police for being a part of the situation.

I also remember a time with the police when they questioned me when I was out in my mom's Chevy S-10 Blazer SUV. It was the most prized car she ever owned and I was using it to pick up my friend and a pizza. We stood beside the car talking with the pizza sitting on the hood.

A man from an apartment above the pizzeria yelled to me to "get that pizza off the roof of the car."

I responded with, "Excuse me?"

He repeated his words a second time. In my innocence, I told him it was my car. I didn't even think about the implications of that. I learned much later the necessity for me to see myself through other people's eyes.

It is those moments that help you understand how you should react. There comes a point that you have to take a stand. You have to think about how you will create advantage for yourself. You must shield and protect your yourself wherever you are. It is important to be aware of the friends you choose, what clothes not to wear, and how you speak. Preparation is key. What will you do when you are in a situation that might have bad actors associated with it; police or friends? How will you react when the situation is unjust? You have to be quick on your feet with a response and dress to reflect the "part."

You must think about what you will teach your children to thrive in an environment that may prejudge them, to keep them safe. You may need to tell your child that he is at the age that he should no longer wear a hoodie because it might reflect something negative about his character. There is certain jewelry that should be avoided because it reflects a profile that you may not wish to be associated, to protect yourself. Even the music you listen too might set you up to be misunderstood.

What are my dreams? I dream that my son is able to raise my grandchildren in a world that does not require him to need to have the same conversation about staying safe, as I have had with him. I dream that he would never have reason to fear that his children won't come home at night, that they would make all the right choices and never encounter a bad actor.

I came across a photo of a beautiful little black girl holding up a billboard that says, "We said black lives matter. We never said ONLY black lives matter. We know all lives matter. We just need your help because black lives are in danger."

Dennis Spoke next from a Millennial's Perspective

My dad was in the military, so I traveled the world up until he retired. Being able to experience different environments overseas and in the U.S. gave me an interesting perspective of life. I had a very broad exposure to different cultures and types of people.

One thing that I noticed was that kids are naturally very perceptive. Even at age six, I was able to understand that there was something different about me. Because we moved so frequently, I worked hard to engage with people, trying to get to know them quickly. I didn't want to be that military child who had not lived anywhere long enough to develop friendships. I noticed that there were moments when my friendships came to an abrupt halt. I didn't know what I did but I knew that I was no longer able to hang out with certain people anymore. I just didn't understand.

As I got older, I began to realize the implications of that. I began to be profiled because of the color of my skin. I remember the first day it ever happened. The police stopped me and told me that I fit the description of someone they had been looking for. I was fourteen years old and was just walking in my very blended neighborhood. They realized I was not that person.

When I was in high school, I was coming home late at night after a show with some of my friends, and we were stopped by the police because we fit the description of people they had been looking for. We were in my neighborhood. This was where I lived. Why did I feel like it had become a place where I was not allowed to be? They once again realized that we were not those people. How can this happen so often?

After enough of those experiences, fear begins to creep into your daily life. I saw what happened to young black men and knew that one misstep, could put me in the same fate that they experienced.

This is 2020. Slavery supposedly ended many years ago but we are continuing to be held hostage by preconceived notions. We are still dealing with the same marginalization.

My dad called me last week to check in on me. He just wanted to hear my voice. I was reminded of my conversations with him about the importance of being aware of my responses when injustices occur. When I am being unfairly questioned, I cannot react like a normal person does. It is human nature to try to escape when someone unjustly grabs you. When you are black, that response can cause you to lose your life.

My oldest son is five years old and when he asks me about the frustration and the protests that he sees on television, it breaks my heart to have to tell him but I do. I want him to be wise to the world so that he can keep himself safe. He asks questions like, "What did that man do?" Most of the time, I really don't know the answer. But I could tell him that innocent or guilty, it was in the man's right as and American to have a fair trial but he was denied that opportunity because of the way people responded to him.

When I wake up in the morning, I am excited about the impact I can have in my life; my family and my workplace, but I also live in fear. I live in fear that the normal things that I do may make me a target. If I am driving and change lanes too quickly, it might bring someone into my life who would misinterpret my behavior and does not have my best interest at heart.

It is sad that there are people all over the world that experience injustice because of the color of their skin. When you are continually shoved down, you begin to believe you are unworthy, and develop a poor view of yourself. Until leadership steps in to bring change and a deeper understanding, it will continue.

It amazes me that there are so many things that people are willing to accept and understand but they do not recognize the fear that people of color live with every day. I have experienced many injustices first hand. It is only because of the opportunities afforded me that I have been able to learn from them and live a fruitful life.

My passion and my purpose is about changing the internal perceptions about people of color. We need to open our minds and listen to one another. Conversations such as these need to happen. Avoiding them because you are afraid that you may offend someone is just wrong. People of color live with this every day. Change will only happen when we begin to understand.

The Last Speaker was Everett

I grew up in Mississippi in the mid-1960s, where you are trained at a very early age, to never look a white person in the eye, to look away out of respect.

I was trained to say, "Yes sir, Yes, ma'am. No, sir. No, ma'am."

Think about how that works in corporate America. In corporate America, you are trained to shake someone's hand with a nice grip and look them in the eye. This was the total opposite to how I was trained in Mississippi, just to stay alive.

Allow me to fast forward to when I had the opportunity to go to college. When I obtained a college degree, I felt really good about myself but injustice continued to reveal itself.

Our society went from Dr. Martin Luther King to Rodney King, to the knee to the neck of George Floyd. Each of these were a step backward for justice. The knee on George Floyd was a knee on every other person of color. Each felt what he felt and anyone that watched that video felt the pain.

Many people asked, "Why didn't the public do something to help George Floyd?"

If a person of color gets involved, there is a good chance that he will be shot.

I raised six kids and the first instinct I had when the protests began was to call each one of them to make sure they were all home safe.

"Please don't go out in the streets," I wanted to say.

But I didn't make those calls because some people need to march, some need to hold up signs, and some to donate money.

This was "de ja vu" for me. I had seen this happen with Dr. Martin Luther King, Rodney King, and now we are seeing it again. Change will not happen when you look the other way. We need to listen and understand what others are experiencing.

You can't help but see the injustice. This is a policy issue. The U.S. government came up with six trillion dollars to help everyone stay home during the pandemic. But every time there is a social program, like welfare, funds are easily cut. I would gladly pay $1,000 more in taxes every year for everyone across America to have healthcare. It's worth it to me. Everyone should have health insurance. Does it cost more money for people to not have it? Absolutely.

In Flint, Michigan, when they discovered that people were becoming ill from the water problem, the authorities knew it and looked the other way for a very long time because the majority of the community were black. But when more people became sick in Flint, it was a tax on the system. We've watched the same injustices happen over and over again.

As Americans, we need to vote into office those people who will represent and support all Americans, those who care about humanity.

Open conversations need to be had. For two hundred years, is the best slogan we have "Black Lives Matter"? Who are we telling it to? I know my life matters. If that is our best shot, it tells us that we have a long way to go.

It's a policy decision. We need as a people to agree and vote what we believe to be true. If we don't, we will never make any progress in race relations.

CEO and President Closed the Discussion

This is only the beginning of the conversation. Many more will need to follow. It is my hope that conversations such as these will bring lasting change.

Restoring Hope

By Carol Marchant Gibbs

A rhapsody of sweet voices dance across the clouds.

In unison, the birds' song announces the new day.

Their utterances speak of freedom to the captives, hope for the future, joy.

There is power in their song and it transforms us.

We wait with hope, oh Lord. Heal our world.

Chapter 3
Living with a Disability

Athletes Serving Athletes

Athletes Serving Athletes is a Baltimore based 501-C3 non-profit corporation whose mission is to elevate the quality of life for individuals with limited mobility, by empowering them to train for and participate in mainstream running events. This experience provides connections, a sense of community, and inspiration for people to lead healthy and active lifestyles. ASA athletes living with a disability are paired with able-bodied runners, most of which are aging and slow, to train and race in running events. The running and the racing is fun but it is really just a means to be part of a community. The benefits to the individuals living with a disability are significant in that they are connecting with people outside of their family and school groups. Inclusion is probably the largest benefit. All people have a need to belong. When you are living with a significant disability, it is difficult to be included in the community at times. In ASA, athletes are brought around great people that they might not ordinarily connect with. It allows the families, parents and caregivers to have a sense of community, as well. They meet people and it inspires them to know that they are not alone. Other families are experiencing similar difficult challenges. There's power in that.

Each athlete is paired with an ASA "wingman." They can be man, woman, young, old, fast or slow. ASA doesn't care about your pace. They care about your heart. It is clear that wingmen get more out of this then the athletes do. They experience "perspective reset." When you are around an individual with a positive attitude that has tremendous physical challenges, and they refuse to give up, having a burning desire to live life with purpose and passion, it is contagious. Wingmen, after being with some of our athletes and families at events, leave feeling extremely thankful.

The Story of Dave

Dave grew up playing sports throughout his life but he has never seen such an emotional impact for all people involved, athletes, families, or spectators, as he has with Athletes Serving Athletes. Even in the preparation for races, gathering, laughing training together is a powerful positive experience. Sports have a wonderful way of breaking down stigmas and creating a sense of community.

I grew up in a family that was unaffected by disabilities. My parents were from the city. We were healthy and there was no one in my immediate social circle affected by disabilities.

I played sports as early as I could walk. It was such a positive influence for me that this continued throughout my life.

I was fortunate enough to go to a catholic high school that focused on building scholars with character, men that would live for the sake of others. I continued my love of sports there.

When I went to college, I played lacrosse there, as well.

Even after college, sports were a large part of my life, but as the realities of living in the working world crept in, time for sports became less and less. I dramatically felt the loss. Sports had been very centering for me and when that was gone, I began to struggle.

When my wife and I separated, I became desperate and the gift of desperation, forced me to face my issues head on. Every area of my life was falling apart. I had two beautiful children that were trying to adjust to the changes in our family, and I no longer liked the person I was seeing in the mirror.

So, I focused on being a good dad to my girls. Being a good dad trumped everything at that point. The books I read about parenting talked about the incredible value of time. I really tried to spend as much time with them as I could. The small apartment I moved into made it possible for me to begin making a home for them when they were with me. I would pick my girls up from school, fix dinner for them and just hear about their day. It was the most important thing I could do.

I had a foundation of faith from an early age but I had strayed and my desperation drew me to God. I confessed the mess I had created in my life, a “fox hole” prayer, and I became obedient to God once again and began t attending church.

At the same time, I realized that I had allowed myself to get out of shape physically. Sports had been a large part of my life and I had neglected what had been foundational to my well-being. It became a refuge of encouragement to me. So that year, I made the decision to begin training to run the Baltimore Marathon. I was never a competitive runner, but I was an athlete and knew that committing to this would force me to train consistently. As I began to feel better physically, I expected that it would matriculate into other parts of my life.

During that time, I was inspired by the story of Rick and Dick Hoyt, a father and son from Boston, MA, who were involved in competitive racing. Rick was born a spastic para-pelagic, and after participating in one race at age 17, while his father pushed him in a wheelchair. He was captured by the chance to compete. He came home from the event and told his father that being in that race made him feel like he “wasn’t handicapped.” Dick, at age 36, had never been a runner but wanted to prove to his son and others that living with a disability did not prevent you from anything. They are still competing today, 43 years later.

I cried as I watched this incredible story and knew that I needed that in my life. So, I began to ask around to see if there was anyone providing racing opportunities for people living with disabilities in my area. After a two-year search, I realized that there was no one locally or nation-wide, non-profit or otherwise. If I wanted this to happen, I was going to have to do it myself.

I approached the William Baer School, which had been serving children with multiple disabilities for 75 years, to see if they believed that some of their students might be interested in participating in races. I introduced the concept by showing them the video of Rick and Dick Hoyt.

When asked the question about interest, they replied, “David, we have two hundred students. When do you want to start?”

As I drove down to the school in the city feeling so out of my element, my concerns were met head on by a beautiful oasis of love. The Baer School was incredible. I initially started working with five students.

It took about a year and a half to get our first athlete in a race, a 5 K. James and I ran our first race together, *Run to Remember.*

He absolutely loved the thrill of the race and a month later, we were at the Baltimore Marathon ahead of the athletes competing professionally. Some were just back from the Olympics. It was an amazing celebration. The mayor was there giving high fives to all of the athletes. People were jumping out of airplanes. There was so much excitement and we were right in the middle of it.

About a year later, as the vision began to take hold, I put a business plan together for starting a nonprofit focused on people living with disabilities participating in races. It was a real leap of faith but I felt called to do it. I had never done anything like this before but I had a good friend, who was a business man advised me. He said that the vison I had for ASA was going to take two years before I could even hope to get a pay check. I had a little bit of money saved and had gotten rid of all my debt so I willingly accepted the challenge. It was almost two years to the day that I began to see others get behind the vison financially.

It was a slow start but the momentum eventually began to increase. The first year we were incorporated, we raised $14,000, $9,000 of which came from spinning a money wheel at the Raven's game. The second year we raised $54,000. The third year we raised $105,000 then it was $152,000. I knew it was going to be a challenge but I didn't care. I thought, if this didn't work, I could always go get a job.

Twelve years later, after having started our program with one athlete, we now work with over a hundred athletes living with disabilities. Over two hundred have participated over the years and we have four hundred "wingmen" come alongside these athletes. We take part in close to one hundred races a year. Seven racing communities have been established throughout the county and city area.

ASA is a powerful experience for both the "wingmen" and for the athletes being pushed in wheelchairs. It changes you. I needed this experience more that the athletes needed me. It is not just a race but a relationship. An authentic connection is built between the athlete and the wingman. When you are running with a person living with a disability, you forget about yourself. The athletes get to participate in something that their physical bodies would have never allowed. Between the athletes, the wingmen, the relationships, the exercise, and the race, something incredible happens when all work together to create this experience. Freedom.

Families benefit immensely from the experience, as well. The racing events are fun and festive but it is more than the race itself. Friendships develop between athletes, wingmen, and parents. When others love our children, it is a gift. The parents have opportunities to connect with other parents and they love and support each other, as well their children. They get involved socially in other events outside of ASA, and offer advice about doctors. Their lives connect. Life is different for our families outside of ASA. It helps to know that there are other people that understand the challenges associated with raising a child living with a disability. It is an opportunity to feel "normal."

There are four pillars on which we build ASA. We desire that all that we do would be safe, authentic, consistent, and sustainable. But more than anything, we want our ASA families to feel loved and that they belong. We are a community.

My personal life has been incredibly blessed. I have four beautiful daughters and a son, ranging from age 20 down to 1½ years old, now. There is never a dull moment in my life.

I met my second wife, Sarah, ten years ago when we were introduced through a mutual friend. My friend thought she would be a great addition to the ASA team. We both played lacrosse and had many friends in common but had never met. At the time, Sarah was responsible for running all of the events for US Lacrosse. Sarah and I had lunch to discuss the possibilities with ASA. She loved the vision and what we were doing but she needed time to think about it. Sarah called a week later and said she was ready to come on staff as a volunteer.

That year, we were planning our first 5K event to raise money for the vision. Sarah came on board to chair the committee to make that happen.

Sarah and I became very close friends over the next few months and after six months, I decided that I had a crush on her. But I waited until after the 5K event to tell her. Our relationship mattered and I really didn't want to mess things up so after the 5K race, we went out to lunch and I told her how I felt. When I told her I had a crush on her, she replied, "That's wonderful. I am leaving to go to England for a year. I got hired for a job." Shortly thereafter, Sarah went to England to work for the *English Lacrosse Association.* While there, she ran the Men's World Lacrosse Championships in Manchester.

It was clear that despite her decision to leave, we did feel the same about each other, so we spent our first year of dating apart.

Fortunately, she did return a year later and continued to volunteer with ASA. We resisted actually working together for two years. Then, she came on board as the director of Operations.

ASA has been a success because of all the wonderful people who have served; employees and volunteers alike. Our greatest asset is our team of people. They are passionate about the cause, and are committed to giving all that they are to the vision.

I am thankful for the success of the ASA. I think I got my entrepreneurial spirit from my dad. I watched him as he ran his small auto repair shop. I knew there would be successes in a new work but I was not naive to the challenges. The purpose behind ASA is what drives me forward.

There is something about the "gift of desperation." When we are forced to reflect on our lives and our greater purpose, it changes us. It is easy to fall into living a life of mediocrity if we are not motivated to do otherwise. I have worked for large companies with great people but I never felt like I was living my purpose. I am thankful for how the vision for ASA has changed my life forever.

It is my hope that I would not let the occasional challenges of life discourage me but that I would press on to be faithful to all to which I have been called. I want to celebrate every joy in my life. I want to be a great dad, husband and executive director of ASA.

On celebrating our 10th year of ASA, one of our board members made a comment that said it all. "You won your first Super Bowl. Congratulations! Now what are you going to do?"

I thought a lot about that. What are we going to do? Is it ASA? Is there life beyond that?

At the same time, because it was our tenth year, Sarah brought a book to my attention, Brand Raising for Nonprofits. The book talked about the importance of communication and how difficult it can be. As a nonprofit, the first thing you need to know is how to communicate your vision well. I pulled out the original articles of incorporation and bi-laws, mission, vision and values, and proceeded to revise them. I discovered that they were vague and I wanted the documents to reflect what we had been experiencing.

Currently, ASA is in eight geographical areas, and we are serving people with all abilities. Our board president undertook the daunting task of leading a strategic planning initiative to evaluate our program. For three months, the board studied our program, talking to as many stakeholders as they could, in order to identify common themes. They created a forty-page document with eight main recommendations, charts, objectives, tasks, who was responsible for the tasks, and a timeline for completion. We had the document published and posted it on our website.

There were two main themes that came out of this study. The first was that we were only going to focus on running events and the training for those events. For ten years, we had been focusing on "multi-sport" events which included triathlons, biking, running, and swimming in some combination, and swimming. Training for those events was complex. But, as we grew, it became even more difficult and safety was being compromised. This led us to the decision to do running events only.

The second theme was the most difficult decision we had to make because it involved the community that we served. We decided that for our community to be safe, authentic, consistent, and sustainable, we had to focus on those people with limited mobility. Meaning, we would serve those who used one type of equipment, a racing jogger, pushed by an able-bodied person. We grandfathered in those who had been in the program to that point, but anyone beginning our program had to fall under that parameter. Our desire was to serve as many individuals as we possibly could while remaining true to our value to keep them safe. Safety was primary, and when you try to serve everyone, it becomes more complicated; engagement, equipment, storage and transportation of the equipment, and insurance. It was a very difficult decision to make. We feel that focusing on the things we can do well will ultimately allow us to serve greater numbers of people.

Currently, five out of the seven areas that we serve have a waiting list to receive athletes living with disabilities. We need two captains per athlete to make the ratio work. They are all volunteers.

Sarah is responsible for marketing, encouraging new people to engage. But, it's not as easy as it sounds. A background check is required for each person who becomes involved, and between that and training, it takes time.

I feel so passionately about what we are doing and what our team created, that I would like to see it in other areas. I am trying to be patient as I look forward to growth. I think we are about a year away from expanding to our eighth and ninth areas. We need to do things the right way so that we are poised for the next ten years.

Our greatest asset is our staff and I want them to stay around. It's important that they feel cared for. We are like family. The goals set for the organization are the same for them: safe, authentic, consistent, and sustainable.

Because this is a new concept and the need is great, people all over the country desire to set up a similar program. Where we can advise others on what we do, we desire to closely oversee each of the areas where we have responsibility. Establishing our program elsewhere is not something we are committed to do presently. Our desire is to create a program that is safe, authentic, consistent, and sustainable.

As Executive Director, I am challenged to be a better leader. I read a great book, Business Secrets of the Trappist Monks, that I found very inspiring. The author of the book was a successful business man that sustained an injury and spent some time in recovery at a monastery. He observed the success of the monks in their business endeavors and asked why. He discovered that their focus involved three values. The first was that each person desires to engage in a "transformational experience." Innately, inside of every person, is a desire to be transformed from being selfish to selfless. The second value was "authenticity." You can't fake being authentic. It takes commitment and hard work. The third was the value of serving in community. People need one another to thrive. I was extremely thankful to see that their values were consistent with what we had discovered in our evaluation of our organization.

Community has been a primary focus for us. Our athletes living with disabilities are sacrificing for the good of the community. Their commitment has been instrumental to transforming the lives of those who have come to serve.

ASA has transformed my life and brought my family together. My children enjoy going to races to connect with athletes. We are particularly close to one of the athletes that comes to our house often just to hold our babies. It is beautiful to watch the relationship between them grow. Two of my girls are older now and are attempting to change the culture in their school because of ASA. It brings tears to my eyes to think about the principal's response to one of my daughters when she went to sit with a student living with a disability at lunch. Her heart for others was so evident and I believe it is because of my children's exposure to people with disabilities. They are not afraid to engage with them in and outside of ASA.

Athletes Serving Athletes has created a community of people that have grasped the vision and supported all of the efforts from the beginning. That's pretty amazing when you are starting a nonprofit and the needs are immense. When the question was asked, "What do you need?" The answer that followed was "Everything!" and people didn't run away. They have been consistent in their support from the beginning. Some have even become board members. It is because of the community that the dream of ASA is coming true today.

The Story of Paul

Families of children with disabilities can potentially live very isolated lives absent the love and compassionate support of others. It is often those closest to them that care the most and take on that mantle of support. But what happens when a group of strangers make it their life's work to create athletic opportunities for those living with disabilities? Athletes Serving Athletes has made dreams come true by making what appears to be the impossible, possible.

My husband and I were beyond thrilled when we discovered that we were pregnant with twins in March of 2011. The pregnancy was as expected for the first seven months and as uneventful as a it could be when carrying twins. Despite my efforts to take care of myself, a routine ultra sound revealed that I was in labor at 28 weeks and had, simultaneously, developed severe preeclampsia, resulting in swelling and high blood pressure. The doctors attempted to stall the labor but I became increasingly more ill, making it necessary to deliver the twins by emergency c-section under general anesthesia. My husband, Charles, and a couple of family members were able to be present during the delivery, watching the birth through an observation window. The early arrival made it necessary for our young twins, Paul and Emma, to be immediately swept off to Neonatal Intensive Care, but they were both healthy.

I, however, was too ill to see my babies for the first day and a half. When I was feeling slightly better, my mother took it upon herself to locate a wheelchair and roll me to the NICU. Too weak to stand, I propped myself up to see the babies for the first time. They were beautiful and absolutely perfect. It was a very special moment.

All tests indicated that the babies were doing well. The brain scans were totally clear. They were both very small, as many twins are, Paul was 2lbs. 2 oz. and Emma 2lbs 7oz., but they appeared to be on a healthy course.

Over the next few weeks, Paul had more starts than stops, indicating some minor complications. He had problems with his bowels but for the most part, he was doing fine. Then, a few weeks later, tests revealed that Paul had developed a septic staph infection. He recovered quickly from the infection after a regiment of antibiotics. Simultaneously, Paul began to exhibit epileptic behavior. A Pediatric Neurologist examined him and concluded that he was just having some spasms. He was not worried. But, after a month and a half in the hospital, a second brain scan was performed that revealed extensive damage to the white matter of Paul's brain. It is believed that this is what triggered his brain damage but no one knows for sure.

Emma was thriving. Though she was born with a hole in her heart, which is not uncommon to premature babies, she was doing well. The hole did close up as she grew.

The babies continued to remain in the hospital until November. They were home before their actual due date of December 12. Emma was discharged a week before Thanksgiving, and Paul, the night before Thanksgiving. Other than the brain damage and visual impairment, Paul had no other issues.

From the beginning, the children's grandparents have been there to love and support us. Charles' mother, a former nurse practitioner in neonatal intensive care, has monitored Paul very closely, making all of his formulas and blended foods as he got older. My parents kept him company and entertained with the potty humor and silliness small boys enjoy.

The grandparents have been consistently encouraging, and are always excited to hear about what Paul is doing. They talk about how smart and very funny he is. It's encouraging when people say wonderful things about your child. They have been amazing.

But, if you would ask us who our greatest source of encouragement is, we would tell you that it is Paul himself. When you see someone with such a love of life and an excitement to do things, it really makes you want to help them experience the world.

A whole new world was opened up to us when a friend of Charles' from high school, Sue, recommended that we investigate getting involved in *Athletes Serving Athletes.* Sue is a runner and involved in the program as a

Wingman, pushing joggers in races. It sounded wonderful to them but Paul was only three years old and very small. We were concerned about how he would react to going off on a run with someone who he really didn't know well, so we waited.

After two years of waiting, when Paul was five years old, we reached out to *Athletes Serving Athletes* and they invited us to bring Paul out for a training run. Sue's son, Alex, was a high school student at the time and became Paul's wingman, and remained so throughout his high school years.

Alex is quite a remarkable young man. Many people shy away from the disabled community out of fear of not knowing what to do or say to them. Alex committed his time to giving back to his community by serving people living with disabilities. Alex was always kind, the youngest wingman in the group and very fast, so Paul loved running with him at every training run. Alex and Paul continue to be good friends despite Alex's attending college in Colorado.

Running has been a fantastic opportunity for Paul. From his first training run, he loved going fast and experiencing the bumps on the trail. He smiles the entire time. This far exceeded our expectations.

One training run led to another and before we knew it, Paul was entered into his first *Runfest.*

Athletes Serving Athletes' sense of community has touched our entire family. Not only has Paul benefitted from being surrounded by people who care about him, but the family has been lovingly embraced by the ASA community.

Each member of the family does their part to support Paul's participation in ASA. Charles and Emma typically take him to the training runs. On arrival, Paul is warmly greeted by his wingmen then ushered off to run. Emma and Charles spend their time riding bikes on the trail and connecting with other families while they wait for Paul to finish his training. So not only do the people involved in ASA know Paul, they also know Emma and have watched her grow up.

Charles has experienced ASA as an opportunity to feel like a typical family. In ASA, you are just one of the group. You are one of many families with children with disabilities sharing a common experience. There are many parents there that have been on this journey of caring for a child living with a disability for a very long time. They freely offer practical advice and encouragement.

I am not a runner but strongly support the races. I am not an early riser either, and the races are *super* early but the motivation to participate in such an incredible event is there and I presses through the early hour for the benefit of our family.

It is an uplifting experience going to a race. All of the ASA events are well organized and a joyful atmosphere surrounds the day. Athletes and parents are greeted enthusiastically and there is always time allowed for parents to talk prior to transitioning their children into their race joggers. I really enjoy connecting with people I have met at previous races and meeting new ASA members. We spend time talking about our children. Then the race begins. At the end of the race, I encourage Paul to thank those that have supported him with a big smile.

My husband and I are intentional about taking time to prepare and celebrate Paul's upcoming races and encourage others to do the same. They inform his teachers at *Maryland School for the Blind* so they can talk about the race with him. They have grandparents and other family members talk about the race, as well. Then after the race, they talk about how great the race was. It is an important event in his life and we celebrate every moment.

Paul has learned to love everything about the races. He loves it so much that I take him to races all over the state so he can meet different ASA communities.

We have experienced the kindness and compassion of the people of ASA as they have cared for our family. There have been times that I did not dress Paul warmly enough for a run and he would return from the run covered in jackets. The team gave up their coats to keep him warm. They have also been wonderful in their care of Emma and have included her in special ways.

ASA has a beautiful way of including people at their social events, too. It's difficult for parents to find inclusive activities for children who don't have the mobility. The social events encourage everyone, instilling a sense of pride in the athletes. Paul smiles going into ASA events knowing that it is for him and the other athletes. Our family is there in a background role.

We have always been very active outdoors and have learned ways to continue those activities with our family. We push Paul in a special needs stroller on hikes, go kayaking, and put him in a bike trailer to go biking…in between races.

Our family couldn't be more grateful to *Athletes Serving Athletes* and Dave and Sara Slomkowski, for the ways they have loved and supported the community and Paul in particular. ASA is breathing new life into families with children living with disabilities. They are making the dream of being an athlete come true for those who would never have that opportunity.

Paul loves ASA! He participates regularly in training runs and has run in fifteen races since that very first time. He loves everything about the race, the interaction with people and accomplishing something together as a team. There is often a "Team Paul" whenever he races and it makes him proud. There can be a lot of joy in living a different life. Even though someone may have a disability, there are ways to live in this world and thrive. ASA has helped Paul and his family do just that.

The Story of Marie

Marie grew up in a small town of five thousand people in New England during the baby boom. Her family lived in a highly catholic area which affected greatly the way she was treated because of her disorder. She was diagnosed with the epilepsy at the age of four.

I remember reading passages about demons being cast out of a child with epilepsy in Sunday school class when I was in third or fourth grade. They would use the words "epileptic" and "demon-possessed" interchangeably. I don't know what version of the bible it was in but I found it very offensive to hear the church's response to epilepsy was an exorcism. That was enough to turn me off to the Gospels for a long time.

This response to epilepsy was prevalent throughout the church. Churches would withhold medication from epileptics and pray over their seizures. People were dying as a result. It frightened me that it appeared that most of the children with epilepsy were girls. There was much judgement and the church worked to exorcise the devil out of children.

I never experienced the church's attempt to "cure" my disorder but I do remember my mother giving me more medication than I should have had so that I would be more compliant and obedient so it wasn't just the church that contributed to my feelings of shame. My family's response was far worse.

I came from a large family. The second of five children, I had an older sister, twenty months older, a younger brother, eighteen months younger, a younger sister, three years younger, and the youngest brother, seven years younger. My mother was highly educated, graduating from college with a degree in Journalism. She worked from home so she could care for our family. My father left college a few courses shy of graduation and worked his way up the ladder in the finance department of a hospital.

My parents had all of the necessary resources available for them to lovingly manage my health but it didn't appear that way. They took me to neurologists so they were not lacking in knowledge but there was a stigma associated with the disorder. Their negative attitude about epilepsy spread through our family and was passed down to my siblings. I was treated as an outsider. My epilepsy was an invisible barrier that alienated my family. My siblings teased me while my parents totally ignored me. I sensed their animosity from the very beginning. I was different and very ashamed for something for which I had no control.

It wasn't as if everyone was perfectly healthy either. My younger sister grew up with asthma but her illness was treated differently than mine. When my sister would need to be hospitalized, there was compassion and care expressed. My parents appeared embarrassed by my disorder and my hospitalization drew attention to something they wanted to pretend didn't exist. My sister grew out of her illness later. I did not.

I am so thankful for the people in my life who *did* demonstrate kindness and compassion toward me, like my extended family. I spent a great deal of time with my six cousins growing up. They had a beach house close by so our entire family would go for the day.

Time with my cousins was wonderful because they didn't judge me. My maternal uncle was very affirming and I adored him. He made me feel loved. My aunt was also very kind and nurturing. I longed to be part of their family instead of my own. But because I was made to feel responsible for my epilepsy, when I thought about being part of their family, I was afraid I would *ruin* their family like I did mine.

I was especially close to my oldest girl cousin, Kathy. We were born six months apart.

Kathy and I were the favorites of our maternal grandmother. Our maternal grandmother was the one we could always depend on.

My grandmother's love and support was important to me growing up. She was the person to which my epilepsy didn't matter. Everything was okay with her.

At one point, I tried to use my epilepsy as an excuse for something and my grandmother told me, "No. You are not special because of your epilepsy. You are no different than anyone else. I don't love you any different than anyone else." She loved me unconditionally.

But despite her efforts to speak into my life, I grew up feeling less than everyone else. I don't ever remember feeling acceptable.

By the time I was ten years old, my grandmother had had several strokes and was incapacitated. She was in her mid-seventies, at the time and moved into our house. The living room was converted into her bedroom. She needed constant care so my family started leaving me at home from outings to take care of her. I didn't realize how inappropriate this was until I was older. I felt excluded and always wondered if my being left behind was related to my epilepsy. I never felt like a part of the family anyway.

I attempted to win the affection of my family by being a very obedient child. Everything my parents told me to do, I did. I would do anything to be accepted by my family and was taken advantage of as a result. This was not the case for my siblings. They basically ignored my parents until they were paid to do something. While my siblings were indulged with material things for the acts they did at home, I received nothing. So, I responded by trying even harder to do everything perfectly. I didn't understand the discrepancy.

In my family, epilepsy was treated as a curse. I remember being in a store shopping with my family and there was a young man having an epileptic seizure near a rack of bikes. I was very concerned that he might hit his head on the bikes and get injured. I knew there was not a whole lot we could do but I didn't understand my parents' reaction. They pulled me by the arm, removing me from the situation and took me to another part of the store. They didn't even alert anyone to help him. They just ignored what was happening. I thought, if this is how people who knew about seizures reacted, how are people that don't know anything about epilepsy going to respond. That could have been me on the floor. I saw my parents do this many times. Yet, if they saw someone having difficulty breathing, they were the first to alert someone.

The same unkindness happened in school. My older sister was friends with the group of students that constantly tormented me. She would actually join in with their teasing. They told my sister lies about me which she believed and reported back to my mother. I was punished for things I did not do. The punishments were harsh and sometimes physical. It was not until my sister moved in with me many years later that we talked about this experience. She could not believe that our classmates would spread lies about me then or years later. She has never understood the damage that was done. It made me more aware than ever of my place in the family but I was still unable to change it.

I could understand the reaction of my classmates. They'd seen the seizures and were scared because no one explained it to them.

My own family didn't help the matter. Their tormenting of me just seemed to spiral out of control.

There was one person who took time to be kind to me at home. Linda. Because our neighborhood was newly established, everyone was new and looking for friends. I became fast friends with Linda, who lived next door. Linda and I would explore the neighborhood, play hide and seek and participate in group games with the other neighborhood kids. My siblings played games as well, but I was only allowed to participate because Linda was on the team. Linda was from a large family of six girls. Together our families made up a whole team. Linda and I were six years old when we first met and have remained friends to this day.

Medication inhibited many aspects of my life. I wasn't very athletic and would struggle through the games. I had no eye-hand coordination and was often hit with the ball. There was no chance I would attempt to play sports in school. But Linda didn't care about that. She continued to include me in the neighborhood games.

Another side effect of the medication was that concentration was difficult for me. I had to work extra hard to achieve academically, spending most of my time alone studying. In high school, even if I didn't have any homework at night, I would bring every book home to study. That's what it took to get the grades that I did. My siblings didn't have to do the same thing. I never understood why it was so hard for me.

I learned to do sign language when I was in eighth grade so I could volunteer at a school for the deaf. In ninth grade, while attending my own classes, I would volunteer each week in a classroom for the intellectually challenged.

After school, I was volunteer director for one of the two plays my youngest brother's class was staging. I loved this and it set the stage for my major in college, Elementary Education with a minor in Special Education. I had always had a heart for those having disabilities.

I found joy in many extracurricular activities. I participated in my school's dramatic productions, and played the clarinet in the band. This really added an element of fulfillment to my life.

Linda continued to be a faithful friend at home and at school. Her friendship made life tolerable for me. She was very popular so when she came out as being gay during senior year, it didn't change anything for me, or anyone else in our very small graduating class of seventy-six students. She was just as popular as ever. I would have never survived school without Linda's kindness and her faithful friendship.

In 1978, when I was 20 years old, my family decided to move out-of-state and decided to leave me behind.

They said, "We are moving and we are not taking you."

They sold the family home and planned to take the rest of the family with them.

The weekend before the move, everyone in our family had a going-away party to attend but me. I was not invited.

That morning, I found myself talking to the police. My brother had been really struggling. He was on drugs and had gotten my sister on drugs as well. He had just committed grand larceny, taken off with the family car, and fled the weekend before my family was supposed to move. The police came to our home and I was the only one that would answer the door. No one else wanted to deal with it.

My parents required that I go to their new home town so that I could register my two younger siblings for school. My father had been already working there. That made it necessary for me to quit my job. I registered my siblings then had to babysit them until the rest of the family arrived later. Unfortunately, this wasn't too out of the ordinary because I had spent much of my time raising my youngest brother but I wasn't even permitted to move with them.

During my time before school started, my mother called to say that my brother, who was struggling, had spent all of the money he stole and wanted to come back home and move with the family after all. They agreed. But, I, who supported the family in so many ways, was not welcome.

When my family finally arrived, they loaded me into the car and drove me back to our old home state, leaving me on the streets of an unfamiliar city. The only belongings I had was what I could carry.

I was homeless and took residence in a "drunk" hotel that I paid for by the night. It was called such because of the patrons that occupied the rooms. It was a terrible place to live but I could not afford anything else. The man next door beat his wife constantly. I could hear the thuds through our adjoining door. I was terrified to leave my room to use the shared bathroom that was in the hallway. You could often hear a drunk person banging on the locked front door, trying to find shelter. I was twenty years old.

My parents were very financially comfortable but I didn't have the same luxuries as my siblings. All of my siblings went to college and were helped by my parents except for me. They had a home base and would come home from college for a weekend to do laundry. They were taken out to dinner, and would come home during the summer break. I was not welcome. The only person I could depend on was myself.

I went to two years of college, working three jobs to pay the tuition. I knew I couldn't afford another year, I had many loans, so I planned to take a year off, work full time, live at home and save money so I could go back the following year. All that went out the window when my family moved many states away without me.

I couldn't find a job right away, so I started attending night classes, paying tuition from what I had saved over the summer. Then I was able to enroll full time. I couldn't apply for financial aid because I had to be twenty-one years old to assume that debt myself. Because my parents lived out of state, having them help me apply for financial aid meant that I would be considered an out-of-state student. Tuition would be much more.

I was able to press on in life because of some of the special people who took time to really encourage me. Another one of those people was Ellen. Ellen had been my freshman high school English teacher. She was a dear friend in my life and remained so after graduation. She always made me feel like I had value. I wasn't damaged goods.

I did my first two years of college in Cambridge and lived in the dorm not far from where Ellen was going to law school. She and her husband had me over for dinner often. We'd get together for coffee now and then. Sometimes I would take them out to dinner to reciprocate. It was fun to live so close.

Living in the same city, I was able to spend a great deal of time with them. I was invited over to their apartment for dinners and Ellen and I would go for walks in the park next to their apartment building. It was wonderful to spend time together. When I moved, I would take the train to visit, or she would drive in to visit me. We would walk around town and go for coffee as she pushed her oldest son Jonathon in an umbrella stroller. He would want me to pick every dandelion that he saw as we walked toward the center of town. It was not as if we did extraordinary things together, but she was like an older sister that my sister never wanted to be to me.

My epilepsy continued to be an issue. I had a seizure in one of the office buildings one day while at college. I knew one of the people who was present. She told the dean about it and the next thing I knew, I received a letter from the dean telling me I was going to be thrown out of school. I was shocked!

I said, "You can't do this!"

They told me if something happened to me while having a seizure, if I hit my head and got really hurt, I could sue them. I told them I would sign a document that said I would not do that. The result was that I was forced to sign an agreement that said that I would wear a helmet on campus simply to attend classes. Not only did I have to wear it on campus, but I had to agree to wear it taking the bus to campus. The helmets that they had for seizures were several hundred dollars, so much more expensive than other helmets, so I resorted to wearing a football helmet. I was paying my own tuition and my own rent, I couldn't afford anything else.

I was quite the sight in a football helmet while wearing my skirts and dresses. People couldn't help but stare. I will never forget going into a class the first day after signing this agreement. The professor made such a hurtful remark in front of the entire class, all I wanted to do was cry. I went up to him after class and explained that if I wanted to go to college, I had to wear this helmet because of my epilepsy. I chose to live through the embarrassment so I could continue in school. "So thank you for making the remark you did," I said.

All he could say was, "Oh, sorry."

There was another reason that I fought to stay in college. I had heard of another student who was experiencing what I did because he also had epilepsy.

He was coming to speak at the Epilepsy Association. I met him there and we shared our experiences. It made me feel less alone.

I volunteered at the Epilepsy Association and found a safe place in the Disabilities Group on campus. I became friends with many of the students there, all of which had some type of disability. They elected me president and I was instrumental in bringing famous speakers in each year; the first official winner of Boston Marathon, wheelchair division, Bob Hall, and Ted Kennedy, Jr.

Sadly, I couldn't stay at the school because I could not continue to afford the tuition. I left school and found myself working in a shoe factory. After three weeks, I was promoted to the office to do payroll. I did this for nine months and was unexpectantly laid off. I heard later that lay-offs happened often at the shoe factory.

I moved on to working in the finance office in the local hospital for four years. It was supposed to be part time but I excelled and they created a full-time position for me.

Unfortunately, my medication was changed so many times while there that my health was affected and I had to leave my job.

During this time, my older sister suddenly moved in with me. From what I could gather, she had a major fight with my father and that prompted her to move out of my parents' house. It was only supposed to be a visit so no ground rules were ever set initially. She continued to order me around, treating like she always had. She would come and go as she pleased and totally ignored our "no pets" agreement. One day, she brought home a cat from a friend's house and never returned it. To make matters worse, she was gone from Friday afternoon to Sunday night or Monday morning every week and was not there to care for the cat. That became my responsibility.

It was only in the last three or four months that we were sharing the apartment that my sister came to appreciate and value me as a person. Someone had lent me a copy of the Sears "Wish book" Christmas Catalog, during the holidays. One night, Ellen and I were sitting together at the kitchen table as I thumbed through the catalog after dinner. Occasionally, I would make a comment regarding something on the page, not really to her, more just aloud.

When I got to the kids' section in the catalog, I said aloud, "Oh, I wish we had kids in our family."

When I finished leafing through the catalog, my sister asked me why I made the comment I did. I explained to her that I would find great joy in buying toys for kids.

It was at that moment, my sister informed me that she was pregnant. Our conversation about the Christmas Catalog initiated a heart-felt discussion that changed the course of our relationship. I was able to ask her deep questions about her stage in life. Did she want to continue the pregnancy? Did she want to keep the child? Did she want to get married? Then, I explained that I would be there for her every step of the way, no matter what decision she made.

I did just as I promised. It started with me standing beside her as she called my mother to tell her she was pregnant. I supported her as she planned the wedding, helping to draw up the guest list. I was there when her morning sickness was unbearable. For the first time in our lives, we became very close. Even after she married and moved back to the shore, she would often call me to discuss concerns about her kids or any number of other things.

My father died when I was twenty-two years old. It was a chaotic time for our extended family prior to his death. I had just been laid off from work at the shoe factory and had not yet gotten the job at the Hospital. My second youngest cousin, Stephen, was hit by a van riding his bike to school and suffered severe brain injuries and was in a coma for several months.

When the accident happened, my cousin's older sister, Mary, called me to let me know. I immediately called my father. My grandmother had been living at my aunt and uncle's at the time. When my father called my aunt, his sister, about the accident, my uncle insisted that my father come down immediately to pick up my grandmother. My father agreed to drive down the next day because he had an important meeting that evening. My uncle was very angry about my father's response to his request and told my father that he could never talk to my aunt again. My father had spoken daily to my aunt. Meanwhile, since I lived nearby and was currently unemployed, I stayed at my aunt and uncle's house taking care of my grandmother and my youngest cousin, Amy. Amy was eleven at the time, prepared meals and took care of the house. This freed up my aunt, uncle and two other cousins to spend all their time and energy at the hospital. After about a month, my aunt informed me that they no longer needed my help. I was dismissed. My aunt said they could handle everything on their own.

When I went to visit Stephen in the hospital with Mary, my aunt and uncle informed me that I was not welcome there. Not only could I never see Stephen, they never wanted to see me again. I was shocked and never attempted to contact them. My father agreed to never contact his sister as well. It was a sad time for our family.

The next thing I knew, my father was dead. This all happened within a four-month period. My aunt and uncle did come up for the funeral. It was terrible. During the course of the week, my aunt accused my mother of driving my father to suicide. He had drowned but evidence pointed to murder.

Our extended family became even more fractured than ever after my father's death. The week after the funeral, my siblings and I came up to celebrate my mother's birthday. My cousin, Mary, had told both my older sister and I earlier about her mother's belief that my mother drove my father to suicide. I have no idea what she based this on but alcohol may have played a role. However, my sister relayed it to my siblings as if I was the only one present so I was the one grilled about it at the dining room table by my family, including my sister.

After dinner, my mother called my aunt to question her about the comments she made and she denied it. Once again, I was made out to be a liar even though my sister was present for the whole conversation with my cousin.

What we do know about my father's situation is that as Assistant Hospital Administrator of the regional hospital, my father had discovered that the Medicare money was missing from the account. He talked to a friend in the hospital about it and started a quiet investigation. Shortly after that, my father went missing and was found dead three days later. Immediately, the Hospital Administrator and the hospital attorney, confiscated all of the records, making it difficult for my father's friend to complete the investigation. Then, the Board of Directors of the hospital met to discuss the matter. A friend of my mother happened to be on the board and after meeting, came to see my mother. The Board wanted to change my father's death certificate to say he died by suicide. Fortunately, the medical examiner was the only one who could determine the manner of death. The death certificate read "death by drowning" but many people in town believed they knew the man responsible. The district attorney and state's attorney did some investigating but the evidence that my father was collecting had gone missing, making it impossible to prove anything. At one point, the district attorney accused my father, after his death, of stealing the

Medicare money himself. My mother had to allow access to what had been their joint accounts to show that there was not an excess of money there.

Eventually, the Hospital Administrator moved on to another hospital after his contract was up because the hospital refused to renew it. After working at the new hospital for a while, mysteriously, money was discovered missing from their Medicare account. Again, nothing could be proved so he faced no punishment of any kind. Almost 40 years after my father's death, we are left with no more answers than we had then.

I always had a complex relationship with my father. I was treated very severely by him but during the four months prior to his death, I really began to feel compassion for him. That brought some healing.

I lost my job at the hospital because the medication I was taking had serious adverse side-affects. They said I was rude and disrespectful and appeared intoxicated at times. I explained that the medication was the cause of this negative personality change but they were not willing to work with me. There was no protection for employees back then, so I was released.

I had been experiencing several sinus infections, running high fevers and needing medical care at that time, as well. A friend, aware of my dysfunctional relationship with my mother, contacted her to tell her that she needed to take me into her home. A ticket was purchased for me and I quickly moved into my mother's home. That was a complete disaster for me.

I lived in my mother's home for six years. She did not want me to pay rent because she wanted to claim me as a deduction on her income tax, saying she paid more than half of my expenses. I paid for all my own medical, prescriptions, clothes, dental, transportation but she still claimed me as a deduction. I also did all the housekeeping, cooking, sewed new curtains, ran errands, and fixed appliances. My siblings felt the need to speak into the situation, saying that I should be paying rent to Mother. I explained to them that it would be better for me to do that but she did not want me to. She wanted to claim me as a deduction. They felt I should pay her rent under the table. In other words, I would not benefit at all, despite her receiving the deduction. My mother was in a fine financial position, having a decent investment portfolio and traveling to Europe once a year for vacation. They still did not understand.

It was hard to maintain my friendship with Ellen when I moved into my mother's apartment. There was no privacy there and I could not use the phone very often because my mother needed it for her journalism work.

My mother's home was a very unhealthy place for me to be and I knew I needed to leave. The therapist I had been seeing recommended a hospital for me to receive better treatment for depression and Post Traumatic Stress Syndrome but it required me to move south. It just so happened that the hospital was located where my friend Ellen and her husband were living. They kindly offered for me to stay with them when I was discharged from the hospital until I could get established in the new city. After six weeks in the hospital, I moved in with Ellen and her husband for three and a half weeks until I was able to rent a room not far from them. I lived there four and a half years.

It was wonderful reconnecting with Ellen and her family. I often went into the city to meet her for lunch and we talked on the phone. They would have me over for family dinners and we would share meals out. I spent Chanukah, other holidays, and family celebrations with them.

I've known Ellen for forty-five years so when I moved away and we lost contact for a while, it was quite a loss. I stopped calling her because my aphasia, loss of ability to produce or comprehend speech, became so bad that it was difficult to use the phone. I tried to contact her later but her number was changed. After an extensive search, I was finally able to locate her and we have rekindled our friendship, once again.

My family really has no idea the extent to which they have hurt me. At my sister's wedding, my brother, two years younger, apologized for the many ways that he mistreated me.

He said, "I know we don't have a relationship. It's my fault and I am sorry." But it was short lived.

I came to my mother's 90th birthday celebration last year because I hadn't seen my family in a long time. My mother was getting old and I really didn't know how many opportunities I would have to see her. I didn't want to have any regrets. It took much courage for me to put myself in such a vulnerable situation. The reaction from my family was as expected. My brother's response to me showed that, despite his apology years before, things had not changed, even after fifteen years. That weekend, he paid a kind compliment to each of my siblings. At the dinner table, in front of the entire family, he made a horribly hurtful comment about me. I expected that a criticism might happen that weekend, from he or my mother, so I prepared emotionally for how I would respond, should it occur. In the nastiest way imaginable, he criticized the fact that I was on disability.

He said that I "expected the world to take care of me."

It hurt, but I was able to respond unemotionally and with the facts. I said, "Yes, I am on Social Security disability, but I don't have a lot of choices. I have not had the advantages that a lot of the people in this family have had." This made him even angrier and he stormed out of the house.

There have been many experiences that have confirmed my position in our family. I thought I was close to my youngest brother but a few years ago, he had the family for Thanksgiving and forgot to invite me.

Mother paid for a family vacation a few years ago but did not invite or pay for me.

My brother a few years younger, has all of our siblings on his cell phone bill except me. I can't even afford a cell phone.

If I could openly share with my siblings, I would like to ask them; Why? What have I done? What's wrong with me? Why do you exclude me? I have tried to be there for each one of you. Yes, I feel guilty about not being able to support myself. Up until ten years ago, I was still having seizures pretty frequently so I had to go on Social Security disability. I had no other choice.

My family did not see anything wrong with the way they treated me. I can't imagine how they could not be aware of the pain they have caused.

I just want to be treated just like everyone else. I want my family and others to know that I have feelings just like everyone else. The things that are said, the things that are done to me, and the times you exclude me, hurt.

People who are struggling with a similar situation, know that I feel your pain. You may need to protect your heart. Keep a distance from those who hurt you. Fight for your rights. I wish I would have fought more to move with my family. Though, I am not sure that that would have been better for me. I wish I would have fought for my jobs more and not gone on disability.

Believe in yourself. You must be your own advocate.

Believe in the True God. The God I know now is not the one I was brought up knowing. Coming to the Lutheran Church has been a salvation for me. I have been attending there sixteen years.

I used to have an amazing network of friends. Recently, over an eight-month period, I have lost many people in my life. have moved away, and others have died. I've tried to keep up with those who have moved away but it has never been the same.

Marie has many acquaintances in her life but not many friends. There is not one person she can call if she needs to talk. There is no one to call in a crisis...but God.

Epilepsy Foundation

The Epilepsy Foundation is a non-profit national organization, established in 1968 "to lead the fight to overcome the challenges of living with epilepsy and to accelerate therapies to stop seizures, find cures, and save lives."

The most common causes of epilepsy are: brain trauma, brain stroke, brain tumor and brain infection. Other possible causes include: metabolic, genetic, and congenital malformations. However, there are many cases of epilepsy where the cause is unknown. 6 out of 10 people have no identified cause.

There are sixty-five million people living with Epilepsy in the world today. 3.4 million are in the United States alone. Between four and ten out of every one thousand people live with active seizures. One third of those people have no treatment available to them.

The Epilepsy Foundation exists to give a great understanding of epilepsy and available therapy. Through education, care, advocacy, research and new therapies, they are striving to improve the quality of life for those living with epilepsy, and in some cases, they are saving lives.

The Epilepsy Foundation is headquartered in Landover, Maryland and has a network of 59 affiliates. (8301 Professional Place West, Suite 230, Landover, MD 20785 | 1.800.332.1000)

Heaven Comes Near

By Carol Marchant Gibbs

The beauty of the morning captures my soul.

I am transported to a place where the value of people extends beyond their geography.

All cultures are embraced with reckless abandon.

There is no poverty or lack.

The challenge to respond to the needs of others is met with overwhelming joy.

The beliefs of others are not challenged but serve to teach us.

It is a place where the One True God is Father to all and His goodness is celebrated by all for eternity.

Heaven Comes Near.

Chapter 4
Life as an Immigrant and Asylum Seeker

The Melting Pot: My Story

Between 1890 and 1924, America experienced one of the greatest influxes of immigrants to this country. Millions of people, many fleeing hardship, came with hope of a better future. America quickly became known as a "Melting Pot" of many nations. A term coined by an immigrant, Israel Zangwill.

People quickly changed their names as they walked through the gates of Ellis Island and other ports, fully embracing their new identity and exciting future. All people were considered Americans and everyone wanted to learn what it meant to be so.

My grandparents were included in this population of immigrants. My grandmother was only three years old when she arrived here with her family from Sicily. Most of her memories were made here, very few remained of her home in Italy. They came because the financial situation in their little fishing village had become bleak. America offered the hope of a new life.

My grandfather came much later. He was seventeen years old when he boarded a boat to America. He was fleeing similar circumstances. Poverty cast a shadow over his village, and organized crime attempted to offer a better life. My grandfather refused to succumb to that lifestyle and came alone to a country he knew nothing about. He did not speak the language but arrived with a piece of paper in his pocket, having the name and contact information of his closest relative here.

When he arrived at Ellis Island, he too altered the name he was given to become more "American." He quickly located family, got a job, and enrolled in English lessons.

My grandfather was never allowed the privilege of going to school in Italy. At a young age, he would help to work the family farm to help make ends meet.

So the fact that he became proficient at learning the English language that he would substitute for the instructor on occasion, was quite extraordinary. He was very proud of this accomplishment.

When my grandparents met up again in America, they fell in love, married and began their life together. Connecting with relatives between New York and Baltimore and in search of employment that would support a family of four children, my grandparents traveled some before settling in Baltimore.

This is where my story begins. My parents met in Baltimore, fell in love, and raised a family of five children.

I've often thought about my grandparents and where I would be if they were unable to immigrate to America. Would I even exist?

When I think about our present state as a country, it saddens me to see that the "melting pot" that use to be a symbol for our all-embracing nation has become a boiling cauldron of intolerance, promoting a society divided by race, religion, nationality, and gender identity, resulting in blatant persecution of those who are different. The words "and justice for all" appear to becoming less of a reality.

How do we respond as we experience one of the greatest influx of immigrants in the history of the United States?

Compassion develops as we begin to get to know someone. Hearts and attitudes change when we hear about the life experiences people have had. Personal stories give us a clearer picture of someone's life and we are able to understand them more fully.

Where does your story begin? Are you the child or grandchild of an immigrant? How would your life be different if your family was unable to come to this country? "…I was a stranger and you invited me in." Matthew 25:35.

Asylee Women's Enterprise

Tiffany is the Executive Director of The Asylee Women's Enterprise, an organization that welcomes and supports people seeking asylum in the U.S.

The *Asylee Women's Enterprise* provides social services to asylum seekers and other forced migrants. However, the manner in which they do that is different than most organizations.

When you arrive in a strange country and are fleeing danger, finding a safe place to land is critical. The *Asylee Women's Enterprise* provides a safe community for asylum seekers to build safe and meaningful relationships.

The day program offers a place for asylum seekers and their children to gather every day with the AWE staff and volunteers. It is there that the asylum seekers learn to regain trust in others. It is a place of mutual support that feels like a family.

The *Asylee Women Enterprise* provides a variety of services to assist with the adjustment to living in a new country. Through the program, people are able to have access to housing, food, medical services, English classes, computer training, and assistance with applying for asylum. Each day, they have coffee and work together to prepare a meal.

Last year, AWE served 438 people; 218 women, 181children and 39 men. Most of the people they see are single mothers.

AWE does have an open-door policy. While they focus on asylum seekers primarily, they welcome refugees and other immigrants, as well. Refugees do have work permits so some services are not provided them, such as housing, but the community day program is open to anyone.

The Story of Tiffany

Tiffany is a social worker by profession. Before coming to AWE in 2016, she worked for the U.S Committee for Refugees and Immigrants with asylum seekers and unaccompanied children traveling over the border into the U.S., for ten years. Most of her time was spent advocating for children.

I was set on this career path by my participation in a study abroad program in Ecuador while in college. My family really didn't travel much so I had only been out of the country once before. The experience in Ecuador really changed me. I remember, vividly, the condition of the airport as I emerged from the airplane. The airport was very rustic and much of it was under construction at the time. The baggage claim was open to the outside, the ceiling was unfinished and there was dirt and dust everywhere.

Our team of students quickly climbed into the bus provided and began our trip into town. As we rode along, we noticed street kids that had climbed the light poles so they could reach into the bus to ask for money, food and other needed items. As a fairly privileged, sheltered college student, it was more than I could process. Even now, I remember that vividly as if it was yesterday.

I attended a language program there but it became secondary as the school was more interested in protecting the students' interests by getting all of us connected to the local community.

Because I was a senior social work student, I was placed as an intern with a day program for incarcerated women and their children. In this part of Ecuador, when a woman has a child and is incarcerated, usually for petty theft from trying to provide for her children, the children are placed with their mothers in jail. As an intern, I helped care for the children, cleaned the facility or worked wherever the staff needed help.

I also worked in a school for children living with disabilities. The support for these children was very limited in 2003 and many were not welcome in public school. This organization was providing care, music, art and basic educational skills to the students in its care.

Over all, the people in this country had so few financial resources but appeared generally happy. They were very family oriented and warmly welcomed me. I became acutely aware of the privileges that I had in the United States and realized that my priorities were off, placing more importance on material things and less on relationships.

The people were so kind there and offered to help us readily. "Where are you from?" "Where are you going?" "Can I show you this?" "Can I show you that?" They were extremely interested in our culture and were eager to share their culture with us.

I have encountered two types of societies in my lifetime; individualistic and collectivistic. People living in the U.S. are individualistic, desiring to live for themselves. I saw a collectivistic culture in Ecuador, where people looked out for each other. It was refreshing. They cared about their neighbor and the community as a whole. They embraced shared spaces, gathering at the Plaza on Sundays, listening to the music with people that they didn't know. The family was valued and every Sunday, they gathered for dinner religiously. It was mind-blowing.

I was only in Ecuador for a two-month program, but every minute was an amazing experience. People were always out and about there and valued community highly. When I returned home, I missed the Sunday dinners with the host family, the music, the cooking together and all of those things that I never did in the U.S.

I returned to the U.S. in the dead of winter which was very difficult. We were closed up in our homes because of the weather and it was quite depressing.

I found that my experience overseas opened my mind to other ways of living. I developed a desire to travel, live and work abroad.

Venezuela became my next adventure. I lived there for a year, working for a non-profit that offered education to children living with disabilities. Such children were not welcome in the public-school system there.

The mobile school, for which I worked, went into some of the shanty towns to offer education to those who were unschooled. The mobile school would move into the neighborhoods and offer school to the children a few times a week.

In addition to those with disabilities, there were undocumented children from Brazil, children who were working during the day and children whose parents worked in the mines for weeks at a time. These children were charged with guarding their homes and caring for their younger siblings. Six and seven-year-old children would cook, take care of the house and watch their siblings. That was a lot of responsibility for young children. It was amazing the ingenuity that they possessed taking care of the daily challenges that arose. In the absence of an adult, they survived well. While the education piece was very important, I feel like our being present as trusted adults was really important.

In some ways, I could relate to these young independent children because I was raised by a teen mom who was a single parent for many years. My mom was a hard worker and as a result, I became very independent. As an adult, I really appreciate that experience because it taught me how to be self-sufficient. My mom worked all day when I was seven and eight years old, so I needed to learn how to make my own meals. I understood that if something happened, I could figure it out. I saw that same independence in the children in Ecuador.

This is probably why I felt at peace about backpacking alone in South and Central America. My relatives and peers thought it was crazy to do such things but I had the self-confidence and the wear-with-all to keep myself safe. I did t the things that interested me and made me feel whole. I credit my mom for that.

When I was twelve years old, my mom got married and I suddenly had a step-brother. We weren't raised together but we saw each other a few times a year.

Since I was raised as an only child, my desire to be in community with others became very strong. My mom called me a "party coordinator" because I was always trying to find ways to bring people together. Where can we go? What can we do? Who can we get together with? That is probably why I am doing what I am with AWE.

As an independent child, I liked to cook, spend time with family, and read. I was a good student and people pleaser.

My grandparents were very present in my life and helped nurture my interest in cooking and other interesting skills. They taught me how to drive the riding lawnmower, and how to plant and tend to a garden.

When I was in sixth grade, we moved a few times. It was hard to start over twice in one year but I weathered it well. Sixth grade is a difficult age for anyone and being a new and kind of chubby kid made fitting in a little harder.

In the summer, because my mom was working, I would spend time with my grandparents who lived nearby. We became very close, as a result.

My grandfather was a truck driver so he and my grandmother would take me with them in his eighteen-wheeler. We'd drive long trips, like to California and would tour the country as we went, stopping at landmarks to play tourist when we could. On one occasion, before cellphones, the truck broke down in the wee hours of the morning in rural Pennsylvania. From the highway, my grandfather spotted smoke from a chimney across a field. We walked over to the house together to find a kitchen full of Amish women baking bread and pastries for the Amish market that morning. The women agreed to watch me while my grandfather walked to the gas station/mechanic down the road. They seated me at a long table where they were preparing baked goods for the market. I sampled the hot baked goods as they came out of the oven. They were delicious. Traveling with my grandparents created some of the happiest moments of my life.

Sometimes, in the summer, we would go to the beach in North Carolina with my extended family. It was a wonderful gathering. We didn't do it often but have cherished memories from the times we did. As an only child I loved being with my cousins, always having someone to play with and to whom I could talk. We would have barbecues other times of the year but the beach was special.

I volunteered in high school and established a group called *Best Buddies,* with a friend. The group aimed to provide social connection and authentic friendships for students living with disabilities. We would have lunch together a few times a week and social gatherings outside of school. I enjoyed doing things like this. I really enjoyed getting to know these students that were somewhat isolated from the mainstream student body. That is when my social work calling began to reveal itself.

I had a wonderful group of friends in high school, though we weren't the popular people. We kind of blended into the background. My friends had good solid character and we had a similar interest for compassionate outreach. I was very fortunate to be surrounded by people who were such a good influence on me.

I was raised in the Southern Baptist Church. As I got older, I began to see inconsistencies in what was being taught with what I experienced in real life. The world I saw was different than what the church presented, so I stopped going.

Today, I have continued on my spiritual journey and am content with my relationship with God. I align with the beliefs of the Lutheran and the Unitarian churches.

When I was in college, my heart for outreach continued as I majored in Social Work. I volunteered with *Habitat for Humanity* and would tutor international elementary students in English.

After graduation, before going to graduate school, I went to Costa Rica and to Nicaragua for three months to volunteer with an immigrant rights group. The organization was doing advocacy in Costa Rica for undocumented Nicaraguan migrants. Even there, the parallel to how we treat Central Americans in the U.S. was evident. Nicaraguan migrants are a very important part of Costa Rica's economy and agriculture but are unkindly talked about and treated poorly.

The misunderstandings around the profession of a social worker in our society made my focus very misinterpreted. Many people believed that most social workers were involved with child protective services and our focus was strictly case management. My worked primarily with refugees and immigrants so an explanation was often needed. An important part of what we do is advocacy for clients.

As advocates, not only is it important to meet the needs of the asylum seeker but it is also important to reach the hearts of those who are opposed to immigration. Many people believe that asylum seekers should not be allowed into our country, that they don't deserve to be here. Much of my time is spent engaging with people who do not understand the "Why." We do outreach by hosting presentations at churches and with other organizations on asylum seekers and refuges. It is our hope that when people hear the stories, they will begin to understand the circumstances that surround asylum seekers and other immigrants leaving their homes to come to the U.S. We want people at these presentations to ask the difficult questions so we have an opportunity to clarify the reasons for people leaving their home country and tell them about the arduous process they encounter.

Asylum seekers come to this country because they have experienced persecution for a variety of reasons; race, religion, ethnicity, tribal affiliation, political opinion, member in a particular social group, disability or sexual orientation, but they can also struggle with their perceptions of others within the asylum seeker community. People are persecuted for anything that sets them apart from the "norm" in their society. We have seen quite a few asylum seekers that are pursuing protection from persecution they have received because of their sexual orientation or gender identity. Even among asylum seekers, this group is misunderstood. The religious or tribal affiliation can determine how they see people from this orientation. For example, a transgender asylum seeker is not easily accepted, and even persecuted by others seeking protection.

I have always realized the value of community but for asylum seekers and all of those fleeing their country, it is even more important. They come to a country where many do not know the language, culture, or have any personal relationships.

I love my country, but everyone else loves their country, too. No one leaves unless they are unable to stay. Asylum seekers miss their home countries and would still be there if they could be. They were persecuted and forced to leave their home and families. Many have experienced much trauma and the journey of working through the trauma is often very painful. To have a safe place to go and friends to encourage them is critical to their survival. When you level the playing field, and people are treated more as friends than clients, that's when authentic relationships are formed and healing happens. They need a safe community, all human beings do.

It is important to recognize that people coming to the U.S. bring many talents and skills along with them. The language barrier can be very deceptive, giving a view that they are not capable or competent. Many come and are very educated but are not permitted to practice in their field of study because of certification.

When an asylum seeker wins their asylum case, we celebrate the victory. Though that was the goal from the beginning, there is great loss in that, the asylum seeker may never set foot in their home country ever again. All ties are severed. Much of their family, they will never see again.

Once an asylum seeker has reached this point, they can apply to have their spouses and other children come to the U.S. but it is a very long process. An asylum case often takes many years to be decided. It could be another year or more to bring their spouse and children. It is required that the children you are bringing over are minors and not married. If you have children that are ten, fifteen and twenty-two years old, the twenty-two-year-old child may not be permitted to come.

It takes another five years to get citizenship. At that point, you can petition to bring other family members to the U.S. but it can take many years, depending on the relation to the person and government processing times. The Trump administration was trying to prohibit this from happening, calling it "chain migration." An elderly parent would be dead while they "wait in line" for family reunification with a relative in the U.S. that has been granted asylum.

Asylum seekers carry a lot of guilt from leaving others behind. They are safe but in many cases their family is not.

One of the highlights at AWE is, every year, we have college students come during "alternative" spring break and the summer to do internships. The interns come with a passion for advocacy. Not only does it energize the asylum seekers, but it energizes the staff as well. The day to day demands can be exhausting for all of us. This line of work can be emotionally very taxing. The interns help to give an emotional boost to us to press on with vigor.

The group of college students were quite extraordinary this year. The time together allows for them to share their journeys and what has drawn them to this type of work. Two of the students were children of refugee parents who came to this country twenty-five years ago. Their parents never shared about the experience so they had no idea the process that their parents had to go through to get here. Two other students were from Asia and talked about the discrimination they experienced when the coronavirus came to the U.S. It was interesting to hear about how family backgrounds led each of the students to have a heart for this line of work.

It is Tiffany's hope that AWE will continue to be a welcoming place for asylum seekers, refugees and other immigrants and that this spirit of welcome continues to be cultivated in the wider community. When we get to know people for who they are and take away the labels, there is greater understanding and acceptance and it becomes a place where everyone can share their gifts.

More about the Asylee Women's Enterprise

Katie works as the Program Director for Asylee Women's Enterprise. Her position involves that she acknowledges the needs of the organization by her presence in the community. She identifies the need then connects with the volunteers and partners of Asylee Women's Enterprise to present how they can better support the organization.

Asylum seekers are those people who have endured severe persecution in their home countries and are fleeing to another country for protection. These people have made the decision to leave their homes, their culture, their families and their community for a safer life. Everything that they know has been left behind in order to save their lives and the lives of their children.

AWE has created a program specifically designed for supporting asylum seekers through the process. They are coming to this country legally to seek asylum in the U.S. but the process can be quite rigorous. The asylum process can take about five years for it to be fully complete, for the seeker to be granted all the rights of asylum. Within the first year of arriving in this country, asylum seekers are required to submit their application. It is not until a few months after submitting their application that they are eligible to work. This can take up to a year.

So, for the first year and a half, asylum seekers are in a type of limbo. They typically don't know anyone in the country or have access to any benefits; food stamps, temporary assistance to needy families, or medical care. They have no resources available to them. This is where AWE steps in to assist.

The AWE day program is a safe place where asylum seekers are provided assistance to navigate their first two years in the country. Isolation can be a real challenge for people coming to this country. The day program focuses on community and empowerment. They experience community with other families that have had similar situations in their home countries. They are allowed opportunities to build relationships with the staff and volunteers. As a community, we cook lunch and eat together every day. This becomes a special time to share about our experiences, families, kids, and what we are learning in the English classes and elsewhere. Moms come with their young children that are not in school yet so this process provides an extended family for the children. They acquire many aunts and grandmothers through the program. It becomes like a huge family where people offer support and encouragement to one another.

The program also serves to empower asylum seekers by preparing them for employment. We focus on the skills that they already have, then teach them English, how to use computers, help them adjust to the new culture, and offer shop readiness training. It is comforting for them to know that they are not going through this process alone. Once they get their work permit, they are on their way to self-sufficiency.

AWE has a housing program for the asylum seekers that provides places to live throughout the county. Some families are invited by other families to live with them so they are doubled up in homes. Some choose to move in with a distant cousin or relative. The program has expanded dramatically over the past two years so it is our hope that additional housing will be available in the near future.

Each asylum seeker's situation is different. Sometimes families come together. Other times, women are actually fleeing their husbands and they come only with their children. Some women come alone. It is not unusual for family members to join the asylum seeker many years later.

The Story of Katie

I grew up in a family of five in the northeast. I have two brothers, one is four years older than me and one is four years younger. We lived together with our parents who happened to be happily married. Being the middle child and the only girl, I became a "mommy's girl," and a "goody two shoes."

My mom was originally from Germany, coming to the U.S. when she was six years old. The U.S. was a big adjustment for her. She did learn English and make friends easily so that helped with the transition. It was to her advantage that physically, she looked like everyone else in America.

I grew up understanding that my mom did have an immigration experience. Fortunately, it was much easier for her then it is for those immigrating today.

I had many interests growing up. I was a girl scout for twelve years, all the way through high school. Many of my friends did it with me. I really enjoyed the service activities and selling girls scout cookies.

Serving others became a large part of my life. I received much approval for my efforts. I grew up believing that this is what we were supposed to do.

I tried some other activities without much success. I was not very athletic but did gymnastics for a while. I, also, played the clarinet but didn't really like that.

My mom stayed at home and was very involved in all of our lives. I saw in her a heart to selflessly love other people. She was always willing to go the extra mile to support someone. I admired that and wanted to be just like her.

When I started high school, I found that I really enjoyed studying French. I continued that in college and studied in France for a semester. I have found this very helpful at AWE since many of the asylum seekers speak French. It is encouraging for them to be able to communicate with me in their native tongue.

I didn't realize, until I was in college, the impact my mom's heart for others had on me personally. Service just became a natural way of life.

I went to a very homogenous school and lived in a homogenous neighborhood, so I never witnessed any vulnerability. Persecution was not really anything that I experienced growing up. I knew that there were people in society that did not look like me and were from other cultures but I never was exposed to them.

My first exposure to persecution was when I was in college. I developed relationships with many people who were different from me and had the opportunity to go on a cross-cultural trip to China for five weeks. We traveled to an area where a Muslim minority group lived that was being persecuted by the Chinese government. We were partnered with other students there with the hope to develop cross-cultural relationships. We became roommates and language partners for the duration of our trip. They taught us their language and we taught them English. We ate meals together and explored different areas of the city.

The woman I was paired with was a little older than me and had a very funky personality. I was surprised at how well we got along because we were so different from one another. I wanted to learn everything about her and her culture. We really grew to love each other. It was an incredible experience.

My time in China gave me the confidence to pursue a profession that involved working with other cultures. I saw that I really could have an impact on someone's life. Before that, I didn't have any vision for my life. That experience set the course for my future.

After I returned from China, I started teaching English as a second language with several organizations one or two days a week.

My major in college led me in a different direction. I was in business with a focus on hotel hospitality management. I liked planning and helping people so after graduation, I naturally worked in a hotel. After two years, I found that I really wasn't using my gifts and my heart wasn't in it.

While still working for the hotel, I took an internship working for the International Rescue Committee, a refugee resettlement agency. Eventually, I was hired by the IRC to be a youth case worker. I was an economic empowerment intern that worked with individuals who needed jobs. I sat with them, went through their past work experience, and helped prepare their resumes. I helped them develop a budget and a worksheet with goals. It was nice that I was able to use the business I had learned in college to help others. I really liked working with individuals, writing resumes and giving them space to talk about their goals for work and their goals for their families. I met with one to two people each day during my internship. That was the beginning of my exposure to the refugee community. I spent time with them and developed close relationships. It was important for me that each person was seen and understood. It all began to come naturally. I remained in that internship position for a year.

I also took an internship position on the Women's Economic Empowerment Appointment team for the *Youth and Women Employment Program*. This program was specifically designed for single moms with young children to find employment. We had a training program where they could learn about different cultural practices while working in the U.S. My position required me to visit childcare sites to help moms determine which was the best for them. We helped them to find appropriate childcare, giving them vouchers to help with the payment. I really enjoyed this internship. This was a part of IRC at the time but is no longer.

I was then hired into a temporary position as the youth case worker with the IRC. I worked with families with children for the purpose of getting them settled in the U.S. Many of the families were Congolese, from Tanzania or the Democratic Republic of the Congo. Others were Burmese and a few were Afghani families. We would do a school orientation for the families, talking about important school practices in this country. We shared about what children could expect going to school and how to communicate with the teacher. We also helped parents to know how to best contact the teacher and inquire about how their children were doing in school. We supported them through the whole enrollment process through the first day of school and made sure they were prepared with uniforms and supplies. As a youth caseworker, I then became an intermediary between the school and the family. When the administration changed, the organization lost much of their funding and many positions were terminated. I worked in this position for three months.

I transitioned to working retail for six months but my heart really wasn't in it. I took time during this transition to evaluate my life and respond to the healing that needed to take place in me. This was one of the most difficult but very necessary times in my life. I learned that I really needed to pace myself and not let the demands of my job exhaust me. That can be challenging when you are working in a people intensive position.

From there, I took a position at the *Asylee Women's Enterprise*, where I am currently employed.

I am surprised that I have not experienced much negativity toward me or the goals I am attempting to accomplish. My family has been very supportive of my position to empower asylum seekers. I was a little nervous about that because my parents are scientists and my brother is an engineer, which is much different than what I am doing. My dad was concerned about how I would support myself, especially with my decision to attend graduate school in the Fall. I am pursuing a Masters in Social Work. Other than that concern, he has been very supportive.

My focus of study will reflect my heart for the relationship between family and child and the development of each child. It is my hope that despite their circumstances, the families I come in contact with will be able to see their family as a whole.

Many moms and children come into AWE every day that have already experienced severe trauma in their lives. They are fearful and need a safe place to heal, learn and grow. It really matters to me that they have access to quality care, specifically childcare. My next step is to create a childcare program for all.

I have learned that it is wise to take time to care for yourself. Faith enters greatly into this for me. I realize that I cannot do this demanding job on my own strength. It would be easy to be overwhelmed by all of the needs of the people around me. I could believe that I am responsible for doing it all, but I remember that my strength comes from God and I have constant access to Him. I am also learning about the timing of responding to the many needs before me. Is it something I must respond to right now? Or, is it for later? That is a healthy change for me.

I have been able, with God's help, to conquer fears in my life because the desire to accomplish the goal has outweighed the fear. Allowing myself to go forward has caused me to grow personally and professionally.

Katie hopes that people will begin to be more welcoming to the community that she loves. Her greatest desire is that they would be seen and understood by leaders throughout the country and the world.

The Story of Katrina

Katrina has committed much of her life to the empowerment of internationals all over the world. She has witnessed the hardship that many have experience when forced to leave their country of origin. Katrina is an ally for refugees.

Internationals are not always welcomed well by many countries and the United States has become one of them. Over the last few years, it has become increasingly difficult for internationals to seek asylum in the United States. It's Katrina's hope that the stories she is about to share will give a deeper understanding of the challenges internationals face, and create compassion for those who are living in such circumstances that they must flee their homes. May the way we welcome others be transformed by her words.

I am currently preparing to work with refugee women in a small city in Europe. Many of the women there are escaping dire circumstances in their home countries of Syria, Iran and Iraq. They have been through considerable challenges and need a sanctuary where they can regain their dignity and self-worth. Katrina and her team will be providing a safe place for these refugee women to gather to share their experiences without the fear of retribution. Through the Café, they will have opportunities to grow relationships and become involved in programs that will help them to live independently. As their physical survival needs are met, emotional, spiritual and psychological needs usually begin to rise to the surface. Many of the women have experienced extreme trauma on multiple levels. This will all be addressed as well, through trauma healing.

When refugees leave their home country, they leave everything behind; house and belongings, culture, and even family members. Sometimes their faith is shattered by their dire circumstances. It is of primary importance that we assure them that God cares for them and will continue to be for them despite all that they have experienced to this point.

The effort will be called *Hephzibah*, meaning, "She is my delight." This is taken from Isaiah 62:1 where God is reminding the people that despite their propensity to wander from Him, He loves them and desires to bless their lives.

"You will be a crown of splendor in the LORD's hand, a royal diadem in the hand of your God. No longer will they call you Deserted, or name your land Desolate. But you will be called Hephzibah,...for the LORD will take delight in you..."

I will also be involved with efforts to encourage those people who are followers of Jesus, through a faith-based discipleship program. Because the country is highly Christian orthodox, not only are we encouraging refugees to seek God wherever they are, we are also teaching the residents of the country to do the same. Many of the refugees are in camps so it is important for them to know that they do not have to be in a church building to seek God.

The life of a refugee is very unstable. The systems at the United Nations and on the national government level are so overwhelmed with the number of applications, over the past several years, that it can take two to three years for applicants to get a decision. The people in the camps are waiting to hear about their asylum applications. The vast majority are rejected. Then, there is a process of appealing the decision and that can take even more time. Once there is a final decision, accepted or rejected, they are moved to another location. People who are rejected move back to the camps and live there "extra-legally." The people who have been accepted for refugee status are typically relocated to other cities and towns.

What I have learned is that there can be many misconceptions about refugees and asylum seekers if you do not know them personally; Who are they and why are they fleeing their country of origin? Hundreds of thousands of people were leaving their country and fleeing to Europe. Countries are not always prepared for receiving refugees. When they arrive in another country, they are often mistreated because they are misunderstood. People do not know what they have been through. Even allies who work with this population are continually learning about the people and the process.

But it was God that got my attention and opened my eyes to the plight that many people were enduring. I found myself in relationships with people that were struggling in their own countries and feared for their lives and it changed me. That is what guided me into this line of work. Here are a few stories that have spoken to my heart.

I lived in Central Asia for a time and some friends of mine were visited by a middle-aged couple from France. The people were very anti-refugee. Soon after meeting the woman, she freely expressed her bitterness about the refugees coming into France.

"Why are they coming here? We have our own problems. There are not enough jobs for our own people. Our young people can't get married because they don't have enough money and can't find housing. These foreigners just walk in and are given everything. If they have a war, they should stay in their own country and take care of their problems themselves. In France, during the war, we helped each other," she said.

I thought to myself, *This is different because during the war in France, you had a common enemy. People fleeing from the middle east, are in a civil war and have no idea who they can trust.*

While in Central Asia, I was constantly watching to see what was happening with the refugee situation. The people were in danger and they were desperate to get to safety. They and their families would get into overcrowded small boats to get to Europe, many of which never made it. My heart went out to them.

I soon became friends with a young refugee family from Afghanistan. The young man's father, a high government official, had sent him to Saudi Arabia to do Islamic studies. While in Saudi Arabia, the young man had an encounter with Jesus and became a Christian. When he returned to Afghanistan to his wife and son, he eventually told his wife about his experience. He did not tell his father. Somehow, his father found out about his son's new faith and wanted to kill him. Instead, his father imprisoned him in the family basement for a year, trying to get him to turn away from his new faith and come back to Islam. His wife and son were living in his father's house and were allowed to visit him on occasion. During that time, his wife became a Christian, as did his mother and two sisters but it was all kept secret because the father was working with the Taliban. After a year of imprisonment, his mother came to her son to help him escape because his father was going to have him killed. The young man left with his wife but his son was not able to go with him. The couple fled to Central Asia.

I met the couple at the International Church that I was attending in Central Asia.

They were very fearful because they believed that the father was going to send people to try to kill them. Because of the circumstances, people were afraid to befriend them. No one would take them in or provide aid because they feared for their own lives.

Eventually, the father's men found he and his wife in the capitol city. They did not harm the couple but returned to Afghanistan with his phone number and the father began making threatening phone calls to them. The father told his son that he needed to return to his home country immediately. The son tried to reason with his father but the father persisted to threaten him saying that if he did not return, he would kill his son. Soon after that conversation, the father did as he promised and killed his own grandson. In response, the young man's mother told the father that he was a horrible person and that she and his daughters had become Christians, too.

The young couple later did get asylum for religious persecution, moved to Canada and have had other children.

Religious persecution is not uncommon in many countries. I met a young twenty-two-year-old woman in Central Asia who had recently become a Christian and was in need of asylum because of religious persecution. While home visiting her family during the summer, she was stolen by a young man from her village. This is not an unusual practice. When women are stolen and forced to stay overnight, they are shamed into staying with the perpetrator. Her family didn't care that she was a Christian and neither did the man. Staying overnight with a him made it mandatory that she remain under his roof. She did try to make it work but the man was horrible to her. He was often drunk and raped her constantly. Even her own family did not come to her defense. When the couple was married two months, the man beat her so badly, he thought he killed her and threw her in the lake. The young woman mustered up the strength to swim to safety, left the area and went on to live a new life. Years later, she met a kind Christian man, they married and made it their life's work to serve God in ministry together.

The woman had applied for refugee status because of religious persecution years prior to her second marriage. Eventually, she and her husband were contacted by the American Embassy to come in for an interview. When they were approved, they quickly moved to New York with their four children. It was a real struggle for a while because the wife didn't speak any English and the husband was in poor health.

After many years in the U.S., they are talking about returning to Central Asia to serve God there. They believe that God wants them back in their home country to continue their ministry. Returning to Central Asia would mean they can never return to the United States. They have already started raising money to make the move.

One of the dangers for some refugees is that some countries send agents to find their countrymen and either bring them back or kill them. They use the family members left in country as leverage to get the refugees to return.

The reasons for people applying for refugee status are many. In some countries, religion and the government are deeply intertwined and you cannot separate the two. Many refugees come very disillusioned with their country's religion. Where some people are escaping religious persecution, others are escaping family control, some fleeing war, and some poverty. All of the situations are very dangerous.

Many of the refugees are going to Europe because most of the more affluent countries in the Middle East are not receiving refugees.

People fleeing war often settle just over the border from their home country waiting for the war to end. This can take many years and when they can return, their countries are often so devastated by war that there is nothing to return to when it's over except rubble and many of the remaining family members have perished.

Much of war takes place in the neighborhoods of war-torn countries. Men, women and children are shot going to the store to buy bread. Some people just disappear never to be seen again. If families lose their older sons when they serve in the military, many families will run away just to prevent from losing any more sons.

It is believed by many that refugees go to another country because they are economic migrants but that is not always the case. When people leave their home, it is usually under severe circumstances; there is no food or work in their country. It becomes a life survival issue.

Some refugees do come to America because they believe it is the land of opportunity, a fairy tale. It is the dream of some to come to America but not everyone's dream. I spoke to a Nigerian family that wanted to come to America because they believed that everything was paid for there. They ended up going to Europe. It is not as easy as many think to receive permission to come here.

American television contributes to many misconceptions by those who are seeking to come to this country. It can be very difficult for refugees when they arrive here because their reality is much different than their expectations. Europe is also thought about in a similar way.

It is so necessary for host countries to evaluate their strategy for receiving people as well. How can we better welcome refugees? Welcoming starts with being intentional about building relationships; a willingness to be a friend. That could mean helping refugees get connected to services; learn English, apply for employment, find a place to live. Being an advocate for a refugee family could mean the difference between surviving and thriving.

It can be very difficult on arrival to enter a country where the language is unfamiliar. *Google Translator* can be very helpful in communicating until they have an adequate mastery of the English language.

Schooling for children can be a challenge. I had an experience with a young family in France that had come from Syria but because they did not speak the language, they were unable to register their children for school on their own. A friend from mine befriended the family and helped them to get acclimated. He assisted the family so they were able to register in the country, get housing, and enroll their two oldest children in school. The first day of school, he took the father and the two children to school to meet the teacher and explain the family situation. The teacher assured them that he would take good care of the children. The father and teacher exchanged phone numbers should the family have any problem and need to connect with him.

The father began to cry as they left the school explaining that this was the first time his children had ever been in school.

Unfortunately, since the government was supporting them, after a time, the government decided that they wanted to move the family to another town. The family didn't know anyone in the new town, nor did they speak French well. Their friend and ally went to the church for support. He explained the situation and then went to the government to petition on the family's behalf. he explained that the family was doing well there. To move them would be detrimental. The government officials were flustered by his plea and told the family that if the father could get a job, they could stay. Someone from the church got him a job as a cook at a local restaurant.

Cultural misunderstandings happen constantly and I witnessed this firsthand. There was a motel in France on the outskirts of town that was a home to several refugee families. My colleague and I went to the motel to befriend some of the people. After sharing about his life, a Nigerian man explained that he had been in the country for one year and no one had ever asked him to share his story. My colleague told me that the French would never ask for that information because they feel that it is respectful of their privacy. If they ever did ask, they would need to have known them for a very long time.

Though it is very difficult to speak a language poorly in an unfamiliar country, the culture can be even more confusing. Not only does the language need to be translated, the culture too needs to be translated.

We can all be helpful with this process. Take time to notice the refugees around you. When you see someone struggling in a store or elsewhere, patiently help them with interpreting the language and the culture. This is so encouraging to them.

The opportunities to serve in organizations that support refugees in our country are endless. Inquire about how you can help in a city near you.

Katrina's heart for refugees is now taking her on an assignment in Greece.

The Story of Fariborz

In 1976, when Fariborz was twelve years old, the decision to come to the U.S. for his education was in the foremost of my mind.

Fariborz was born in Tehran, the capital city of Iran. Tehran is an advanced metropolitan city, very much like Washington DC. He had everything he wanted and needed there.

My job, at age twelve, was to be a good student. We were required to carry a rigorous course load so it could be very difficult. Because classes were not optional, I took the same classes as everyone else. Each year we studied Math and variety of sciences, Chemistry, History and Literature. A craft or technical class was included, as well as other miscellaneous classes. It was mandatory that you pass every single class or you would be required to repeat the entire year again. They did allow for students, at the end of the summer, to retake the test of the class that was failed. If you passed, you could go on to the next grade, if you failed, you would not. Just to put it in perspective, the Math and Science track for high school graduates in Iran included Math through Calculus and Differential Equations, and enough advanced Physics and Chemistry to pass you through the second year of college in the United States. I only went to one year of high school before moving to the United States though.

My studies were my top priority and I would get my work done immediately after school but I always found time for other activities. I played soccer in the neighborhood leagues and on the streets with my friends. I also loved music; listening to, playing and singing. I played Melodica and Keyboards, primarily. The Melodica was a mini keyboard that you would blow into to play. I never really had any formal training. I started playing Melodica by ear, and taught myself the organ and any other keyboard that was around.

All was well in my world.

The problem was that as we looked forward to higher education, the number of "seats" for college students was very limited, allowing for only a few to attend in Iran. This caused people to try other means to get their sons and daughters into schools. There was much favoritism at the time so if people knew people, their sons or daughters were admitted into college. Entrance exams were very difficult and the results dictated what major you were going to study and where. All of that was unacceptable to my family.

The solution to this educational dilemma was that families who had the means, sent their sons or daughters abroad to go to school. The plan was to receive a higher education away and then return to our home country to live the rest of our lives. We weren't wealthy. We were middle income, but our family could afford it, so that is what we did.

At the same time, we were observing the students in our neighborhood who were going through the process of attending school abroad. As they returned home in the summer, and we could see the change in them. They were fluent in another language, kind of cool and very fun. That is what we looked forward to doing.

Two years later, on July 13, 1978, my brother and I, along with a group of students and two chaperones, landed in California. I was fourteen years old and my brother was fifteen. The original plan was for each of us to live with an American host family...separately. The hope was that this would force us to speak English, learn the culture quickly, and ultimately go to high school and college, always with the goal to return to Iran.

My brother and I lived apart for a while but it didn't go as well as we had hoped. It had nothing to do with the host families. Living without our parents in a new culture was too much of a shock.

It was a real challenge that we found the Iranian and American cultures to be so different. The families we were living with appeared very dry and impersonal. It felt more like a business than a family environment. We struggled with learning the language, behavioral expectations and social etiquette. At the same time, we were quite homesick and because of the housing, had to spend time away from each other. My brother and two friends were housed somewhere else.

Telecommunications were very expensive at the time, so the cost of calling home to Iran was $3 per minute. That was not something we could afford on a routine basis.

One of the students who was a little older than my brother and I, faked an ID and moved into an apartment in Fresno. They were no longer part of our group.

That really appealed to us so my brother and I did the same and settled in the suburbs of Los Angeles, in Riverside. We followed our friends and enrolled in the same High School. The grown-ups that we were living with were our friend's relatives and welcomed us, gladly signing-off as our guardians, completing all the school paperwork. What seemed ideal at the time was very short lived. We thought the adults were watching out for us, but later discovered they were taking financial advantage of the money our parents were sending. When we discovered this, we decided to take a different course of action and moved out.

Our journey landed us in a very small town in West Virginia. One of our younger uncles, about eight years older than we, had just moved from Iran and was living there. We made the decision to move and live with him. He certainly would be more trustworthy than the people with whom we had been living.

On arrival, we went through the process of registering for school and lived together with our uncle temporarily. Later, we rented a mobile home and lived there while going to High School.

The town we lived in was so small that it only had one stop light. There was no McDonald's or Wendy's, either. The closest fast food restaurant was forty-five minutes away. It did, however, have a high school and a state college.

Language became an interesting challenge in West Virginia. While in California, I started to feel comfortable with English but moving to West Virginia was like starting all over. I had studied English in school and was pretty decent in grammar but speaking was a challenge. Terminologies and pronunciation were so different in West Virginia that it felt like another language. I responded to everything people said to me with "Yah."

I managed to go to high school and was able to take several classes at the same time; Sophomore, Junior and Senior English, Civics, Math and a variety of sciences. I had never taken many of these classes in Iran but seemed to manage well. I completed all of the required courses and graduated when I was fifteen.

Studying science was very easy for me but far more challenging were English and Civics classes. I was fairly strong in English Grammar from my Iranian second language education but writing and speaking was another story. My classes went so well that some of the American kids would copy my answers during senior English class exams.

Overall, people were fairly welcoming but many had never interacted with foreigners. Every time my brother and I went to the cafeteria for lunch, people would stare and questioned our presence.

My brother and I graduated from High School the same year and went to college together.

My primary focus in college was Political Science and other Sciences. Prior to my admission into the university, I was required to take several Political Science classes as well as general electives; French, Geography, Speech, College English, Math and Science classes. I was very prepared for the academics of college.

In college, I did the majority of my studying at the library. Sometimes breaks were needed, so I found myself frequenting the audio-visual rooms there. The lounge was equipped so that you could listen to music on records or watch television.

One night while taking a break, I was alerted to the quickly changing political climate in Iran. The Shah's regime was beginning to topple and it was at a rate faster than anyone anticipated. My friends and I watched the entire process together as we gathered around the television. Each night, we met to watch as the Iran we once knew, became something we no longer recognized. The streets were filled with people demonstrating against the government. There was nothing we could do about it so we continued to focus on our school work.

Then, the breaking news came that changed everything. A group of Muslim students in Iran stormed the American Embassy and took the diplomats as hostages. We were shocked! It was serious. When you do that to an embassy, it is like invading another country.

We were surprised by the reaction that the people in West Virginia had to this incident. It became obvious that many of the students and the residents simply did not like foreigners. They viewed us as threats and held it against my circle of friends and the other Iranian students at the college. We looked like the people they saw on television every night.

The press was very anti-Iran at the time and that didn't help. This really stirred emotions and the people rallied against us as if we were involved in what had taken place in Iran. We were clearly outnumbered and had to be very careful about our surroundings and how people would act on their emotions.

Of course, anytime there is a situation like this, the U.S. government is obligated to respond. The first thing President Jimmy Carter did was to freeze all of the Iranian assets. We were no longer going to receive any money. This included the money for our education. We had to live on what we had.

The immigration law for students required that anyone in the U.S. on a student visa must be enrolled in school full-time. If you needed to work to help pay for your education, you could not be employed off campus. You had to work on campus part-time. My friends and I had to support ourselves by doing any job we could find. Fortunately, the cafeteria had a lot of positions available for dishwashers. That was the first job I have ever had in my life. So at 5:00am each morning, I would put on my dishwasher hat and do what I needed to do to survive.

The animosity toward the Iranian students began to increase. It was really difficult to understand because we weren't any different than we had been and we definitely were not responsible for what was happening in Iran. We were watching as the rest of the world did.

Because of the financial burden, we moved with many of my Iranian friends into an old home off campus. It was a two-story house full of rats. At night, we could hear them running through the ceiling. But that is what we could afford, so we did what we had to do. Peanut butter became a major staple in our diet. You'd think that I would have tired of it but even today, I eat a lot of peanut butter.

One evening, we were sitting in our family room watching *Happy Days* on the television when we heard what sounded like a bomb exploding. Suddenly, we were covered in glass. A gang outside of our house disapproved of our living there and had thrown a large rock with a nasty picture and some very colorful language toward us. It was frightening.

We began to experience persecution on campus, as well. Banners were hung in protest against us. There was horrible profanity toward the Iranian students sprayed all over campus. People carried signs on their cars having horrible claims against us. It was quite shocking. The perpetrators were actually proud of their actions.

I was a fifteen-year-old college student, without my parents, working as a dishwasher, just trying to survive. Students would even harass me in my Political Science class. Big football player size guys would sit near me and verbally assault me. Of course, I couldn't respond to people that big.

Some of the hostility was also directed toward the Iranian students at my workplace. It was my job to take in all the trays and wash the dishes. The same students from my Political Science class would come into the cafeteria, make the biggest mess they could on their trays, stick a fork in their mashed potatoes, draw an American flag on their napkin and hang it from the fork. When they returned their trays to the kitchen, they would spit on it, throw it at us, saying something nasty as they walked away. All for the purpose of harassing us. Their message was loud and clear. It was a horrible situation that we just had to live with. There was no way out of it.

As a fifteen-year-old starting college, I was really scared. It was difficult to know how people would react to the news that was being communicated by the media. I didn't respond to the harassment because this was part of the country where many people legally carried guns. So, I lived in fear.

My brother and I stayed in touch with my parents by phone. It was expensive to call so that limited the frequency. We kept our conversation on the lighter side to protect them from the seriousness of our circumstances. It was interesting how my brother and my roles with our parents had reversed. They were unable to advise us on life because they were unfamiliar with the culture in the United States. We advised them. It was not because they were incapable, it was just too complicated to explain our situation when they could do nothing about it.

Our original plan when we came to the United States was to be gone from Iran during the school year and return home for the summers. My parents were going to financially support us but when all of the turmoil happened, plans changed. We were unable to travel home.

In the midst of this dark and gloomy time came the Gaspers. Glee Gasper, known to many of us as Mom Gasper and her husband Don couldn't be more politically opposite from one another. Mom Gasper was a liberal Democrat. Don was a staunch Republican. But when it came to my friends and me, they were on the same page, extremely welcoming. They "adopted" us. Their door was always wide open and they made sure we were cared for. The Gaspers took time to get to know us and vowed to be our protection. They said that if anything politically or otherwise happened, we were going to come to live with them until everything stabilized. Mom Gasper really meant it, too. She wasn't from a wealthy family but she had a big heart. Caring for us was really important to both of them. It was a breath of fresh air, a blessing, to have that experience after all we had been through.

I wondered why the Gaspers were different. We lived in the same community with others who persecuted us. Why did the Gaspers love and support us? As I look back, I realize that Mom Gasper really embraced diversity. She strived to get to know those who were different. She understood why we were there and respected our choice to go to college in their town. They valued our differences.

The others in town, were afraid of getting to know something different. I know they were very good, hard-working, honest people, but we didn't speak like they did or look like them. The media painted an inaccurate picture of us. That didn't help the situation. So, many feared us without even getting to know us.

This had a direct impact on the entire community. The media continued to create a real bias against us and poisoned a lot of minds that were easily influenced. The people in our town were brought up with a lot of tradition and lived in communities that looked a lot like they did, not like us. Had they not had been exposed to so much negativity, perhaps they would have gotten to know people that did not look like them or speak like them. Perhaps they would have chosen to learn from others, expand their circle of friends and grow. This was taken away from them and ultimately impacted us. It limited what we could do safely.

After I graduated from college, I moved to Baltimore to attend University of Maryland School of Pharmacy. I lived by myself in the downtown area on the west side, a few blocks away from the school. It was a fairly dangerous part of city. My brother planned to stay in West Virginia for a couple of years to complete his Bachelors in Psychology. I managed to convince him to change his major to pharmacy and move to Baltimore. I felt this would be a better future option for him than psychology. He went for it and moved to Baltimore and we lived together until after he graduated in 1988. When he got married.

Once we were in the United States and unable to travel outside of the country, our destiny was determined for us by our circumstances. After a few years of living here, we learned the culture and appreciated all that it had to offer. We loved the diversity that we came to experienced.

I did not see my mother and sister again until after I graduated from Pharmacy School in 1986, ten years later. Because Johns Hopkins Hospital offered me a job, I was able to obtained my Green Card and was finally able to travel. I coordinated with my parents to meet them in Turkey, a country that they could travel to easily without a visa. I could not go inside Iran because Iran was in the middle of a war with Iraq and I would have been drafted to go to war. I simply did not believe in that government anymore. We met in Istanbul, Turkey for a three-week visit. It was a wonderful reunion.

I met my wife in December of 1994.We had a mutual friend who had come from Iran to stay with my family for vacation. When she asked to spend time with some of her relatives, my wife and her sister came to pick her up. That was the beginning of a beautiful life together.

I have learned many valuable lessons from my experience. Many of which, I learned from Mom Gasper and have continued to practice in my life today. She taught me the power of compassion and the importance of it being first and foremost in everything we do. She taught me about embracing diversity, and getting to know people that are different than we are. Mom Gasper also impressed upon me that we should not only do good, but look for the good in everyone. If we look for it, we will find it, even in people with which we disagree. These lessons have carried me through life.

I traveled back to Iran for the first time after seventeen years from the date I had left the country. Being back in Iran was a heartwarming experience. It was amazing to see all the countrymen, women and family. But I also came to realize that I had spent most of my life in the United States. I discovered that living in Iran was not easy for me anymore. My way of life had changed and there was much about Iran that did not make sense to me. I had become accustomed to life in the United States.

When I listen to the news today, I see history repeating itself over and over again. It may be a different nationality or the demonizing of another people group, but the fear of the unknown continues.

It is important to mention that all of the Iranians that I attended college with have grown up to make considerable contributions to the world today.

They are influencers and are now hiring those people who once persecuted them.

I realized after completing pharmacy school that there was no doubt in my mind that the United States was home for me. I saw the potential of expanding my family's experience and professional life here. I will simply be visiting Iran from now on.

Fariborz works in a pharmacy in the northeast that he and his brother co-own and manage together. He is married and has two grown daughters who clearly reflect the values that he learned many years ago.

The Imprint

By Carol Marchant Gibbs

An incredible canvas stretches across the world.
Vibrant colors and textures reflect the beauty of every being.
All different but each carrying a light within.
The imprint of the Creator.

Chapter 5
Life in the LGBTQ Community

Spiritual Direction

When people of faith begin to recognize that their sexuality is inconsistent with what they have been taught, they have several possible choices. They can choose to walk away from the faith they have known and live an authentic life without faith. They can ignore who they really are and live an "acceptable" life in the church. One that others have created for them. Or, they can cling to God and reconcile the feelings they have deep inside, allowing Him to direct their path.

The Story of Bridget

It was through her deepening faith that Bridget began to recognize and appreciate every aspect of who she was created to be. The profound effect that Bridget's spiritual director had on her inspired her to do the same for others. Today, Bridget devotes much of her time to accompanying individuals on their spiritual journey, exploring their faith and growing in relationship with their God. But to begin doing that, it was first necessary for her to reconcile her faith with her sexuality. Bridget was gay.

I grew up in a Roman Catholic family, the youngest of seven children. My siblings and I are very spread out in age. There were four children, then a fourteen-year gap before the next three came along. My oldest brother is twenty-four years older than me. Of the three youngest children, my sister was born seven years before me and my brother four years before me. By the time I was born, the four oldest children were out of the house.

The age span of the seven children made our family dynamics quite unique. My oldest brother, oldest sister and my mother, were expecting babies all at the same time. Because I grew up with aging parents, my older siblings had a considerable amount of influence in my life. I was the same age as some of their children.

Many of my childhood memories are of being with my oldest sister Rosemary's family. We would play outside as much as possible, riding bikes and having adventures when the boys were involved. When it was just the girls, we would play dress ups and with dolls.

Television was also a big draw in the early sixties. My brother Mark and I spent many hours after school watching TV and eating our snack from a big can of Charles Chips.

My parents were much older, forty-four and forty-eight when I was born. Raising children for twenty-four years was exhausting for them! They became grandparents a month after I came along. They were tired, but had enough love for each us. I always knew I was very loved, although not necessarily a welcome addition at this stage of their life.

My mom and sister Rosemary were very close since they both had young children. As a result of my mother's age, Rosemary became like a second mother to me.

My mom was full of life, however; loving, very generous, and always involved in activities. She was an extrovert and loved being with people, talking on the phone, and riding anything that went in a fast circle at Hershey Park. She adored her children and grandchildren and would do anything to be with them. Not too many kids can say this, but I was good friends with my mom even as a teenager. I remember playing hooky from school so the two of us could get our ears pierced together.

In a different time and place, Mom would have been quite the business woman. Though she was a stay at home mom when I was a kid, she worked as a salesperson at Hutzler's Department Store when my older siblings were young to help put food on the table.

Mom continued her love of sales her entire life by becoming an Avon Lady. As a little girl, I would go with her on Avon sales calls and play with the sample lipsticks while Mom encouraged women to buy cosmetics and perfumes.

My dad was just the opposite. He was an introvert. Dad was very loving and adored his family, and very typical of men from his generation. He worked long days and expected dinner on the table when he got home. Dad was an avid reader and very self-educated so no one would ever know that he only had an eighth-grade education. His father died when he was eighteen months old and his mother struggled to survive with three daughters and a baby boy. He quit school to help support the family getting a job parking cars. He remained in the parking industry his entire life, eventually managing a large parking company in Baltimore. Dad worked well into his seventies before retiring.

Church was a large part of my Irish Catholic family's life. We went to mass every Sunday and were very involved in the church community. As large a family as we were, there was always a baptism, first communion, confirmation, wedding or other event that brought us together with church at the center of the celebration.

My sister, Mary Margaret was the youngest of the first four kids and twenty years my senior, is a Roman Catholic sister. She was in seminary when I was born. We often visited her as a family when she lived in the area. I remember the fun of playing hide-and-seek with my siblings, nieces and nephews in the cemeteries and other "holy" grounds at the mother house.

We did a lot of things together as a family and were close and loving, though at the same time, many subjects were taboo and feelings were rarely discussed or explored.

There were many tears when my sister Rosemary's family moved across country. I was twelve years old at the time. This was a significant event for my family. No one had ever left Maryland before. My heart was broken. I missed my big sister, beloved brother-in law and their five children. I especially missed my nephew and one of my closest friends, Bob. Bob and I wrote each other regularly for many years and are still very close.

Being an introvert, I did not have a large circle of friends nor was I involved in many activities. I was very close to the friends that I did have and remain close to a couple of them today.

I spent a considerable amount of time with my best friend from middle school. Most of my summers were spent swimming in her family's pool. We enjoyed sleepovers at each other's house where we spent most of our time talking about boys. We shared a special liking for Friendly's chocolate ice cream sodas and French fries. Our friendship continued through high school.

I enjoyed Girls Scouts from elementary school through high school. It was more of a social activity as I got older. The troop leader was a really cool mom and made everything extremely entertaining. We hiked, camped and had sleepovers at her home. Girl Scouts was a safe place for me and I loved it.

I made another close friend in high school, Rose. A group of us worked together at the local Hardees after school, on weekends and in the summer. We would often close the store and then hang out drinking and solving the world's problems. I was the designated driver before we knew that term. which simply meant that I had a car and perhaps had one less beer or swig of Boones Farm. Somehow, we all survived. When I dropped Rose off at home, I would often sit on the front porch with her while she sobered up a bit.

Rose continues to be one of my best friends today. In 2013, after same-sex marriage was legalized, I had the honor of being Rose's *Best Person* when she married her partner, Pam, after 29 years together.

When I was in high school, my dad's depression became more noticeable. Apparently, this was a struggle that he had dealt with for years. A tiny, daily pill helped him cope with life. It was never named as such or talked about but I remember times when Dad would come home from work on Friday night, go to bed, and stay there until Monday morning when he went back to work.

My parent's relationship was often unpleasant to be around in those days. I was the last one at home and was often drawn into the middle of their arguments and dysfunction. I heard from both parents why they were not happy with each other and often found myself trying to be the peacemaker between them. It was a time when people chose to stay together at any cost and I'm glad they did. I believe that they reconciled in their own way. Their love for one another was evident as they grew old together.

My happiest memories are of our family camping trips. When I was young, I would go camping with my sibling's families. After I left home for college, my parents bought a pop-up camper and joined in the camping fun. We started a family tradition of having an annual camping trip at a campground near the beach. It was a huge group. Our family would occupy an entire campground circle. It was a perfect environment for us because every family had their own space and we could roam from campsite to campsite. The kids were able to play freely, while the adults relaxed and enjoyed each other. We hiked, swam, fished, went canoeing, played games, told ghost stories around the campfire, and enjoyed the best ice cream at the campground store.

I never really understood what "gay" meant until I went to college. We certainly never talked about it in my family. In high school, when others were going on dates and to dances, I didn't. I just wasn't interested. I had friends both boys and girls but no dating relationships. I was "Mother Slinky" – always taking care of everyone and being the designated driver. I believe people were drawn to me because I had a calming presence; was a good listener and a good friend. I was well liked, but the absence of a dating life made me feel different. I didn't have the highest self-esteem so I chalked this lack of dating relationships up to, "No one must be interested in me. I must not be pretty enough. I must not be this or that." I thought there was something wrong with me. It wasn't even on my radar to consider that I might be attracted to girls. College was a different story.

My parents weren't paying very close attention to my decisions when I was graduating from high school so I needed to figure out what was next on my own. Should I go to college? If yes, which one? What major? Because things were tense at home with my dad, Mom felt I should go away to college. This was her way of protecting me. At the same time, there was no planning or money to send me to college. It really was not on their radar to consider what I might do after high school.

Given that lack of planning or forethought to my college experience, I decided to look at a school that my brother-in-law's sisters attended. It was only an hour away. You could enter the college and not declare a major until two years after being there. With Mom's Avon money, my savings from Hardee's and the first of many college loans, I applied to the school and was accepted with an "undeclared" major.

The college I attended was in the northeast and excelled in Physical Education and Music. There were many lesbians in the Phys. Ed. program and many gay men in the Music program. The LGBTQ community was clearly present everywhere on campus, including my girls' dorm. I had never seen same-sex relationships before, nor did I believe that they were okay. Still, as I observed these relationships for the first time, I began to wonder if this was who I was. It had never occurred to me before.

Eventually, in sophomore year, I fell in love. It was a new experience for both Shelby and me. We muddled our way through, hiding our relationship from everyone. From a spiritual perspective, we both experienced tremendous guilt. She was very involved in Campus Crusade for Christ and Young Life. I didn't feel comfortable around the people in those ministries, they kind of freaked me out, but I too carried the burden of guilt. We stayed together for a couple of years until the hiding and guilt became too much so the relationship ended.

My faith was important to me, though I wasn't in church very much after I left home. I would dabble in different Christian groups and bible studies on campus, often with Shelby.

I never heard about being gay in church growing up. We just didn't talk about it so it never occurred to me that maybe God created me this way. At the time, I believed that being gay was just a flat-out sin. I should never allow myself to be involved with a woman or to be influenced by the wrong people. At least, that is what I heard from the Christian groups on campus. They worked very hard to keep everyone out of the sinful lifestyle. Being gay was just wrong and the sin was unforgiveable.

I needed to work to pay tuition, so in my second year, I continued my career in fast food and took a job at McDonald's. After a short time, I became a shift manager and continued to work there through college. I excelled in my position and was recruited to go to *Hamburger University*, a management training program for McDonald's, after I graduated.

A kind woman who also worked for McDonald's and had become my mom-away-from-home, discouraged me from attending *Hamburger University.* She suggested that I consider talking to her husband who worked in the insurance world. I did and got my first job as a claims processor. That was the beginning of my career in health insurance.

I stayed in my college town for a few more years after graduation then moved back to my hometown to continue in the insurance field. I was hired as a claims manager despite my lack of experience, and worked my way up to Vice President of Operations. For the last five years, I have been supporting the COO and other Operations leaders working thirty hours a week from my home. I have been working for the same company for thirty-one years.

Shortly after graduating from college, I entered into another relationship and again began to wrestle with my sexuality. Nancy and I moved in together and relocated back to Maryland for her job. We were together for almost six years and out to her family, but were still hiding our relationship from mine.

It was difficult to reconcile the faith of my childhood and my sexuality. The Catholic Church was very much a part of who I was even if I no longer attended mass.

Nancy was the complete opposite of me. She was a computer programmer and an atheist, as was her family, so she had no religious struggle with her sexuality. Years later, I realized that not being able to share my faith and have Nancy support my struggle was a huge obstacle for me personally and for my growth.

My faith made it a real challenge for me to commit to being gay. I was conflicted, often trying to deny who I was. It was not really what I wanted. It was too difficult and too wrong. Eventually, my lack of commitment led to Nancy walking away. My vacillating became tiresome and she just couldn't continue to try to convince me of our relationship.

After the relationship ended, I dated a man for three months, poor guy. It started as a blind date. He was nice and kind, but it didn't take me long for me to realize that he wasn't right for me. I struggled for years reconciling my two relationships with women, but I knew in three months that I did not belong with a man. I always feel badly when I think about him. I was just trying to do what I thought I was supposed to do and I broke his heart.

I did not hear from Shelby for six years after college and then one day, I received a letter. She had gotten my contact information from some friends. We talked on the phone and I accepted her invitation to come to Pennsylvania for a visit. She was dating a man at the time, so I thought I was safe but I was wrong. Our love quickly rekindled and we began a long-distance relationship.

A few months later, my mom was diagnosed with lung cancer. She had been a smoker until a heart attack prompted her to quit. I was in my sophomore year of college. Unfortunately, Mom's heart was weak, and she had a heart attack that took her life just as chemotherapy was to begin. This was one of the saddest moments of my life.

It was also a wake-up call for me. I could no longer continue to live with the guilt and uncertainty of my sexuality. Shelby and I agreed that we needed help each other to reconcile our struggles and confirm our truth. We entered therapy separately and each emerged with the realization that we were indeed gay and it was okay. It was not only okay with us but it was okay with God, as well. God created us and loved us. From that point on, I never again questioned if being gay was a problem with God. We were both finally at peace.

We never really became active in the gay community. We just had a few close friends who were gay. That was enough for us.

Shelby and I realized through the counseling process the importance of the presence of faith in our relationship. Faith was very much a part of each of us and Shelby especially missed a church community. She had grown up in a very active Lutheran church. The church was a huge part of her life and most family activities involved the church in some way.

We resisted going to the "gay" church, Metropolitan Community Church, for a while but ultimately did go. It was like coming home. We were not hidden or just tolerated. We were celebrated as individuals and as a couple. The church was Christ centered and, for me, the rituals were familiar to my Catholic spirit. We became very involved in the church for many years. I was on the board of the church and Shelby sang in the choir.

Part of the therapy experience encouraged me to tell my family about my sexuality. My mom had already died and I didn't feel a need to tell my aging father. I didn't think he would really understand. He simply loved Shelby as another daughter and never questioned me about her.

I did tell two of my three sisters; Mary Margaret and my sister closest to me in age, Barbara. I was twenty-nine and even at that point, I think my sisters thought my being gay was a phase that I would outgrow but they really were not surprised. They embraced and accepted my news but we never talked about it again. I believe it was my wonderful brother-in-law who reminded my sisters when they needed it that this was my life and they would have to let me live it.

Shelby was definitely part of our family and warmly included, but we lived in a "don't ask, don't tell" world. I worked hard most of my life to keep my true self hidden and to avoid making others feel uncomfortable. If you keep your life hidden, you will not be discriminated against or hurt. It's an exhausting way to live.

Shelby's family was different at first. They had known about her sexuality when she was younger and got her "help" to fix the problem. When she told them about our relationship and how we were moving forward, she was told I was not welcome in their home. This was devastating for her because she was very close to her family. That didn't last very long for Shelby's mom. Shelby did not go home for Christmas that year and her mom decided that she was not going to live without her. She needed Shelby in her life. It took two years for Shelby's father to speak to me. Even when I would sit next to him at the kitchen table or play games with the family, I may as well have been invisible to him. This changed over time but those first two years were very difficult.

Shelby and I were together for fourteen years but because marriage was not an option at the time, we never married. Most of those years were happy and I'm sure we would have married if that had been an option. Over time, the busyness of our lives took its toll on our relationship. Our priorities became skewed. I was always busy at work, committing much of my time to an extremely stressful job and Shelby put her energy into a vacation rental property at the beach that we were building. I was completely oblivious to the fact that we were growing apart.

Then one day, Shelby expressed that she was unhappy with our relationship shortly after our beach house was finished being built. We separated three months later. We continued to own the beach house together for the next ten years and were both deeply saddened about the fate of our relationship.

Although it was difficult to own a beach rental property together and no longer be a couple, the house became a wonderful vacation spot for my family. It was like the camping of my childhood. Every Easter and every fall, my siblings and I would retreat to the beach house. It was extraordinary time together. Shelby used the house with her family at other times in the same way.

I was devastated by the break-up of my relationship with Shelby. I thought we were going to be together for a lifetime. I had counted on Jesus to not let the separation happen and I felt like He let me down. My body, mind and spirit were broken. I quit my job and blamed it for the stress that was occurring in my life. My body was in pain, eventually leading to my hospitalization and surgery. I longed for a God who would make things better again.

As I recovered from surgery and wondered what to do next, I thought maybe if I took a religion class at seminary, it would help me to find God again. Through education comes understanding, right? My intention was to only take one class but the next thing I knew, I was enrolled in seminary. I went back to work part-time and started school as a full-time student in the Masters of Religion program.

I loved the experience of being in seminary but it was very difficult as well. I was in the same classes as many of my friends in the Masters of Divinity program, but I was not receiving the same spiritual formation, support and direction as those peers. My classes spoke to my head and the academic in me. They did not speak to my heart and the longing for the God who was absent.

On graduation day, I wondered if I was the only one in my class standing in that church who no longer believed in God. My academic pursuit messed with the faith I was trying so hard to cling. I knew there was a God intellectually, and I was deeply disappointed in Him. And Jesus, He had definitely disappeared from my life. Everything I believed about Jesus was seemingly a lie. I wasn't angry with Him anymore. I just felt nothing, and nothing felt a whole lot worse than anger.

The funny thing about this Mystery we call God is that the questions about Him never go away. That longing for Him had always been with me. So, I went on a search to fill the lack in my spiritual life.

A few years later, I stumbled upon a program with the Shalom Institute entitled, *Personal Spiritual Deepening*. The commitment involved five hours one Saturday a month for nine months. Every student was also required to work with a spiritual director during their entire time in the program.

I was familiar with spiritual direction but had no previous experience with it in the past. I contacted my former therapist, Sophie. knowing she was also a spiritual director in hopes that enough time had passed since my therapy. All was well so she agreed to meet with me in a new capacity. Sophie welcomed me warmly and accepted without judgement as I shared about how God and church had *seemingly* disappointed me. She listened to my stories, doubts, fears, and longings, and gently encouraged and challenged me to explore and respond to them. Sophie also recommended a simple and out of print book entitled, Jesus, A Disciples Search, by Murray Bodo. Written by a monk searching for Jesus, it took me a year to read this little book. I joined Murray, sitting under his imaginary fig tree near the Sea of Galilee and met Jesus anew. He was no longer the savior of my sin and my soul, or of my relationships. I was able to develop an authentic relationship with Jesus as the Wisdom Teacher of my life. Several years later, we met at the Sea of Galilee and shared a laugh as I offered my tears to the sacred water.

As I moved from learning *about* God to developing a relationship *with* God, I began to recognize the Loving Presence had always been with me. I allowed this Presence to fill the emptiness in my soul.

The gift and impact of spiritual direction in my journey of transformation and growth has been enormous. Nine years later, Sophie continues to listen deeply and gently challenge me as I walk my spiritual journey.

Eventually, I explored, and responded to the call to become a spiritual director and offer my support to others. I enrolled in a two-year training program that consisted of a monthly intensive weekend with classes, spiritual formation, verbatims and supervision. Over time, my body, mind, and spirit has healed.

I knew from the first weekend that I had found my people and my calling. Six years later, my ministry has evolved to include individual spiritual direction, small groups, and retreats. I continue to be humbled and grateful to those who trust me to accompany them on their journeys.

I was fortunate to be able to continue working for the same company that had once caused me so much stress and now was in its rightful place and priority in my life.

As a result of my healing, I decided to take a chance on love again. I met Robin in 2016 and discovered what love looks like at 50-something versus a 20-something relationship. It's been a beautiful thing. Robin is a special education teacher who has creatively joined her degree and gifts in art with her passion for education and enjoyment of history. She has a huge heart for her students and for all creatures great and small. Our home has been a welcome rescue and resting place for bees, butterflies, crows, geese, cats, and dogs, just to name a few. Robin is from a small family and though our backgrounds are different, we share the same love of family and creation, and the same desire to make a difference in the people and world around us.

Robin was aware that she was gay at a much earlier age then I was and did not have the same struggles coming out. Her mom sadly passed away when she was only sixteen so she never had the opportunity to tell her. Robin told her father she was gay when she was in college. He was busy with his own life and, though he struggled to understand at first, he accepted Robin's life with little resistance and a great deal of love. Today, Robin talks to her ninety-three-year-old dad every day and lovingly cares for him in every way possible during this horrific pandemic. I am grateful for the gift of her in my life.

Sophie has often said to me, "Nothing is ever wasted." Reflecting on my story, I understand this simple statement as a profound truth. The twists and turns of my life have created who I am in this moment and continue to shape my awareness of the God with whom I dwell and who dwells in me.

This *Mystery, Presence, Wisdom* and *Love* that some call God is big enough to embrace all and intimate enough to know each of us by name. In the midst of the chaos surrounding us in 2020, I am more grateful than ever for this deep knowing and for the opportunity to walk with others on the journey.

Bridget works part-time as a consultant with the insurance company she has been with for thirty plus years. Part-time allows her time to develop the things that she cares most deeply about in her life. Spiritual direction continues to be a passion of hers. She loves working with individuals, meeting with two small groups each month, and leading retreats. She hopes to one day lead and encourage a group of people from the LGBTQ community. Bridget feels very blessed to have all of this in her life.

The Q Christian Fellowship

The Q Christian Fellowship is "a diverse community of people with varied backgrounds, cultures, theologies and denominations, drawn together through their love of Christ and belief that every LGBTQ+ person is a beloved child of God." Their mission is to "cultivate radical belonging among LGBTQ+ people and their allies through a commitment to growth, community, and relational justice."

I met Kim at a *Q Christian Fellowship* Conference in 2019.

The Story of Kim

For many years, Kim attempted to live the life that was expected of her…as a straight woman. Kim married a man, and continued to be active in their very conservative church. She may have appeared to be fine on the outside but inside she knew that she was living a lie. It was an excruciating way to live. When her husband left her, Kim realized that she couldn't live the lie anymore. Everything she had once believed to be true began to change.

I grew up in a small town in the Midwest in a family of five children, having three sisters and one brother. I was directly in the middle. My parents separated when my youngest sister was born so my mom was left to raise us on her own.

I have very few memories of my father living with us but the ones I do have were difficult and I remember them vividly. He was a very stern man and he used fear to keep us in line. His spankings were intense and I tried to avoid them. One of the most troubling things that happened to me as a child was when my father made me sit outside on the front porch in the dark as a form of punishment. I was terrified that somebody was going to kidnap me. I just kept looking around from the left to the right so I would be ready to respond quickly if I saw someone. Shadows and unfamiliar sounds gripped me. Though I don't know how long I had to sit there, it felt like an eternity to my four-year-old self.

My parents' relationship was very troubled. I remember my father physically assaulting my mother. He just kept screaming at her. When would he stop? I was so frightened. My mother would try to defend herself but he hit and pushed her even harder. When the police arrived, she showed them a handful of the hair he had pulled from her head. My father wasn't around much after that. He moved out and we only saw him a few times a year.

My grandparents worked hard to maintain a relationship with our family after my dad left. I was close to my grandparents and saw them fairly often. I remember Grandpa bringing food for us to eat. I would help him skin the squirrel, rabbit, and pheasant, and prepare them for cooking. My grandparents tried to support my mom as much as they could. When I was old enough to visit them on my own, I saw them more often. I was especially close to my paternal grandmother despite not seeing my father very much.

My mom raised her five children on state aid after Dad left. She didn't have a job so she was home much of the time for us. We eventually moved in with my maternal Grandma who lived in a small two-bedroom trailer. Grandma owned a house next door that she rented out so after a short stay with her, we were able to move into her house. Grandma took care of us financially and in every other way.

My grandma was a very caring person. I remember being sick for four days, once, and she told my mom to take me to the doctor because something was seriously wrong with me. When Mom finally did, they sent me to the hospital immediately because my appendix had burst. I received an emergency appendectomy to prevent anymore poison from spreading through my body and remained in the hospital for two weeks. A draining tube extended from the incision in my stomach for the majority of my stay. I am thankful my grandma recognized the severity of my illness.

It was a challenge to get close to my mom. Though she appeared easy going, taking life as it came to her, raising five kids on her own was stressful. Mom just tried to survive her day to day life. She was very busy keeping up with the chores of the house so I spent my childhood tending to myself, with my siblings, and running around the small town where we lived.

I really admired my oldest sister and tried to follow in her footsteps. We were the athletic ones in the family. We didn't play together much because she was five years older but we were both tomboys and if I was going to play catch with anyone it was going to be her. Even in high school, I wanted to have her sports jersey number. When it came time to apply to colleges, I attended her alma mater.

My second sister was two years older than me and more of a "girlie" girl. I would have to bargain with her to play catch with me. If she played catch with me, I had to play dolls with her. I hated playing with dolls but it was worth the sacrifice sometimes.

My brother was four years younger than me. We played together some but our age difference and interests made it difficult to determine what we could play. He was the favored grandchild so he spent a lot of his time next door with my grandma in her trailer learning how to play the piano.

My younger sister was five years younger than me and I rarely did anything with her because she was too young. I think I was jealous of her because she was the baby and appeared to get most of the attention.

Most of the time, I played with my best friend, Rick. Rick lived down the street so we were able to spend most of our time together. Everything was a competition between us. We would throw rocks at bottles on the railroad tracks to see who could break the most, and snowballs at telephone poles to see who could hit the pole at the highest point. Even chopping wood at his house became a competition. We won an equal amount of times.

My mom was usually unavailable to me so a wonderful woman in our town took an interest in my well-being and filled in the gap. Martha and her husband were very supportive as I was growing up. Martha was like a second mother. We did many fun things together. I especially remember riding bikes with her. She and her husband had a paper route so when they were away, I would cover their route and watch their house. When I was old enough, they were the ones who taught me to drive in their car. Her husband even took me to get my license. When they had a son, I would be the one to babysit for him. I was very close to Martha but my mom never seemed to mind at all.

My dad was one of eleven children so I had quite a few aunts, uncles and cousins. I didn't see them very often but we would get together occasionally for family reunions. I became closer to my extended family when I became a teenager and started to make my own money. That allowed me a way to visit them.

I grew up attending a very strict Baptist Church. We were in church every Sunday and for other activities during the week. It didn't take long for me to figure out that I really needed to pay attention to my behavior, even as a child. There were things that you did and things that you did not do. Everything outside of the "dos" resulted in "hell, fire and brimstone."

Some of the most frightening memories that I have had as a child are related to my church experience. One day, I remember coming home and finding no one there. I thought the rapture had occurred and I was left behind. It was terrifying because I was taught that if I was going to "catch-up" with everyone in Heaven, I was going to have to deny the antichrist, accept Jesus as my Savior and have my head cut off. We actually saw movies about this at church. It was horrible and it caused me to be very anxious any time I came home to an empty house.

I gravitated toward the activities that I enjoyed the most; sports, cards and chess. Being a good athlete and very competitive, I participated in every sport activity that I possibly could. Every year, I played little league baseball and was the only girl on the team. In the 70s, it was a big deal that I was the pitcher. The boys on the other teams used to make fun of me until they found themselves at the plate receiving my pitches and failing to hit the ball. I would throw anything I could throw, and played often down by the creek skipping stone.

I learned at a very early age that if I wanted something, I would have to work for it myself. In the summer, I would "walk beans." Walking beans meant that I would use a hoe and cut out the weeds in the farmers' fields. I also mowed yards, cleaned houses, babysat, and had a paper route. I did anything I could to make money.

As my oldest sister matured, we spent less time together. She committed herself to babysitting other children and doing odd jobs for people in the church so she could make money. When she wasn't working, she was with her friends. There was not much time for me.

Some of the happiest memories of my life involved Easter Sundays. Mom tried to make them special. We would always attend the sunrise service as a family. Then, one year, I don't know how she did it, but Mom bought new fancy dresses and bonnets for each of my sisters and me, and a nice little suit for my brother. It really made that Easter special. Every Easter after that, I would get my two older sisters' hand-me-downs.

A week at the Bill Rice Ranch made summers really fun. My mom would stay up very late the night before, sewing culottes for each of the girls in our family because we couldn't wear pants there. The ranch was a Christian camp that provided opportunities to participate in many activities like horseback riding, cookouts on the mountain, swimming, sports, and hiking. Riding horses was my favorite activity there. We heard a lot of preaching that week and we actually enjoyed it.

I don't ever remember hearing anything about homosexuality at the camp. I believed it was considered a sin of adulthood and we were just kids.

My very conservative upbringing became increasingly more difficult for me as I aged. The pairing of couples in church was the first time that I noticed an attraction to the same sex. I heard in church how same-sex attraction was wrong and those who chose that lifestyle were damned to hell. While I didn't have any sexual awareness during my younger years, I do recall sitting in church during the service pairing up couples. I was probably around eight to ten years old and I did this only with adults. Married couples were always paired together, with one exception. A lady, who was married and had five boys, I paired up with me. It wasn't a sexual thing, it was a couple's thing. I thought she should be with me. I knew that I was different from the other girls but I just thought that I was a Tomboy. At least, that is what people would call me. I had heard many times about the "sin" of same sex attraction in church; men with men, women with women, Sodom and Gomorrah. They were all damned to hell so I tried not to think about my fascination with the same sex.

There were many other difficult moments in my childhood. I was often on my own and remember getting lost while riding my bike one day. I was only five years old and just couldn't find my way home. I became so upset I stopped in the middle of the road and started crying. A man working in his garage came out and tried to point me in the right direction but he really wasn't very nice about it. I did manage to find my way back home, eventually.

It was frightening being at a friend's house down the street when his dad molested me. We were playing in the backyard and his dad took me into the shed and put his hand down my pants. I didn't know what he was doing but I knew enough to stay away from him after that happened. I told no one about it.

My father was very unreliable and that caused me a great deal of angst. I remember waiting, for what seemed to be all day, for him to pick my siblings and I up for our visits. There were two ways to get to our house and I would ride my bike back and forth and back and forth, waiting for him to come. Eventually, I would go home and call my grandma's house only to find that he hadn't left yet…but he was getting ready to leave. I would repeat my ride back and forth until he finally showed up. I saw my father only a couple of times a year and usually for a week or so in the summer.

Another difficult moment involved my neighbor. I used to clean house for the lady across the street to make a little money. Her husband had a motorcycle and he liked to give me rides on it. I loved riding the motorcycle because it was bigger than the little mini bike that I owned. One day, he began to enjoy the motorcycle ride too much. He used it as an opportunity to play with my breast as I steered his bike. I learned, once again, that he was another man I needed to avoid.

We didn't have money to do any traveling as a family, or anything else for that matter, so time with friends was my only entertainment. When I wasn't in school, I spent most of my time outside with my friend, Rick. I would leave the house early in the morning and return when the street lights came on. Sometimes, I would stop in at home during the day for a peanut butter and jelly sandwich, then I was off again.

Friendships were an interesting challenge in school. I spent most of my time competing with the boys in sports. When I entered the sixth grade, I physically couldn't keep up with them so I backed off and started hanging out with kids that were younger than me. They thought it was cool to have an older student befriend them. I became like a mother figure to them, looking out for them on the playground.

When I got to high school, I really started to struggle with same-sex attraction. I had never had any close friends in school up to this point and now one of the few that I did have I had become very attracted to soon after meeting her. Alice was my first serious girl crush. I began to develop this deep affection for her and desired to be with her and touch her. It was very confusing because she was my best friend. Alice was quiet and very shy at school but did things to tease me, not understanding how serious I was about her. She was feeding right into my fantasy to be with her and it was a struggle for me.

Each day I battled my desire for my best friend. It was a challenge because we were together all the time. We would go down to the lake, sit in the car and talk for hours. I loved being with her. I always enjoyed the sleepovers at her house. When we weren't together, we were talking on the phone. Time just seemed to fade away when I was with her. And though she appeared to be somewhat aware of my feelings for her and would give me subtle encouragement to tease me, I would never give any reaction. I was scared to death that she would figure out just how serious my feelings were for her and she would reject me. I kept my feelings to myself for fear of being "outed." I knew the consequences of being labeled a lesbian. That would be devastating so I kept my secret hidden. I was fifteen years old, and the voice of the church kept ringing in my ear. It was so negative I did all that I could to avoid thinking about it.

I attempted to distract myself from these deep feelings by dating a guy from church, Thomas. We only saw each other on Sundays or at other church activities. When he and his family moved away, we stayed in touch through letters. We continued our long-distance relationship even through his service in the military and then we got engaged. The whole time, I was struggling with my feelings for Alice.

When I was a senior in high school, I moved out of my mom's house and into her car. I'm not sure why I did that. Mom didn't really care as long as I was buying groceries and bringing them back to her. It was pretty obvious that I was homeless because most of my clothes were in the car. One day, the principal noticed. When he questioned me directly about living in my car, I denied it because I was afraid I would be in trouble.

When others heard I was homeless, a very nice family who had a daughter my age offered me a place to stay. I went to the same school and played on sports teams with their daughter so I had gotten to know the family fairly well. After staying with them for a few days, they invited me to come live with them. I accepted and stayed there for the rest of my senior year of high school.

After graduation, I continued with my plan to get married to Thomas even though we had never dated. He had been away for four years, and we did not really know each other. I believed that getting married would cure me from my attraction to Alice, who I knew I could never have. It was "against nature" as I had been told all my life.

Thomas and I began planning a wedding for the December following my graduation from high school but he called me a few days before the wedding and told me he wasn't able to take leave to be there. What? He couldn't get his schedule together to come home for a wedding that had been planned for over a year? Finally, the lightbulb went on in my head. I was about to marry a guy that I had hardly seen. Our relationship was built on the letters we had written for four years. What was I doing? This was the first time in my life that I didn't go along with the plan. It was an eye-opening experience for me. I wrote him a letter and called off the whole thing.

Despite my more stable living situation, I went downhill after I broke off the engagement. Now that I wasn't going to get married, I turned my attention to Alice but quickly became frustrated because she was dating a boy that she was probably going to marry. I responded by sleeping around with twelve guys over the course of a year. I wasn't old enough to get into bars, but there was a college town nearby that I could get into on the weekends. I would find someone to buy me drinks then pick up by some random man for a sexual encounter. It was empty. I never enjoyed a moment with the men. I was attempting to neutralize the feelings I had been suppressing for Alice. I continued this pattern until I went off to college.

My oldest sister had returned after three years of college and moved in with my next oldest sister and her boyfriend's family. Only two of my siblings remained at home. I stayed where my older sisters lived sometimes but mostly I stayed with the family that had taken me in while I was in high school.

The mom in the family, Clara, had become very instrumental in my life. Not only did I graduate from high school, but she made sure I went to college, too. She knew the marriage plans had fallen through and she encouraged me to consider going to college. Clara helped me fill out the application, complete all the financial forms, and get together everything I needed to go to school. I wish I had listened to what she was telling me more carefully but I chose to go to the Christian college where my older sister had gone. It probably wasn't the best choice for me, but I was determined to go there.

In fear, I continued to internalize my same-sex attraction. There really was no one I could talk to about it. I don't ever remember hearing any derogatory remarks in school but I knew it was definitely frowned upon. I was aware of how gays were persecuted. I had seen and heard about it on the news so I remained silent.

My conservative church certainly made their views known. The homosexual community was a major topic of discussion there. They were an "abomination." Any and all who participated in such sexual perversion were damned to hell for eternity. The condemnation I heard was so harsh that it prevented me from disclosing my secret. The fear of anyone ever finding out about me was overwhelming and I swore to keep it to myself no matter what.

I hoped that going far away for college would cure my attraction to my best friend, Alice. She was planning her wedding to the father of her child. I wanted to believe that distance would help.

I went to a Christian college convinced that it was going to "fix" me. I majored in Psychology with a plan to become a high school guidance counselor.

Clara continued to be active in my life. It was wonderful to receive the packages that she sent every month. She knew I didn't have any dresses, which women were required to wear, so she sent a steady stream of dresses, food and money. She was amazing.

My attraction to women only increased my first year of college. I would attempt to fight against my desires by sleeping on the floor or going without food. It was a punishment for how I was feeling. I tried to change the way I was thinking to no avail and continued to struggle.

After my first year of college, one of my friends, Dana, wanted to come to my hometown to take a Philosophy class with me at the local college during the summer. I remember feeling very anxious about her coming to stay with me. I was excited and fearful all at the same time. The plan was for her to live at my house for the summer. The second week she was there, she made a pass at me. I didn't know how to respond. I was entering into unknown territory.

Though I tried, I didn't have a clue of what I was doing. I'm certain it was very disappointing to her. She had been sexually active with her boyfriend for the past two years and I did not meet her expectations.

The next day, I wrote Dana a very long letter to tell her I really cared about her, that I loved her. My delivery of the letter probably wasn't the best timing. I gave it to her during class. I was ready to let it all out, especially after what had happened the night before. She read the letter, put her head down on her desk, and left the class when it was over. She refused to talk to me about what had happened and moved out to live with my sister's husband's family for the rest of her time that summer.

Dana was the first person I came out to. Now, we would go to class and she wouldn't even look at me. My lifelong fear of telling someone blew up in my face. I felt rejected, alienated, devastated, and defeated.

The turmoil of finally revealing myself had just begun. We lived in a small town so news of it traveled through my friends and family quickly. Coming out was a humiliating experience. My sister's father-in-law sat me down and told me it was just a phase I was going through. So the remainder of the summer, except for going to class, I managed to keep to myself. I just stayed at home not wanting to face friends or family. I feared the conversations and the condemnation an interaction would bring.

I made it a point to see Alice a few times that summer. Much to my surprise, she did not reject me but was very supportive. Alice had her own life now. She was married with a baby. My affection had turned to Dana so my past attraction to Alice was not an issue anymore.

Unfortunately, Dana and I had signed up to be roommates for our sophomore year. I anticipated it to be extremely awkward but after driving thirteen hours back to college, the result of our encounter was far worse than I ever expected. On arriving at school, I was stopped at the gate and told to go directly to the Dean's office. The dean explained that I was not going to be allowed to go to school that semester.

"Turn around and go back home," he said.

Dana had told the administration that I was a lesbian and she didn't want to be my roommate so I was kicked out of the school. Homosexuality was not permitted on the Christian campus. Dana had neglected to tell them that she made a pass at me first.

I left college, devastated once again, and began the thirteen-hour trip home. I had never been so humiliated in my life. Everything was lost, my integrity, my education, my friends and family, everything that was important to me. I felt like my life was over. I was the lowest I had ever been in my life. There was no reprieve, no way to redeem myself, my reputation, or my life. As the tears flowed down my face, I remember traveling through West Virginia and wanting to drive right off the cliff. I truly wanted to die and end the hurt, pain, and rejection. I certainly didn't want to go home and explain to everyone why I was not permitted to enroll for the fall semester. I saw only death as a resolution.

Only God could have stopped me from driving off the cliff that day. It was a wonder that I didn't do it. In those moments of despair, God convinced me that taking my life was a non-negotiable choice. I fought through my tears and my sadness and I chose life.

I made the decision to move in with my father instead of going to my hometown to live with the family that I had lived with prior to college. I just couldn't face all my family and friends.

While living at my father's house, I remember thinking about how important the decision was that I made that day. Life isn't always easy, but no matter how bad things get, suicide would never be an option for me again.

I was determined to fight back and do whatever it took to get back all that I had lost, so I "reformed myself." That is what I had to do to go back to school. I got down on my knees, prayed and read the Bible. I became everything they wanted me to be. I had letters written from myself and others that stated that I would be an asset to the college and I was allowed to return the spring semester. Probation was a requirement for returning the first semester back and I had to be in my room by 7:00 pm every night. I was required to go to counseling and managed to convince the therapist that I was straight. I came out "smelling like a rose." I realized that choosing to be who everyone in the Christian community wanted me to be made me feel loved and accepted. It made me worthy to be actively involved in ministry. I was reformed and had turned away from my "wicked" homosexuality… for the time being.

I tried to do everything by the book, exactly like the administration wanted, all the way through school. I worked my way up the "totem pole" and became the Spiritual Life Director the second semester I was back. I continued my reading and memorization of scripture and became a spiritual pillar in the dorm. The next year, I became a Resident Assistant which awarded me the last three years of tuition free.

I continued to struggle with same-sex attraction on the inside but kept my mind in check and rejected any thoughts that might take me down the path of my desires.

After the first year of being a Residence Assistant (R.A.), I went on a summer inner city mission trip with other college students to New York City. It was an eight-week trip where we ministered to and helped meet the needs of many in the inner city of Manhattan. It was fulfilling and I have great memories from that summer.

Ironically, the second year that I was an R.A., I became roommates with Dana, despite her "outing" me to the Dean. We had become friends again. I don't know what I was thinking because it was a very difficult year. Although nothing physically happened between us, I struggled with being near her. A constant battle raged within me. The things I had come to believe were "unnatural desires". They haunted me and battled against my desire to be pure and righteous before God. By the end of the year, I was an absolute mess.

I stayed several days in my dorm room after Dana left school. I had entered a "zombie state" and tried to regain my composure. It was a phone call from home that broke through my despair. They were wondering why I hadn't returned home from school. I didn't tell them of my struggle.

I graduated that year but had another year of free tuition so I returned in the fall to take extra courses.

My inner battle raged on but as I began to take down the barriers I had placed around my thoughts, feelings, and emotions, I began to open up to new opportunities. I started a relationship with a woman in my dorm my last semester on campus, Kaylee.

Kaylee was from the northeast so after graduation, I went to live with her family. We did our best to keep our relationship a secret from everyone but it didn't take long for her mom to recognize our attraction to one another. When she told me that I needed to move out, Kaylee moved out as well, and we got an apartment together. We continued to try to hide our relationship, having separate bedrooms for all to see. When her parents would come over, she would make it look like she slept in her own bed.

Kaylee and I lived together for a year but the entire time, we both, being raised in strict Christian homes, carried a lot of guilt. The voices from the past told us we were going to hell because of our relationship. We tried to stay away from each other but to no avail. I was a courier at the time driving three hundred miles a day, and every day I believed I was going to die because of my sexual lifestyle. The only way to save us was for me to move back home. We cried together daily as I prepared to leave the love of my life. The heartache was beyond measure, and we felt it for many years as we attempted to have a long-distance friendship only.

As I reflect on that time with Kaylee, I realize that it was the most beautiful relationship I have had in my entire life. We were so in love and spent every possible moment together. We even held hands while we ate dinner. I couldn't wait to see her each day and she felt the same way. There was nothing we withheld from each other, no conversation we couldn't have. We were one. We were connected but we just couldn't continue because we felt condemned. So in response to our experience, Kaylee ended up marrying a pastor and I married the first man that would have me.

I met a man from my sister's church while visiting home a couple of months before I made the move. I started dating Mitch when I moved back. Within three months, we were married.

Once again, I believed I had found a way to save myself and fix my unnatural desires. This was what I was raised to believe was right. We had the expected church wedding with most of the congregation there as well as friends and family. Everyone was so happy at this joyous celebration of the two becoming one. Everyone was happy but me. I remember crying my eyes out in the bathroom at the rehearsal because I did not want to marry this man. I forced myself to regain composure and continued with the rehearsal. Kaylee was by my side as my maid of honor and it was, I'm sure, the most difficult day of her life, as well.

My marriage to Mitch started off okay for the most part, other than I did not enjoy the sexual aspect of it at all. That was only the beginning of years and years of devastation not only for me, but more so for the children that I would soon bring into it.

In the beginning, I thought about how nice it would be to have someone take care of me for a change. That ended very quickly when I began to realize that I would be taking care of him. It was necessary for me to take over all of the finances immediately so bills would get paid. My new husband was not inclined to work nearly as hard as I had believed when I met him.

Our marriage lasted a year before I left and suffered the consequences from church and family for not being "subject" to my husband, as stated in the wedding vows.

I visited my lost love, Kaylee, a couple of times that year. I was with her once again trying to figure out what to do with my life. Our love relationship continued over that year, although not much in person. Our phone bills were outrageous. I would stay with her for a couple of weeks and then would go back home to my mother's to start counseling at the church with the pastor and my husband. Over my six-month separation from my husband, I visited Kaylee another few times and finally decided I could not handle the relationship anymore. The criticism from the church and my family was too much and I couldn't disappoint God with a failed marriage.

I returned home to my husband and within a year decided it was time to start a family. We had three children together over the next three and a half years; two girls and the youngest, a boy.

After the birth of my second child, my relationship with Kaylee changed dramatically. She had met a man and was planning to marry, too. I made the trip out for her wedding to what was the most difficult day I had ever spent with her. Her future husband was a pastor and she was to be a pastor's wife. She ended our very close relationship and said we could only be friends. I knew that could never work for either of us going forward. I spoke to her one time after the wedding and then never again.

My husband and I stayed involved in the church and I tried very hard to maintain our upstanding Christian appearance as a family. I taught Sunday school, worked in the nursery, sang in the choir and hosted monthly game night for the entire church at our house. I attended Joyce Meyer conferences and listened over and over again about how homosexuality was an abomination. I remained confused about the whole matter but it didn't matter, I was married. My focus was on my family and I wasn't really attracted to anyone in particular so I chose to not dwell on it.

Finances were a struggle over the next several years and arguments about money were continuous. My husband did not contribute much to our welfare because he failed to keep steady employment. Our financial shortfall made it necessary for us to move from our very nice home to a smaller home in an unsafe neighborhood. I was very upset about it. I tried to help remedy the situation by working alongside my husband in our mowing business. We also started a rental property business that brought in some money. Mitch continued to resist full time employment and was always in between jobs.

I attempted to do everything I could to keep the family together. I was helping with the businesses, volunteering at church, and homeschooling two of our children. It was exhausting.

In March of 2001, Mitch came to me saying that he had a dream that I was a lesbian. I was shocked. We had never talked about this before. That day, I confessed to him my secret. I knew that it would either make or break our marriage. I told him all about Kaylee and I, though we hadn't had any contact for five years. Mitch was distraught and we spent the remainder of the day apart. When he came home that evening, he told me he wanted to make our marriage work and things actually did get better between us for a short time.

When I shared with Alice, my best friend from high school, how well things were going with my husband, her reaction was very unexpected. She told me that she had deep feelings for me. Alice believed that one day, we would be together. Well, that was definitely enough to get my attention. The brief closeness I felt with my husband was over immediately and we began to grow apart again, even though nothing was going on between Alice and me.

By August of 2001, Mitch began to accuse me of having an affair with a lady who sang in the choir with me at church. It wasn't true but he left me a week later. I couldn't believe it. I remember being out on the riding lawn mower the next day thinking about how I would never have to sleep with that man again. I felt the weight of duty, responsibility and self-sacrifice lifted from my shoulders. It was a welcomed relief and I was determined to keep him out of the house. He was gone and he was not coming back. I had done nothing wrong. Now, I was free. I was so happy. My girls were five and six and my son was three at the time.

The church made it their responsibility to speak into our separation. We started counseling but I stood firm. I didn't want him back. In order to maintain the family appearance for the church and to keep the family together for the children, I gave him a choice. He could move back into our home but I would never sleep with him again. He had his own terms but I refused and held my ground. The church tried to speak into our relationship telling me that I couldn't have those expectations. Once again, I stood firm. My husband had left me in the first place and I was finished with him. I was no longer willing to live a life that left me feeling empty and violated.

Mitch moved into one of our rental houses and, for appearances, we went to church every Sunday together and sat with the kids between us. I did it for their sake. It was what was expected of us. Don't make a big scene.

The church hoped counseling would save our marriage. During one of the counseling sessions, I told the counselor that I had lesbian tendencies and if I was free from my marriage, I would pursue that type of relationship. The next day, the choir director told me that I could not sing in the choir anymore. So much for confidentiality.

For some reason, I continued to attend that church. I'd just grin and bear it. Every Sunday, it felt like the preacher would say something about homosexuality. I would sit there and just cringe. Then, I finally had enough and left the church.

My kids and I started attending a larger church because we could get lost in the size of it all. I didn't have people knowing all of my business and asking questions about my life. I could go and just be. That lasted for a few years and then I stopped going to church altogether.

My family wasn't very surprised about my divorce since it came out that I experienced same-sex attraction when I was in college. My grandmother, who raised eleven kids, and was a very godly woman, shocked me with her response.

She looked me straight in the eye and said, "If you are one of 'them' I will disown you."

I tried, through the years, to be who I believed everyone wanted me to be. I did everything I could to make my marriage work for as long as I could stand it. I went to church and went on retreats. I did what I thought I was supposed to do and it was always at my expense. I was trying to be someone that I wasn't.

It took four years to get divorced and it was ugly. The court battles were stressful, tiring, and expensive.

Alice was somewhat back in my life. She was getting divorced and we talked about being together. I was really looking forward to that but as the time approached that we could finally be together, she was not ready to commit.

I told my kids about my same-sex attraction after I was divorced. I started seeing a woman, Jane, five months before my divorce was final but I kept our relationship very quiet. The divorce process had taken four years to this point and I didn't want my husband to have another excuse to drag it out. I was also afraid that I could lose my kids if anything came out about me. So, I kept it quiet. When the divorce was final and custody was set, I could relax and it came out that I was dating a woman.

The kids adjusted very well to my new relationship. They were fond of Jane and she moved in and lived with us for six years.

My ex-husband did not take my relationship with Jane well and used it against me with the kids every time he saw them.

He constantly made negative comments about my new relationship. "Your mom is living in sin. She's going to die and go to hell."

In 2008, my oldest sister's husband died and three months later, she married my ex-husband. This just intensified the situation, causing more strife for the kids.

My sister began to join him in his comments about me. "She's living in sin. She's going to go to hell."

This was the sister I admired as a young child.

The situation got even stranger when my sister wouldn't live in her house after they were married. That was where her first husband had died and she did not feel comfortable there so they moved into a camper in the backyard. When the kids would go to visit them on Wednesday nights and every other weekend, they too would be in the very small camper. It was terrible for them. They could hear everything that went on in their father's bedroom. It is beyond me why they would put the children through that. The kids were eleven, twelve, and thirteen years of age.

Visits to see their father were a nightmare. My ex-husband and sister would often have the children in tears, bombarding them with condemning statements about me for being a lesbian.

One day, my daughter screamed out at them, "Stop talking bad about my mom or you can take me back home."

My son also spoke up saying, "Why can't you just leave Mom alone?"

My daughter wanted me to come get her that night but her dad wouldn't let her call me. It was heart wrenching to hear what my children were having to endure.

My girls hated going with their father and would stand at the door crying every time they had to go. This was extremely difficult for me to watch knowing I could do nothing to stop the turmoil they were experiencing. After a while, my girls started making excuses to not go to visit their dad. It helped that the oldest had a job.

My son didn't always like going but he went willingly if they planned to visit my dad. He and his wife had three kids around the ages of mine. They would go over to my dad's house to play and did a lot of fun activities. My son really enjoyed being around my little half-brother and nephew. The rest of my family would join them there, as well.

It is amazing how my family handled the craziness of my sister marrying my ex-husband better than my being gay. Before my sister and ex-husband got together, I would attempt to go to family gatherings but I couldn't bring Jane. I did this for a while because I felt like my kids needed their extended family. I hoped that they would finally accept me and allow her to come but it never happened. Not only did my siblings never accept her but they would do an intervention on me when I would come. They would corner me and tell me I needed to change my ways. I was an abomination living a life of sin and I "was going to hell." They would throw out any Bible verses they could to back up their proclamations. It was hideous. One day, I responded by screaming at them and left. I never went back.

My husband didn't take it well that the girls didn't want to come stay with him. When they would refuse to get into the car, he would call the police and try to have me arrested, saying that I was going against the custody agreement. This led to more court appearances and more attorney's fees. Eventually, the court battle went in my favor and the girls no longer had to go visit their father. The judge ruled that they were old enough to make that decision themselves.

Things were going pretty smoothly at home for a while. Jane's family was very accepting and welcomed my children and me into their lives. They included us in all family gatherings and holiday celebrations. They even bought my kids Christmas gifts and birthday presents. The difference between my church going family, the Christians, and her non-church going family, was stark. Who was more Christ-like?

Jane was great to the kids and we got along most of the time but we had troubles that eventually led to a breakup. It was great to have her in my life while raising the kids but we never developed that deep love that I desired to have with another person. And as my kids got older, it became obvious that the maturity level of my children began to surpass Jane's. She didn't have any children of her own and would become very jealous when I would spend time with mine. She always wanted me to watch television with her back in our bedroom rather than being out with them. I refused to do that so it caused a lot of quarrels.

When my daughter began showing signs of depression, I took her in for an evaluation. The therapist told me that the depression was probably caused by tension in our home, so that was the end of my relationship with Jane. I didn't want the challenges in our relationship to affect my children. We separated after being together for six years.

My daughter continued to be depressed and I attempted to talk to her about it. I understood depression, or so I thought, because I have had many times of sadness myself. I had no idea what was about to come out later, the real source of her depression.

Over the next several months, despite our many conversations, I just couldn't figure out why she was so sad and depressed. One day, I took her for a drive to talk about it. I explained to her that everyone experiences depression at some time in their lives. I tried to point her to God, telling her He was faithful and would help her but she didn't want to believe in God. Finally, it came out. She told me that while her father and I were separated, he sexually abused her from age six until she was eight. It was heartbreaking. I couldn't believe that she didn't tell me when it happened. I worked so hard to keep my children safe. I was careful about who I left them with when they were young because of what had happened to me. The one person I could not protect my children from became the perpetrator. How could I have not seen it?

After my daughter told me this, I called a sexual assault organization in town and they advised me to file a report with the police. I told them that she didn't want me to do that but they insisted. It didn't matter what she wanted. I had to report it. They couldn't help her unless I reported the sexual assault to the police. I filed the report and my ex-husband was arrested. He spent one night in jail and they released him. Of course, he denied it.

The entire family rallied around him believing that I manufactured all of this because I wanted to get back at him for marrying my sister. It was so twisted. What kind of mother would put her child through something like this? In their minds, I was a lesbian, a perverse person, a liar, a sexual deviant, corrupt and desperately wicked. They told me that many times in previous years. According to my family, I brought all of my problems on myself. I was sexually perverted and going against God. They could not see past their hostile opinion of me to even consider the pain and suffering of my innocent child.

Not only did my family turn their backs on me, Martha, the woman who was a second mother to me, stood by my ex-husband saying, "He would never do anything like that."

My daughter had been named after Martha because she was such a positive influence in my life growing up. Now, she had turned against me, and, not only me but the child who bore her name. She told me that I was being very "unchristian," hung up the phone, and we have not spoken since.

I had to have my daughter hospitalized two times to get her through the trauma her father inflicted upon her. She was really struggling, depressed all the time, suicidal and cutting her legs. Eventually, the counseling at the sexual assault organization began to help her. I am so grateful for all they have done.

I also went to counseling myself and it was a great help to me. I remember sharing about the rejection I experienced in my life. Rejection had become the norm to me. I learned to expect that from anyone who knew I was a lesbian. The counselor was shocked by what I had endured, telling me that no one should get used to rejection. She reminded me of the unconditional love of God. This was something I had not felt in a very long time.

It became my responsibility to build a case against my ex-husband. I spent many hours going over past calendars, phone records, home videos, and my own writings to try to come up with any evidence for the sexual assault case against him. I finally pinpointed exactly when the first event happened. He abused my daughter for the first time on Christmas Eve when she was only six years old. The recollection of that assault haunts her every Christmas season, as she tries to understand how someone who was supposed to love and protect her, violated her in such a horrible way.

Ten years had passed since the sexual abuse occurred and the District Attorney told me that out of the four cases of sexual assault in our town involving one word against the other, there had been no convictions. She told us we could continue to the next level, go to another county for trial but cautioned that dragging my daughter through anymore would be very difficult for her. I just wanted to focus on getting her well…and that's what I did.

All of this came out the fall of her sophomore year of high school, making going to school very difficult for her. When she asked me if she could graduate early, I checked into all the requirements and made it happen. She worked very hard, took night and summer classes at a community college and graduated after her junior year.

After I had my ex-husband arrested, I wouldn't let my son go to visit his father. That became another custody battle. It was uglier than any of the other court battles we had been in, and between that and my efforts to help my daughter, I was physically, emotionally, and mentally drained. I remember calling my niece on my ex-partner's side of the family to come help me with the kids one day because I was literally ready to fall apart. I was in tears and had nothing left within me to get through the day. She gladly came to help and I was able to regain the strength needed to push forward.

My daughter decided to change her name as part of her recovery. I had to make it a public record in the papers that she was going to do so and my ex-husband couldn't contest it. She chose to change her last name and remove Martha as her middle name because she no longer wanted to be associated with either of them. Choosing her own unique name made a huge difference in her life.

After much disappointment in the court's handling of the visitation matter with my son, I told my attorney to offer a deal where I would take full financial responsibility, including college for the children, if my ex-husband would leave my son alone and not contest my daughter's request to change her name. He agreed and my three children were finally free from their father.

Although the sexual abuse happened to my middle child, my older daughter was not untouched by her father. She was admitted to the hospital on suicide watch the next year where she talked about the abuse she endured. She had been punched in the face and back handed by her father. She mentioned some sexual abuse but did not go into detail and I did not press the issue but got her into the counseling she needed to heal. Both girls suffered physical and sexual abuse. All three of my children suffered emotional abuse.

My older daughter went off to college, graduated and is now engaged to be married. She works in the school system, teaching students about the effects and consequences of drug use. She is doing her part for the community and has plans to continue her education and get a master's degree to support her efforts.

It has been a steady healing process for my second daughter but her life has moved forward. She graduated from college with a degree in Psychology and is preparing to begin her master's program to become a high school guidance counselor. She works in high schools in the area helping students with college applications and financial aid forms.

My son probably struggles the most. When I explained to him about everything that happened to his sisters, his first response was, "I believe it."

While I didn't want him to see his father, I did give him a choice. But, if he didn't want to, I would fight to keep that from happening. It was all about what he wanted. He decided not to see his father. As promised, I did all that I could to keep him from that.

After my son graduated from high school, he started to blame me for not having a relationship with his father. I explained to him that I did what he asked me to do. He felt that he was put in a very hard position. Now, he was an adult, if he wanted to see his father, he could do that, but once again he chose not to see him.

A year later, when his father became hospitalized because of diabetes, my son decided it was time. He went to the hospital but found his father in a coma. He didn't even know that his son was there.

Several months later, just after Christmas, my son made another attempt to see his father. He and his girlfriend met his father and my sister in a restaurant for dinner. This was the last time he saw him. My ex-husband died a month later choking on a summer sausage.

My son did attend his father's funeral but my girls did not. It was a relief to know that my daughters would never have to worry about running into him again. He will never be able to hurt them.

Even after my son saw his father for the last time, he wasn't sure he wanted to have a relationship with him. He was so torn between his relationship with his sisters and wanting to have a father. As a mother, I didn't want the relationship between my kids to be destroyed but I let him make his own decision.

My ex-husband's death has been very difficult for my son but more and more, I am beginning to see his spirit return. He is moving on. He married his girlfriend last year and lives nearby so I am able to see him often.

The secret life of abuse did not begin with my ex-husband. My father was married three times and when his second marriage ended abruptly, when I was fourteen, I never understood why. I found out recently from my brother that my step-sister, from my father's second marriage, wanted to get in touch with me. We met and she told me the story.

My step-sister explained that my father started sexually abusing her when she was nine years old and when she was older, she became pregnant. I asked her why her mother didn't have my father arrested. She did not have an answer but explained that her mother told her that she had asked her mother not to report him. My step-sister has no memory of that.

I shared with my step-sister my daughter's experience with abuse and how I worked closely with her as she went through the healing process. This helped me understand the trauma my step-mother and step-sister went through. Unfortunately, my step-sister did not receive any counseling to help her heal from the abuse she endured from my father. Now, she wishes she had. She commended me on standing firm with my daughter, for fighting for her and my other children.

I treasure the new connection that I have with my step-sister. We have never been so close. Sadly, the circumstances surrounding it are heartbreaking but I'm glad we are now in contact and can support one another. I feel like I am part of the family I had lost in my earlier years. My relationship with my step-siblings is being restored out of a horrible situation.

From my conversation with my step-sister, I became aware that I have a thirty-nine-year-old brother. I just met him for the first time and we are building a relationship that we were never given the chance to have. He is getting married this fall and has invited me to the wedding. I will happily be there.

I have also spent time with my step-sister, his mother, and we are restoring the friendship we shared as children. They only live three hours away, so I am planning to visit them as often as I can.

My current step-mother's, wife three, reaction to me when I had my ex-husband arrested, was inexcusable but explainable now. My step-mother immediately "unfriended" us on Facebook and told my younger half-brother and my half-twin sisters to do the same. It was too close to home for her. She was an attorney in the county that I had my ex-husband arrested. She knew all about my father abusing his step-daughter from his second marriage, and kept it a deep dark secret. She didn't want to enter into a big mess about sexual abuse for fear that the secret of her own husband might come out, so she did nothing. This amazed me because my step mom had set up a home for people who have experienced domestic violence. She, of all people, should have stood by my daughter but she did nothing. She was more concerned about her reputation as an attorney in the community than doing what was right and standing by her step-granddaughter. I have not had any contact with her or my younger half siblings and they have not contacted me either.

My family knew what my father had done to his step-daughter and what my ex-husband had done to his own daughter and chose to ignore it. They would not have anything to do with my partner and yet they would gladly sit and dine with a child rapist and sex offender. I have had a difficult time understanding the hypocrisy of it all.

My kids have continued to have a relationship with my ex-partner, Jane. She was in their lives for six years while we were together and they love her. Even now, they celebrate holidays and birthdays together. I have been very careful to keep a distance myself from her because I know that she would be easily encouraged to return. That is not my desire.

I haven't dated much since I broke up with my partner eight years ago. I attempted to work towards a life together with Alice. We saw each other a few times a year and spoke nearly every day. We were making plans once again to be together and I held out hope for the past eight years as I waited for her to proclaim that we could finally be together. Our children were now grown and we had no reason to stay apart. I was brokenhearted when I came to realize it just wasn't going to happen. She will never make the move to be with me. It is my bitter reality.

I have focused my life on raising my kids, loving and encouraging them to live healthy lives. I am so proud of who they have become. They are all independent and living successfully on their own.

I have become an empty nester now so I am devoting my time to helping children in difficult situations. I became a *CASA*, Court Appointed Special Advocate, that works with teenage girls that have been taken into the foster care system. I have also been a foster parent for the past two years for a little boy who is now four years old. I enjoy helping children who need a stable caring adult in their life.

My experience with the church has left some scars but God continues to remind me of his love. About seven years ago, a friend invited me to her church on Easter Sunday. My kids were old enough to stay home on their own so I went by myself. During the service, the children came forward and did an Easter program. I just started crying. I missed my children being there. They used to be in the programs at church. All those feelings of loss and rejection came flooding forward as I relived what I had experienced in my former church and in the Christian community that I used to be a part. I was overwhelmed and left the service. I didn't go back to church for a long time after that.

I stated previously that God intervened when he led me to the decision to make suicide a non-negotiable choice. There have been many times where I have been full of despair and felt the overwhelming sting of rejection by those who should have loved me unconditionally. I've been heartbroken many times in my life. Each time the thought of ending it all comes to mind I am reminded of the promise that I made to God. I believe that most people who commit suicide feel they have no alternative to ending the pain. I am grateful that God ingrained in me many years ago that suicide would never be an option for me. So, I quickly dismiss those thoughts as I remember that drive through West Virginia and my commitment to live no matter what.

Through the years, I believe that God has been revealing His love for me and sometimes, I actually see it. I do remember crying out to God in desperation one weekend when my kids were visiting their father during the separation.

I asked Him, "What is the matter with me? Why can't I just be normal? Why can't I be 'right' when I try so hard?"

I'll never forget what happened next. God responded to my cry. My mind was flooded with thoughts about people and how we are all created differently. People are different in their personalities and physicality, in their total make-up. There are men with very feminine traits and there are women with very masculine traits. It doesn't always mean that they are gay, but doesn't it come to reason that these differences can also occur in our sexuality?

Then I felt God say, "It is in your make-up. This is who I created you to be. This is you and you are okay."

I was so thankful to God that night. Joy flooded my soul as I heard from Him that I am okay just the way I am. I know I am fearfully and wonderfully made in the image of God. Ever since that night, I have been accepting of myself and know that I am okay no matter what anyone else says.

Being gay is a very frightening place to be when you are growing up in a religious home, as I did. I strived for years to gain the love and acceptance of my family and the church to no avail. The love that I had in my life was completely conditional. I was loved as long as I did everything people wanted me to do. I remember as a child in school seeing all the "Be Yourself" posters and I wondered what they meant "Who else would I be?" As a young teenager,

I understood that I could not be me and be acceptable in the eyes of others, especially the church and my own family.

When I finally came to the realization that I could not live a lie anymore, I walked away from my extended family. I don't know if my family would have handled my divorce and my ex-husband's marriage to my sister, differently if I wasn't a lesbian. I wonder if they would have handled my daughter's sexual abuse differently?

They would often respond to me with, "You brought all these hard times on yourself."

I know now that it's okay to walk away from people in your life that are not good for you, even family.

I would have lived my life differently if I would have known then what I do know now. I would have accepted myself. Accepting who I am is more important than anyone else on this earth accepting me. God created me as I am. He loves and accepts me and wants me to be me.

We all need to be authentic and surround ourselves with people who genuinely love and accept us. Parents need to allow their children to be their true selves. Listen to them tell the story of their journeys. Children need to know that they are loved and accepted as they are, without conditions. I am grateful for the few truly great friends that have stood by me and shown me unconditional love throughout my life.

My father passed away about four years ago. I did not go to the funeral. I didn't want to see any of my family. I just couldn't put myself in that position with the people who have hurt me the most. I last saw my father the year before he died. After we talked for a while, I gave him a hug and told him I loved him. When I left, I thought, if I never see him again, I am okay with that.

I still have difficulty understanding why Christians can be so hurtful at times. Of all the people in my life, they have hurt me more than anyone else.

I have heard people talk about Christians saying, "If those people are going to heaven, I don't want to go there."

I understand that. They can be hypocritical, judgmental and condemning. I know they have been very hurtful to me and my kids. Their example does not show the true love of God. I am thankful that God has made himself known to me personally and shown me His love.

I have been ready to begin the next chapter of my life with a special woman for a while now. I long for a deep relationship with someone; to connect with them on a spiritual, intellectual, emotional and physical level. I don't want just any person to be with me. I yearn for a loving and caring relationship where both people are appreciated and maintain their own individuality. People my age have a lot of baggage so there will be some things we need to work through, but it is possible if we both want the same things, have the same goals, and work together.

I believe that I have found that very special relationship with Jodi. God has used each of our past experiences to prepare us emotionally, mentally and spiritually for each other. We have been together for ten months now and I believe we have God's blessing. This is the first relationship I have ever had with a woman that I felt surrounded by God's love. I no longer feel judged or condemned. Our relationship is at the very beginning stages but we are growing together daily as we commit ourselves to each other and to Him.

God awakened Kim's faith at the Q Christian Fellowship Conference. An awareness of His faithfulness and love drew her back to church. It is an affirming church and she drives an hour to get there but it's worth every minute. From the moment she entered the doors, she knew it was the place for her. When Kim explained to a church leader how someone at the Q Christian Fellowship Conference had encouraged her to go to that church, she exclaimed, "We sent fifteen people from our church to that conference."

Kim can now be her authentic self in church. The people have been loving and accepting of her since the beginning. So, she has started to commit herself to serving there. She has done the welcome from the pulpit, has made many new friends and has a vibrant social life. And more importantly, God has reminded her of His unconditional love for her.

Kim currently works as a teacher's assistant in a junior high school with children with special needs.

Chase Brexton Health Care Services

Chase Brexton Health Care Services was founded in 1978 in the Mt. Vernon neighborhood of Baltimore, starting as a volunteer health clinic run by gay men. In the 1980s, they took on the challenge to fight against HIV and AIDS.

They have grown tremendously since then, offering a variety of services to all people but have never let go of their heart to provide equal, expert, and affirming health care for the LGBT community. The LGBT Health Resource Center offers specialized behavioral health services to bisexual, queer, transgender, gay, lesbian; focused support groups, education and training for organizations seeking greater LGBT competency.

The Story of Jack

Jack's father died from a massive coronary when he was only forty-two years old, leaving he and his mother all alone. Jack was seven years old. He remembers attending the viewing of his father but not the funeral. Unaware of the magnitude of what had happened, it was years later that he actually cried and expressed grief about his dad's death.

As he and his mother adjusted to the loss of his father, his mother became increasingly more protective. They became so connected that he had difficulty becoming his own person.

After my father died, my mother and I moved from the suburbs of our mid-western town into the city to live with my maternal grandparents. My grandparents took over the daily parenting role that my mother had played for seven years. My grandmother was also very protective of me and could be encouraging when I struggled or was stressed out. My grandfather and I never developed a very close relationship. For one thing, he was not physically well when we moved in with them and I think he may have found the sudden arrival of a noisy emotional youngster an intrusion on his now retired, quieter life style. He did help me learn about paying bills and making memos on "important things to remember." But he was no substitute for my father, from whom I received much warmth and care.

My mother was a social worker and worked as such until I was born. For seven years, she stayed home to care for me while my father worked as a teacher and school administrator. When he died, my mother was forced to return to the workforce. She took a position as a social worker in the public-school system.

My mother was the most important person in my life, despite the challenges in our relationship. I grew up believing that I wasn't good enough in her eyes.

I remember her saying, "There's no place in the world, Jack, for the average person." Or "Well, your certainly aren't the reader your father was."

Her response to me was not only hurtful but surprising. Her parents weren't scholars. Her mother was a housewife and her father worked for the railroad for sixty-five years, as a district freight agent. But they were the only family I had and I loved them.

Life was challenging and filled with loss. As I look back on my early years, I realize that I didn't have any friends. There were photos of my being present at birthday parties but I don't remember having close friends. The move wasn't helpful. Not only did I give up my few friends but I had to give up my dog. We brought him with us to my grandparents' house but it didn't work out. The dog chased cars on the main street so he had to go. I was heartbroken.

Changing schools from the suburbs to the city was a challenge at age seven. Many of the students in the school had been together since first and second grade, so I found it difficult to fit in to their already established scene. As I look back, I realize that I was kind of a "sad sack," depressed and unhappy…not joyful.

I wasn't skilled at sports so I was always last to be chosen when we played softball at recess. I also had a hernia that went uncorrected and I was restricted by the doctor to engage from strenuous activity. Most of the time, I avoided sports like the plague because I just wasn't good at them. So, I didn't put myself in the position to fail.

But it wasn't just sports that was a challenge for me. Industrial Arts was also difficult.

I would like to say that being a "traffic patrol boy," a safety, helped my cause but I don't think that that affected my socialization in school in any way.

Academically, school was okay. I did well in my favorite subjects, English and Social Studies, but I was dreadful in Math.

There were some joys in my life, however. I was exposed to the symphony through the young people's concerts in town, and developed a love of the arts. I started playing the violin in elementary school and acted in the school plays. I was, actually, the lead in one of the plays in 8th grade.

The church was a large part of my life. I was raised in the Episcopal church but baptized in the Presbyterian Church. My dad was Episcopal and my mother Presbyterian. Because my father was not happy at the Presbyterian church with which my mother was affiliated, we began to worship at an Episcopal Church exclusively, when I was four years old. I was very active there, singing in the junior choir, was a junior acolyte, a senior acolyte, and active in the youth group when older. I continued in the Episcopal Church for my entire life.

I was also active in the Boy Scouts but I really didn't like it. My mother thought it would be good for me to have associations with other men and boys. The troop was sponsored by my church which made joining easier, as I knew some of the boys from the Junior Choir. The Scoutmasters were aware of my "loner" behavior and worked very hard to include in the activities. But how I hated the weekend camping trips. On occasion, I would serve as the "chaplain" for the weekend, reading scripture and offering a prayer on Sunday morning. I really like that.

But despite all of the activities, I really didn't develop any close friendships. I tried to have friends in eighth and ninth grades, but I was self-centered and wanted things *my way*. I wanted to make all the decisions and that behavior was not very conducive to friendship. I really didn't have any friends until I was a sophomore in high school.

I realized that I experienced same-sex attraction when I was fourteen years old. It was difficult because I heard what people said. I thought I was an oddity so I tried to ignore it. The jokes were hurtful. "So and so is a queer."

It was in high school that I began to live into my orientation and became sexually active. I was introduced to a same sex relationship by a guy after a high school dance. I actually had a date with a woman to the dance.

My date had wandered away for a minute and the guy said, "Why don't you ditch this date and we'll go off and have some fun?"

So, I did. I ditched my date, telling her to go home with her brother. She seemed okay with this but her mother wasn't. The next day, her mother called to raise hell with me for abandoning her only daughter, calling me irresponsible and ungracious. She was right.

I did go out with the guy after the dance. He drove to a secluded spot and suggested that we "examine" each other, which we did. This was a one-night stand, but it was the beginning of my same sex encounters. While he and I saw each other at school, we never connected again, nor did we ever discuss that night.

Then, I met Samuel. He was the member of an exclusive singing group and was also a very gifted pianist and organist. I was attracted to his musical ability and he was very physically attractive as well. We became friends and frequently visited each other's houses. We would watch some television and engage in sexual encounters in the privacy of our bedrooms.

We had a lot in common. Neither of us played sports but we attended movies, concerts and school dances together, often double dating. Our relationship lasted, in secret, for about two years.

My mother seemed to really like Samuel. They had met on several occasions when he visited our home. I never heard her say one negative thing about him until I finally "came out" to her about my sexuality and my relationship with him.

During this time, I began to feel a lot of shame and guilt. It was such a burden, that I had to tell my mother what was going on in my life.

Her response was, "You must go right away to talk to Father Daniels." He was an associate pastor at our church.

I immediately went to see him. His was not very empathetic.

He said, "I want to get you an appointment with a psychiatrist right away."

The thought of seeing a psychiatrist for this reason scared the hell out of me. The psychiatrist did several tests and I started seeing him weekly. My relationship with my boyfriend ceased immediately and I started living a "straight" lifestyle.

The 30 minutes sessions with the psychiatrist caused a financial burden on our family, so my mother wasn't too terribly supportive. I think she was relieved when I stopped going after a year.

I started dating girls again after I realized that a relationship with a guy was strictly forbidden. Karen was a safe friend for me. She was a little younger than I and we both loved dancing. We would go to the Scottish Rite for the young people's dances once a month. We, also, went to the school dances together. Our relationship was strictly platonic. There wasn't any passion. Even her mother recognized that.

She would say, "I never have to worry about Karen when she's out with Jack."

Karen and I laughed about that when we got together years later.

There were many guys I found myself attracted to but I refused to even go there. There was too much shame associated with it. I never even told anyone about the same sex attraction that I was experiencing. Only my mother, the psychiatrist and the pastor knew my secret.

Surprisingly, I really didn't talk very much to the therapist about my "secret." We primarily talked about my relationship with my mother. I didn't know it at the time, but I was terribly angry with her. During that time period, it was believed that the mother was responsible for her child's sexual orientation so I blamed her for my struggle. I think my mother felt responsible, as well. I made sure of it. After our first discussion about it, we never talked about it again, until much later. It was a very sad time for me.

I do have some fond memories from that time. My mother and I vacationed at the lake for several summers. It was there that I learned to swim and row a boat. I loved the lake and enjoyed exploring the various lakeside communities and towns.

On one occasion, my mother agreed to my inviting Samuel, prior to my coming out to her. We had passed the point of "puppy love" and entered into a new level of affection.

Another time, I was allowed to bring two friends. They were co-workers from my summer job. Memories from that experience are filled with disdain and guilt, however. There was quite a bit of alcohol involved and sexual encounters.

I remember asking the psychiatrist, when I was in high school, if he thought I could change my sexual orientation.

His response was, "Jack, there are many happy homosexuals in this world."

I really didn't want to hear that at the time. I wanted to believe that I could change.

After high school, I went to college in my hometown and lived at home for the first year. I majored in Speech. I was encouraged to go in that direction because my mother believed that I was talented in dramatics and public speaking.

My second year, I moved into the fraternity house. I did have some friends there but no intimate relationships.

I continued to date women, living the life that was expected of me. I was determined that I was going to change my sexual orientation. I was very much in denial.

My teaching career began at the high school from which I graduated. I taught Speech and English and directed the high school plays. I remained on the faculty for five years but was not happy with my career choice. I know now that the road to successful teaching involves planning, and I seldom planned. Day after day, I would go into school without the slightest idea of what I was going to teach. Failing to plan is planning to fail, and fail I did. I blamed my failure on the students, the school, and the community, and believe it or not, I moved on to teaching on the college level.

I taught at the college for one year. This was not a good career move for me to have made. Many of the problems I met on the high school level followed me there. I had a lack of emotional control, insufficient planning and not accurately assessing my limitations. I thought I was God's gift to the teaching profession. This was not a good combination.

While on the college faculty, I continued to date women. There was one in particular who taught Math there that I began to spend time with. I had high hopes that she would help to "change" me. We attended, concerts, movies and faculty parties together. Our relationship became very intimate. Then one day, I shared with her about my attraction to men. I know she was very disappointed in that because she really liked me. Our relationship continued for a year but when I left my teaching position, it ended. We kept in touch for several years by mail, but eventually, lost contact. She was a very fine person but I just couldn't feel love for her.

I was fortunate enough to get a graduate assistantship in Voice and Diction at another school where I began study for my advanced degree. I was strongly attracted to a fellow teaching assistant and at the same time insanely jealous of him. He was a brilliant student, more mature than I and heterosexual. He had no interest in me. After two years, we were ready to write our dissertations. My "secret lover" left the university, as did I, and that ended my close contact with him.

I moved on to another college with the intention of writing my dissertation while on the faculty there but was distracted by my inner life. Instead of writing my dissertation, I used that time to begin to finally evaluate myself and my life going forward. *What are you about, Jack?* It was during that time that I came to the realization that I could not *be* my father as I believed my mother wanted me to be. I really don't think she thought that but it was deeply entrenched in me. I attended a mental health clinic with the hope of understanding myself clearly. Two counselors helped me to identify who I was. I began to look at my life more realistically. But what was I to do?

I made a feeble attempt to identify another occupation after I accepted my failure as a college teacher, but I had no other skills and I had internalized a maxim from my family that life as a professional person was to be desired. Since College teaching was no longer an option and an advanced degree was beyond attainment, instead of honoring who I was, I decided to leave the small college and return to secondary teaching in a large school system on the East coast.

I refused to accept that teaching was not the profession for me, and I found myself in a new teaching position that was worse than the last. It was a horrible experience. I taught students who were not reading on grade level in an inner-city high school. It was impossible and very frustrating. It didn't help that I had very little compassion for the kids. The system had failed them and I couldn't counter that. This teaching experience went no better than the previous ones, but I managed to stay at that school for 5 years.

It helped that I developed a "secret" crush on a male colleague who was not gay. When he married a young woman, I was so hurt and angry that I refused to attend his wedding. Though I was keenly aware of my sexual attractions, I was determined to live a "straight" life.

At the end of my 5th year, I knew I had to leave teaching altogether.

This time I worked more diligently to find something else I could do to earn a living. At that time, the hospitality industry in the city where I had been living was expanding, and I got a job as a trainee in hotel management. While this work provided plenty of stress, I was happier with my career than I had ever been. I did a number of jobs: accounting, guest service agent, concierge. Eventually, I became resident manager and lived on the property.

I developed some friendships there and occasionally, had secret romantic, not physical, connections with men. At the same time, I was trying to be straight. In my forties, I continued to remain in self-denial. I just couldn't accept that I was gay.

I started attending a church immediately after arriving on the east coast because I believed that it had a large gay population. I really needed that community. But instead of dating men, I started dating a woman. She was a nurse, somewhat younger than I, that I met at church. She was a devout Anglo-Catholic that lived with her family. We dated off and on for a period of a year.

We enjoyed going to dinner, concerts, and movies but our relationship was strictly platonic. I didn't find her physically attractive at all. Our interest in church was really the only thing we had in common. Our relationship ended when I tried to pretend that it was more than it was. Even today, I recoil with distaste when I think of giving her the obligatory kiss goodnight at the end of our evening together.

Throughout my life, I have wondered about what God thought about my sexuality. As an eighth or ninth grade guy, and for many years after, I believed God strongly disapproved of same-sex attraction. I believed it was a sin to the greatest degree.

As a young acolyte, age twelve and thirteen, I would often assist the priest at Mass and then he would hear my confession. We would confess our sins to God and to each other. I never mentioned any specific sin to my priest, yet that act of confession was deeply emotional for me. I think it reduced, to some extent, the burden of shame that I was feeling.

I was pretty unhappy much of my life. When I look back, I have so much shame related to my same sex attraction, hostility and lack of compassion in my human interactions. I, also, regret the guilt trip I laid on my mom, who always wanted the best for me. I spent years in pastoral counseling and psychotherapy coming to terms with my deep and intense anger.

My greatest regret is that I wish I could have accepted my sexuality and lived with it, found a partner and had a life that was satisfying.

I believe that there are some people who can accept their sexuality and say, "Well, that's who I am and I am going to adjust to it. I will be fine."

Then, there are others who fight it. I was one of those who fought it.

I am fortunate to be part of an over age fifty LGBTQ support group. I have learned much about who I am and have begun to accept myself more as I hear others share about their lives during our sessions. I know that it is important that we are self-aware and accept ourselves in order to live a full life.

I remember a pastoral counselor once saying to me, "Jack, you have to live in the world. Be inclusive. Don't limit yourself to those persons who share your sexual persuasion." I think that was good advice.

Thankfully, I have made many good friends through the years, at work, at church, and in my volunteer activities, who are not gay. At the same time, it is affirming and sustaining to have faithful friends within the LGBTQ community, with whom I can be totally at ease, and completely open.

At the age of 80, Jack describes himself as a grateful, contented person. He has become "happy as a homosexual," just as was suggested he could be.

The Story of Ken

Ken knew what it was like to experience loneliness as a child. Instead of allowing that to negatively influence his life, Ken developed a heart of compassion that compelled him to stand up for those who are lonely and defenseless.

Over my lifetime, I have experienced both the super-conservative and the extremely liberal aspects of our society.

I grew up in the deep south, in a very conservative family. Life was very black and white with many conspiracy theories. There was no belief in science. We were never permitted to talk about any aspects of it, especially sexuality. Heaven forbid.

I grew up in the Southern Baptist church and tried to live up to the *godly* standards that I was taught for a very long time. Anything outside of the church was highly sinful and had to be avoided at all costs. There were no options, either you were following God or you weren't following God.

Growing up, I spent most of my time with my extended family on my grandparents' one-hundred-acre farm. My grandparents practically raised my brother and me because my mother worked quite a bit, juggling three jobs to support our family. For nearly two decades, our grandparents gave us a place that felt like home and we were safe there.

I was happiest playing with my four cousins on the farm. We were best friends. We'd build bonfires, shoot guns and play with bows and arrows. Manhunt was my favorite. My only girl cousin at the time and I would play house or school. It was a delightful place that brings back many wonderful memories.

Despite my conservative upbringing, my mother was married three times. My parents divorced officially when I was ten months old and my mom remarried a year and a half later. That marriage fell through and when I was thirteen, she remarried to the man who is my stepfather today.

There was not much life outside of the farm. When I wasn't at my grandparents, I often felt very alone. Much of my time was spent caring for my brother even though he was two and a half years older. I always thought he was purposely cartoonish but discovered later that he had a *social disability*. We never talked about it in our family, nor was he ever diagnosed, but everyone knew that he was on the autism spectrum. Since my family was anti-science and anti-medicine, his mental health issues were never addressed. When we were at home, it was often me, my brother and the television, together.

My brother was a real challenge for my mother. I remember their battles during homework time. Mother would scream and plead with him to *please put an answer down* on his paper…*any answer* would do. This would go on for hours. I waited quietly in another room wondering if someone would ever check on me.

Whoever filled the father role for me was the most important person in my life. Unfortunately, I felt like I was constantly losing that father figure over and over again. Youth pastors could often fill that void. Eventually, my grandparents provided that support.

There were not many great options for schooling where we lived. Some of the schools were poor quality and others were simply unsafe.

My brother and I went to a Southern Baptist elementary school then to a Catholic middle school. I was in the school band but didn't play anything well. I basically held the saxophone for six years. I pretended to play and got away with it. I was terrible.

I wanted to play sports growing up but I was very self-conscious about my abilities and my body, so I didn't. My father really wanted me to play sports which made me want to refuse. Now, I wish I would have played sports but his influence was difficult.

Being isolated with my family made everything seem acceptable. I never felt different because of my sexuality as a child because I didn't understand sex until much later. I always liked a wide variety of activities; guns, bows and arrows, playing house, barbies, dresses, trucks, and dinosaurs. I knew that I liked both boys and girls. But I was trained over and over to never disrespect or mistreat girls so I made a conscious decision to not look at girls in a sexual way. I really wasn't interested in them anyway. I found myself going in the other direction and looking at boys instead.

Friendships were difficult to form because you could be friends with girls but they didn't know you weren't interested in them sexually. It always felt awkward. They'd think my friendship was a crush. I thought that was what I wanted. I was supposed to have a crush on a girl.

I was bullied a lot in school because of my brother. Many of the students were very unkind to him and it was difficult to watch. He was so eccentric and uncomfortable to be around for many of the students and much of the animosity was projected onto me. Even some of the teachers were terrible to him.

But I was not without guilt. I had been a bully to my brother for a while growing up. I wonder how he would be different today if I would have realized sooner the impact it had on him.

I was, also, bullied because of my weight. That was especially painful.

It was difficult when I began to discover that I was gay because my upbringing dictated that not only was it wrong but having a conversation about it was forbidden. I was thirteen when I really started to sense that I was attracted to the same sex. I shared that with my mother but she refused to listen.

I shared it again when was sixteen, eighteen, twenty-one and twenty-four and the response was always the same. "Don't talk about it. Don't tell anyone. It will pass. It's just a phase."

When I talk about it, even now she denies that I ever told her. My whole family knew I was gay but refused to accept it.

My circle of friends was from the band and the church youth group. The groups were both girls and guys. I really enjoyed being with my friends but we never hung out outside of church or school.

Some of my happiest memories were of my youth group. We would do *lock-ins* where we would spend the night at the church, play *underground church,* have church camps, do youth trips, and watch movies together. I hung out with my church friends because I thought that that was what I was supposed to do. We became very close for a long time.

High school had some challenges as I continued to conceal my same-sex attraction. I didn't know very many people who were gay. I had one friend who was bisexual but she did not come out to me until she got expelled from school. Another person that I knew at school was very flamboyant and presented as the stereotypical gay man. He got expelled for coming across as gay. Even today, anyone that appears gay will be expelled. Religious organizations can do whatever they want to discriminate against the LGBTQ community. There is no one who holds them accountable for this anymore.

Teachers were also held to these conservative standards. I had one teacher who shared the specific guidelines that were written into her contract one day. It talked about what she could and could not do. She was not allowed to compare animals or anatomies when teaching. She, herself, was not allowed to have premarital sex or be divorced. She could not be LGBTQ or she would be fired. She came out later as bisexual.

In high school, I decided to come out to a family friend who attended our church when we were away for a weekend together. But instead of accepting my being gay, we decided to date, in a *godly* manner. I dated her off and on until my sophomore year of college. We talked about marriage, engagement rings, a wedding ceremony, and how many children we wanted. We were both all-in even though we were both aware that I was gay. We viewed being gayness as a sinful addiction.

I hung on to the verse Psalm 37:4, "Delight yourself in the Lord, and He will give you the desires of your heart." I believed that if I dedicated my life to God and He wanted me to marry that woman that He would give me the desires to please her as a husband.

Our relationship ended sophomore year. Her father had been abusive and she wouldn't allow me to help her, do anything or say anything about it. I just watched her be in pain. It was too difficult.

We have continued to stay friends even though she moved to the Pacific Northwest. Surprisingly, despite our religious upbringing, she too has come out as gay.

My family had hoped that dating a woman would change my orientation…but it didn't.

God was my everything growing up. I so wanted to be the best follower, to obey His words as closely and as literally as I could. I read my bible often and actually believed that I could hear God speak to me. It was my destiny to one day be a martyr for my faith and I thought I was called to be a missionary to Russia and to China.

For so long, I was enamored with the church and wanted to give back to the programs that raised me. I did, for a time. I loved youth ministry but whenever I would seek help for my sexuality, I would be banned from volunteering and asked to leave the church. The only solution was to pretend that my same-sex attraction did not exist. Churches wanted to pretend that the

LGBTQ community did not exist. How was I to get help if no one would talk to me about it?

I pretended that I wasn't gay for a very long time. I thought that if I prayed more and read my bible God would change me. I dedicated all that I was to Him and went through the motions of being a straight man.

Living a very sheltered existence, it wasn't until I was young adult that I realized how little I knew about the world around me. I was segregated into a white Southern Baptist Christian life and I never knew about the struggles that minorities were experiencing around me. I wasn't directly told to hate minorities but I was absolutely told to fear and never help them. My total lack of knowledge about people outside of my life's bubble prevented me from showing compassion or empathy toward people that were different than me. I still feel the weight of many of the things I said and did growing up that may have hurt others.

My background was extremely racist. I was told that if you were black, it was God's curse on man. It was right for blacks to be subservient to the white upper class.

Because our area was very segregated, I was told that if I ventured out of my neighborhood and something happened to me, "It is your own fault."

"You should have known better."

For a long time, I believed what I was taught. I heard the same message in school. I was told by two teachers in high school that the only way to save America during the apocalypse was to lynch President Obama because he was the anti-Christ.

I knew nothing about the LGBTQ community either, though they had been around forever. Conversations about the LGBTQ were forbidden. In the deep south, homosexual acts were a misdemeanor until 1992. There are still people who carry misdemeanors on their records. They are considered criminals just for being gay. This makes it very difficult when trying to apply for employment or even to go to school.

There was also an immense amount of denial. I remember my great aunt telling me after I came out many years later, that "gays had not been persecuted throughout history and the AIDS crisis never happened."

The world around me was racist and homophobic and my eyes were finally able to see it.

I lived out the faith that I was taught, faith filled with ignorance, hatred and judgement. At the time, I believed that I had godly intentions.

I left the deep south and moved north with the hope that I could live a more authentic life and my roommate, Nate, decided to go with me. I didn't realize how much untruth I had been receiving throughout my life until I was far from home.

But I continued to struggle with being gay even after the move. I accepted that I was a gay man but I didn't want to get married to a man and I didn't want to give up my dream to be married with a family.

Nate and I began to attend a local church believing that the we had found a home there. When the children's ministry needed volunteers, I went to my pastor and offered to help. I had had a great deal of previous experience with that and quickly found myself in the position as co-leader for two and a half years.

At the same time, I continued to explore my sexuality and began to accept myself as a gay man. The person who had been my roommate became more than that and I felt like I needed to talk to my pastor about it. My pastor was kind and compassionate and when I offered to step down from my position in the children's ministry, he declined and insisted that I continue. He told me that he didn't know what would happen long-term, what the church denomination would say, but he wanted me to continue serving. That began my journey to share my authentic self.

Shortly thereafter, I got very sick, finding myself in the hospital with an intestinal infection. I thought, that night, if I died no one would know how important my roommate, Nate, was to me. My mother would come up here and take everything from the life that he and I had built together. I just wasn't willing to live a lie anymore. In my hospitalized state, I asked him to marry me. He said, "No." I was hospitalized, dehydrated and didn't really know what was going on. We weren't even dating at the time and he had never met my family.

For the two months after my illness, I continued to ask Nate to marry me and he kept saying "No."

"What is it going to take for you to marry me?" I asked.

He replied, "I have to meet your family and we have to date for more than two months at a time."

I agreed and that same day I bought a ticket to visit my family to come out to them.

I believed that most of my family knew I was gay but my grandparents were a question. When I came out to my grandmother, she cried. I knew this would be hard for them. She told me that she didn't understand but she loved and supported me. My grandfather said he also didn't understand and if he was hearing me right, this went against everything that I had claimed to believe. That stung but when I left them, I was feeling pretty good that my grandparents would eventually come around.

After my return home, I began to receive letters from my grandparents. My grandmother talked about how much I hated women and how my lifestyle was hurting my mother. It was painful to read.

I tried to bring Nate down for Christmas but every time we were supposed to go for a holiday, my family refused to see us. After six holidays passed, I stopped trying.

When we decided to get married, we had a year of planning and my family had still not met Nate. Over and over again, we asked if we could come to visit and were refused. When I asked if they were going to come to the wedding, every single one of them said, "No." Not one person from my biological family came.

I begged my mom to come. "You don't have to go to the wedding itself but please come to meet Nate's family. Please be here." But she continued to refuse my request.

Over that same year, I, also, began to come out to our church congregation. The response was not nearly as loving and accepting as I found my pastor to be. As parents became aware of my sexuality, they began to remove their children from the ministry, taking them to the service. Only half of the children remained.

I was in limbo for two years as I served wondering if I was going to be accepted by the church. The idea that I could be removed at any time from my position simply because I loved a man caused me anxiety. I needed to put it to an end so I stepped down from my position.

For so long, I wanted to give everything to the church. I even wanted to attend seminary. But, June 12, 2016, when the *Pulse Nightclub* shooting occurred, my perspective about the church changed forever. I watched as pastors, church leaders, friends and even my family responded to this horrific event by praising the shootings as God's justice. I even heard them suggest that the world would be a better place if we had more mass shootings of the LGBTQ community. That was it! I was done. I could no longer defend or excuse the church leaders that I had looked up to for such a long time.

I have always been very open to reading the bible and reconciling my sexuality in discussion with others. How does sexuality line up with faith or not line up with faith? When did homosexuality actually enter the bible? What was the context? How do we keep peace but reconcile what we are personally experiencing? But it is when people disagree about issues and judge others because they think differently, that is wrong. That is where the discussion stops with me.

I have had many sad moments in my life but one of the most difficult was realizing that what I had believed about the teachings church was so false and so hurtful to others. I believed I was responding with the love of God but in no way represented His heart. I hurt people with my words and that was wrong. All those people who needed a safe place to share what they were experiencing were met with a conservative Christian response. I missed the opportunity to meet them in their struggle, to minister to them, to encourage them. I had to reconcile these things within myself much later when I became more aware.

The sting of persecution is painful. The church has been the most hurtful but I have also experienced it from family and from my employer.

I joined the fire department because it was consistent with my desire to help others. I never expected to be *outed* so early in my time there. My instructor took it upon himself to inform not only my class, but the entire department. I had been experiencing sexual harassment from another recruit; inappropriate touching in the workplace. It started with him coming up behind me, rubbing my shoulders. It seemed like he was flirting at first. Then, he began to grab me from behind and pull my hips up against his, as he whispered in my ear. This all happened during training in front of the other recruits. When I reported this to the instructor, I asked that he watch out for this behavior but he insisted that I complete a sexual harassment report. He then proceeded to out me to the group and accusing me of bragging about *kinky sexual exploits* in the locker room.

The instructor then told me that I had to write a report to officially inform the department of my sexual orientation. When I asked to speak to another instructor, he reported that I was being insubordinate. I truly thought that I was going to lose my dream job of being a firefighter before I even had a chance. Thankfully, I survived the ordeal and became widely accepted by my instructors and my classmates. Many of my firefighter friends filled the seats at my wedding that my family had refused to fill.

I have not been in contact with my family for the three years I have been married. They made it clear that they never wanted to see me. One of the things that has helped me through has been the love of my LGBTQ family, work friends, and my mentor.

I met my mentor when I began to have flashbacks of my childhood. That was a psychological disaster for me and I needed some help. He took me in and his family offered to be family to Nate and me. He has become the patriarch figure that I have always wanted and needed. We spend every single holiday together as a family.

The dreams I have had for a family have changed somewhat. I have spent twenty-two years believing that I needed to have a family to feel loved. I needed to have a house and children to feel loved. What I am finding is that my family looks different than I had imagined. My husband, brothers from the LGBTQ community, and my mentor's family have become all the family that I need. I have come to realize that I can contribute a lot to the next generation without having my own children.

There are a few lessons I have learned that have served me well:

*Listen more than you speak. Never let someone have the satisfaction of receiving an emotional response from their words of persecution.

*Serve others but remember to take care of yourself. You cannot help someone if you are totally depleted.

*Have open conversations about your mental health and hardships. This is the only way to open conversations and remove stigmas about seeking help. You will find more allies than judgement because we are all struggling in some way.

It is my hope that, one day:

* People will actually be treated equally. That opportunities would be allowed for all people; healthcare, education, general social rights.
* I would not have to fear that someone that I love might be in danger, hurt or killed because they are gay and went into a nightclub.

* I would live in a world where my LGBTQ brothers and sisters are able to afford HIV prevention; treatments and medication.
* Fewer children who are LGBTQ would be living on the streets because they have been abandoned by their families.
* That my trans friends would be able to freely express who they believe they are without fear.
* Children will never have to experience the horrors of "conversion therapy" because their parents forced them to try to not be gay.
* American LGBTQ history would be included in education.
* LGBTQ people would be normalized in movies, books and in schools.
* My LGBTQ brothers and sisters would never be excommunicated from their churches because they are gay.
* My gay brothers who so desperately want to start families, would be able to adopt children more easily. That invitro would be more accessible and absent of discrimination, that they would not be constantly pushed down the list.
* That I can adopt a baby and not have the fear that the biological parents, six months later, decide that they don't want their child growing up with gay parents.
* I would be permitted bereavement and sick days if my gay family member passes or gets sick.
* The church would stop inflicting hurt on the LGBTQ in the name of Christ.
* That Christian leaders would not just accept gays but actually advocate for them, fighting against the harmful and violent declarations of other Christian leaders.

I have started to reconnect with some of my friends from the youth group. After high school, we lost track of each other for a while. I am very curious to know what their views are now concerning the LGBTQ. Were they as hurt as I was by the conservative teaching? I have been surprised by the responses to the church now. We were taught that anything that was not Southern Baptist was evil. Many of my friends no longer believe that.

I have a lot of guilt associated with my life related to my religious upbringing and my response to others. As I have become aware of that, I have tried to make up for the things I have grown to hate about myself, things I had said and done by being kind and displaying a heart of a servant. I believe this began a process of building a compassion in me that I never experienced before.

The more I talk to people and hear their stories and what they have experienced being LGBTQ, has helped me personally. I was not alone in my struggles. It is really difficult to hear people recount all of the people they have lost in their lives since they have come out, by name with photos, in their final moments.

It has also been helpful to understand the history of the LGBTQ community. I had never heard anything about; the Stonewall riots, the largest LGBTQ mass murder when they were burned in the barn, or any of it. I was told that the gay *thing* over the last few years was because of man turning away from God and toward Satan. It would have been helpful to know that gays had been in this country since before the colonization. Much of what I taught was not true. God is not raining fire down upon us to punish us because a man wants to have a family with another man.

Despite the hurt inflicted by the church, I believe that change can occur. Communication is critical. It is my hope that conversations between the church and the LGBTQ community will help to create a deeper understanding. Good or bad, the lack of knowledge or the inability to ask questions, whether in support or not, has only caused more awkwardness. Truth can never cause division. It can only reveal what was already there.

Ken is not only gay but he is an ally to HopeSprings, working to educate churches about the LGBTQ community. He engages in conversations with pastors and church leaders so that they can more fully understand the people represented in that community, then take that information and share it with their parishes. These conversations encourage an open dialog, allowing questions to be answered, clarifying terms and creating a more informed church community. How can we even have a conversation when we don't know the verbiage? What terms are more acceptable? Which are more offensive? The goal is not to convince churches to embrace a different view of sexuality but to begin to see the children of God behind the LGBTQ letters. It is the hope of HopeSprings that the sharing of personal stories will begin to open the minds and hearts of the church community.

Ken believes that there is power in education and the hearing of personal stories. He has studied the history of the LGBTQ community and commits his time to recording and communicating personal stories in order to generate change.

Ken has been happily married to Nathan for three years. Their family consists of two dogs, a mentor, and a plethora of brothers from the LGBTQ community.

The Story of Isaiah

Isaiah was an Evangelical pastor for ten years. During that time, he had his first encounter with counseling someone from the LGBTQ community. He quickly realized that he had not thought deeply about this and was not prepared for the questions this interaction invoked in him. As he heard members of the LGBTQ community share their stories, he began to see that, very often, the church's approach toward the LGBTQ community, did not adequately reflect God's unconditional love. This put him on a journey to pursuing God's heart about what he was observing in the lives of faithful LGBTQ followers of God.

I was raised in an Irish Catholic family with four brothers and no sisters. The response that I get from nearly everyone has been, *Your poor mother.* But the truth is, no one really needed to worry about my mom. She was a very strong and capable woman, well-suited for the family she and my dad were given.

There were many things that were rock-solid about my childhood. My parents were very committed to our family and to raising us well. We always knew that they were there for us. Even though there was tension at times, our home felt secure. No matter how challenging life became, we knew that our parents would stay together. Divorce was never an option for them. Homicide, maybe. Divorce, never. Their commitment was for better or for worse, for life.

Both of my parents were actively involved in our lives, but in different ways. My dad was the financial provider, the disciplinarian for big things the *Wait until your father gets home*, kind of dad, our coach and mentor. He was very positive and optimistic. His life's motto was *Work hard, Play hard.* He enjoyed life, but was very committed to fulfilling his responsibilities.

Dad was an attorney and an executive in the Department of Defense. His expertise was ensuring that companies with defense contracts had adequate security systems and protocols to keep our country's secrets safe and secure. He was scrupulously honest. If he saw one of us with a pen stamped *U.S. Government*, which was commonplace in the Washington, D.C. suburbs in the 1960s, he would tell us that it was stolen property and that whoever gave it to us had stolen it and should return it.

Mom was no shrinking violet. She was very bright. In 1954, after graduating from college, she was hired by Mutual of Omaha into a management development program. That was very unusual for the time because business was a man's world.

Less than a year into her career, my parents met. Their families had lived in Omaha and had become friends. When my dad was young, his family moved to Washington DC, where he was raised. After college, my dad joined the Navy and was stationed in New Orleans. He decided to visit Omaha when he had a few days off, and it was then that he met my mom.

They fell in love immediately and were married about a year later. Children arrived on the scene quickly and Mom stayed home to care for us. Mom did carry some resentment giving up her career, however. While we knew we weren't responsible for her decision, we did hear about it from time to time.

Where my dad was the eternal optimist and upbeat, my mom could be pretty volatile. She was passionate and could readily lose her temper. Dad would simmer when he was angry but when he blew up, he really blew.

There was a fair amount of arguing in our home when I was young. I remember hearing my parents fighting at night, wishing it would stop. I even remember silently praying that they would get divorced, just so the fighting would stop, although I knew that would never happen. It wasn't like that all the time, but it was enough that I remember it pretty vividly.

Watching my parents' relationship evolve and grow during their retirement years was a joy to see. My brothers and I were grown by then and that probably had a lot to do with it. Empty nesting agreed with them. It was sweet. They enjoyed their retirement immensely and spent their free time traveling, playing tennis, and making lots of friends. It was nice to see them enjoying life.

I was the middle child. My brothers were four and five years older and four and five years younger. We were a very symmetrical family. I was on an island by myself as it relates to age. My brothers and I were fairly close. We really weren't best friends, but we definitely played together a lot. My two younger brothers were probably the closest to each other of all of us. They were a year apart in age and had similar interests. They also had friends outside of the family. My older brothers were eleven months apart. I was more on my own being so much younger and older than the four.

My brothers and I were very active. We played sports and did all the things boys liked to do. And while we loved each other, we fought like crazy.

Today, my brothers and I are much closer than we were as children. I know that if I needed help, any one of them would immediately stop what they were doing and come to me. I would do the same for them.

I felt like we were the typical Catholic family. Church and Catholic education were the highest priorities. We weren't overly religious, but missing church was never an option, even on vacation. I imagine it was challenging raising five boys and putting us through private school, but my parents always seemed to manage.

I was a mischievous Catholic school boy. Corporal punishment was generously exercised on my behalf. There is a proverb that says, "spare the rod, spoil the child." Let's just say that I wasn't spoiled. I wasn't a bad kid, but I was a smart aleck. In fifth grade, the Mother Superior, Principal of the School, brought all 105 fifth graders into one of the classrooms and told us that we were the worst class in her twenty-three years of being Mother Superior of the school. She then began to go around the room identifying the troublemakers.

When she got to me, she said, "Isaiah, stand up. You are the worst one. You are the worst kid in the worst class of my twenty-three years at this school."

I acted on the outside like it was an achievement to be proud of, but inside it didn't feel very good. I couldn't say that I experienced the love of God in that environment, but I definitely came to know the nuns' idea of His justice.

Despite that experience, there was never a doubt in my mind that God existed. He was the Creator and overseer of the world. I firmly believed that life was not the result of some random events. There clearly were evolutionary processes, but behind it all was God.

When I wasn't in church or school, I was playing sports. Football was the one I played and loved the most, but I enjoyed anything related to a ball. We played pick-up games in the neighborhood, as well as organized sports through the Boys' Club and Little League. As I got older, I played on my school's teams. I was never the most talented or athletic kid on the team, but I always gave it my all. I made up for my lack of talent with great effort and desire and ended up doing pretty well.

I was very social and loved being around other kids. During the summer when we were out of school, I would hop on my bike in the morning and return home when the streetlights came on. We lived in a large neighborhood, teeming with kids. When we weren't playing sports, we played in the woods and dug caves and tunnels.

Family vacations were another highlight in my life. When I was young, we had a camper and travelled all around. I loved it. One summer, we took a three-week camping trip to Vermont and Canada.

Later, my parents built a small beach cottage. My brothers and I would spend most of the summers there with my mom. Dad would come on the weekends and for some extended vacations. We loved swimming, riding waves, and surfing. A friend of mine had a small boat and I learned to waterski. One weekend, I asked my friend to invite my dad to go waterskiing. It was quite a success. Dad was up on his first try and skied all around the bay. He loved it.

That winter, I'd wake up every Saturday and study the classified section of the paper for boats. I'd circle the boats for sale and show them to my dad as soon as he got up. Finally, when we found a boat that we could afford, my dad paid for most of it, and my brothers and I all chipped in for the rest. We had great times on the boat, waterskiing and riding around. Afterwards, in the evening, we would build bonfires on the beach. One of our friends would play the guitar. We'd roast marshmallows. We made some incredible memories there.

The transition from Catholic grade school to a public high school was a big hurdle. I got off to a rocky start, but high school became one of the best times in my life. In my Freshman year, longing to be accepted, I became involved with drugs. I knew I was heading down the wrong path and during the summer between my Freshman and Sophomore years, I became determined to chart a new course. I threw myself into playing sports, football and tennis on the high school teams, and made friends who were a better influence on my life. As a result, I ended up becoming student body president and captain of the football team.

It was at that time that I became involved in Young Life, a Christian student ministry, and was introduced to Jesus in a way that I never had before. Prior to this, God was more of an idea than a real person; and religion was more ritual than relationship. Through my involvement in Young Life, Jesus became much more personal, accessible, and relatable to me. And, while I was intrigued, I didn't make an immediate commitment to orient my life around Him. I had my feet in both worlds – attending bible studies and fellowship groups some nights and drinking and partying on others.

In college, my drinking and partying went even further. During one stretch of my sophomore year, I was drunk almost every night and grades plummeted. I saw the academic goals I had when I started college becoming a pipedream. My grade-point average one semester was 0.6, not a 3.6 or a 2.6 or even a 1.6, a 0.6. Not stellar. I was nineteen years old and thought my life was ruined and unrecoverable.

Then, one night, I began to think about the gospel message I had heard about back in high school. Alone in my dorm room, I asked God for His forgiveness and told Him that He could have what was left of the life I thought I'd wrecked.

I experienced a spiritual awakening that created some immediate and positive changes. By God's grace, and with His Spirit within me, I was able to turn my life around. I decided to transfer to a school closer to home so I could live at home, work, and finish school. I was invited, by the Young Life Director who had been my high school leader, to become a leader. I didn't feel at all qualified or ready, but it turned out to be one of the best things for me. I was immediately placed in a community of people who were growing in their faith and encouraging others to do the same and it was so much fun. I built friendships that have lasted my whole life. Those years became very influential for my future.

It was through my involvement as a Young Life leader that I met my wife, Grace. I was initially introduced to her by our Young Life Director because she needed some tutoring in Economics. I was a senior Business major at that time and had improved my academic performance and she was a Freshman. The tutoring turned into a friendship that turned into a romance. We were married three years later and have been married for over thirty-five years and have two adopted sons.

When I finished college, I received several job-offers and accepted the one that paid the least, going on staff with Young Life. I ended up serving on staff for eleven years and loved it. My faith grew during that time and Young Life gave me opportunities to invest in the lives of many high school and college students. I was also able to earn a seminary degree at the same time.

In my mid-thirties, I began to feel the urge to try something new professionally. I had a friend who developed and managed large-scale retirement communities so I went to work with for his company. It was an exciting time for me professionally. We grew the company and created healthy communities that served seniors exceptionally well. I learned a great deal and earned a Master in Business Administration degree, during that time.

It was a nice season of life for our family. Our sons were young, and I had the joy of coaching their sports teams. We were also active in our large evangelical church where I served as an elder. We were thriving.

After about thirteen years with the retirement company, the church where I was serving asked if I would consider a full-time position as the senior pastor. This was something I never expected nor was I seeking but I didn't want to end up like Jonah, in the belly of a whale, so I accepted the invitation. This proved to be a wonderful, challenging, painful, and growth-producing time for me.

God had prepared me for this position as senior pastor even though I didn't always see it. There came a point while serving on Young Life staff that I recognized that I really lacked compassion for others. It hit home one day when I was stuck in traffic, becoming late for a meeting that I thought was so important. When I got to the place where I could see the accident, I saw that this inconvenience for me was an extremely consequential event for the people involved in the accident. I thought to myself, *What is wrong with me?* The whole time I had been focusing only on my minor inconvenience without thinking at all about the people who had lost their lives and loved ones in the crash. I really took this to heart and asked God to work in me and give me a heart of compassion for others.

As all of us, I am a work in process. Some would say I'm just a *piece of work* – and they wouldn't be wrong. In my younger days as a follower of Jesus, I saw the world in very clear terms of black and white, and right and wrong. My theology was lined up, buttoned up and right down the middle. I would say that I always had a heart for people wherever they were in relationship with God, but I was very clear on what I thought was right and wrong.

By God's grace and over a long period of time, God has done a real work in my life in this area. Today, when people describe me, compassion and empathy are near the top of the lists they cite. This is truly a testament to God's power to change a life.

There are a couple of key decisions that I made along the way that created an environment for God to do His work in me. The first is being open to change. God generally seems to move when we invite Him and are open to receive what He has for us. Another key part of my journey has been to intentionally engage in relationships with others whose experiences are different from mine. I've learned that it is pretty easy to take a position on things like religion, theology, and politics when it is all theoretical. But, when you begin to know and love people whose experiences, views, and understanding about the world are different from yours, some things can become less clear – and others even more so.

God has used my decision to mentor a young man from a father-absent home in the large city nearby, to create great growth in me. When we began our relationship, Jaquon was thirteen years old. I would go to his home every Thursday and pick him up at 7:00 a.m. to participate in a mentoring breakfast that was part of a program we participated in together. The area of the city where he lived was very under-resourced and riddled with crime. For me, being a suburban, business executive in my forties, knocking on his door at 7:00 a.m. was a new experience. Over time, I got to know him, his siblings, his mom, his grandmothers, and his neighbors. So many things I thought I knew about the inner-city changed in the context of this relationship. My heart for the city and for those who live in the city opened in ways I never would have expected – and I am certain would never have experienced had it not been for this relationship.

Some other areas of change God had in mind for me came to light when I stepped into the role as Senior Pastor. Our church consisted of about 2500 families and had been known as one of the larger, welcoming, evangelical churches in our area. Many people found faith there. We were a place where people who had been beaten down by life could come and, in a very non-threatening way, find space to come to know Jesus.

Shortly after becoming pastor of the church, people from within the congregation began to find their way to my office to tell me their stories. What I began to learn was that not everyone's experience at the church was easy. Some felt like they were swimming upstream, that the current of the church was running against them. It was not easy to get connected, fit in or find a place there.

One of these communities experiencing isolation were the families who had a child or family member affected by a disability. It seemed to me that Jesus spent a disproportionate amount of His time with people affected by disabilities. I heard from family after family that churches in general and ours in particular were not always easy to navigate for these families. The children's programs were designed to meet the needs of the many, much better than the needs of the few. When your child has a disability, it is more challenging for them to participate in the typical Sunday school program. As I heard these families share their stories, I recognized that something needed to change. If I was going to be the pastor of the church, I needed to be the pastor of the *whole* church. I was determined to do everything I could to welcome those who came to our church who had a family member affected by a disability. We vowed that these friends would not only be a population for the church to serve, but they would be welcomed as full participants in the church. We began to see that every person, regardless of their disability would have an opportunity to serve in the church, as well as being served by it.

An amazing transformation took place in our church through the creation of a Disabilities ministry. Literally, hundreds of members from the church volunteered to serve there and were deeply blessed by being involved. The church and the broader community celebrated our commitment.

Another community in our congregation with whom I had little personal experience but who found their way to me were members of the LGBTQ community. I didn't realize it at first, but God had a training program in mind for me and He set up a series of "divine appointments" that were transformative for me.

Early in my time as pastor, a young man who was an intern at the church and training for the mission field, came to me to share his heart. He was a super sharp, very committed follower of Jesus, from a wonderful family in the church, and very excited about serving in the mission field. He related that he was becoming increasingly aware that there were some things that were true about him that would make it impossible for him to affirm the *Statement of Faith* that he would be required to sign by the mission organization he was planning to join.

As we met, he began to open-up and share about his sexual orientation. He spoke of how, when he was very young, he began to sense that he was attracted to other boys, rather than girls. Initially, this was a painful discovery for him. He "knew" from the teaching of his church that these feelings were "wrong." And yet, despite his prayers, God didn't remove these longings. It became very clear to me at the time that this young man didn't choose to be gay, he discovered it. And now, he was becoming more honest with himself and others about what he knew was true for him. It was an eye-opening and moving experience for me to hear him speak of his faith in Jesus and love for God – and the realization that he was gay. Prior to this, I had always believed that these were mutually exclusive ideas. And yet, in him, they were both very present. It was at that point that my heart began to sense things differently.

Another such appointment was with another young man who had grown up in a church in a different part of the country. He emailed me and told me that he had recently moved to our area and asked if,

"As a gay man, can I be true to who I am and be accepted at your church?" He asked.

I wrote him back and said, "I want nothing more than for you to be true to who you are and be accepted in our church, let's meet for lunch."

We met and I listened as he shared his story. Some aspects were similar to the story of the other young man. He clearly did not choose to be gay. When, as a young teenager, he discovered his attraction to other boys, he cried out to God to change him. He said he experienced shame and self-loathing and told his parents about it. They were committed church people and placed him in a *conversion therapy* program. He was determined, through that program, to live his life as a heterosexual.

When he got older, he met a young Christian woman and got married. A couple of years into their marriage, he again began feeling sexual attraction toward men. He did not act on these feelings but, instead, went to his wife and confessed this to her, wanting to seek counseling. When he shared his feelings with her, she shared that she had been having an affair with another man for several months and that they should get divorced. His wife had been working full-time for the church they attended and he volunteered in the youth ministry.

The church rallied around and supported her in her desire to become divorced, even though she had been unfaithful. He was told to repent from his gay inclinations and leave the church. They also conducted an investigation to determine if he had molested any of the children in the youth ministry. In their minds, anyone who had same-sex attractions might also be a pedophile.

As he shared his story with me, I couldn't believe it – and yet, sadly, I could. I asked him why in the world he would ever want to be involved in another church after the way he was treated?

He said, "Because I love Jesus and I know He accepts and loves me."

I was floored! Such faith! I told him that I hoped he would be loved and accepted in our church, but I also told him that, unfortunately, he would need to be very discerning about with whom he shared his life. Our church did not affirm same sex unions at all. We were loving and welcoming, or at least we thought we were, but our theology was clear. Marriage was ordained by God to be between one man and one woman for life.

Then, there was a woman who sang on the worship team at our church. She was a truly gifted artist and songwriter who played guitar and sang beautifully. One day, she came to me to share about the same-sex attraction she was experiencing. I listened as she shared her story and the dissonance she was feeling between her sexuality and the teachings of our church. She tried to ignore what she was feeling and then she came to the realization that being gay is part of who she is. She ended up leaving the church and moving south to pursue her music career. She didn't feel like she could remain part of a church that wouldn't affirm who she believed herself to be.

In each of these interactions, I took the posture of a learner, not a teacher. Their life experiences were *their* experiences. I wanted to listen, and learn, and love them – right where they were.

As I listened to their stories, some recurring themes kept coming up. One thing I learned was this: If an LGBTQ person grows up in an evangelical church, there is great fear in being honest about one's sexuality – and for good reason. The church often refuses to even have an open discussion about the LGBTQ. When they do, it can be quite judgmental. Sadly, when people come out in the church, they don't find the love and acceptance that they long for, so they distance themselves from the church altogether. As human beings, we gravitate to the places where the dignity of our humanity is affirmed. For our

LGBTQ friends and family members, this is rarely found in the evangelical church.

Another transformative experience for me began when a woman my wife and I knew from our Young Life days reached out to us. She, her wife and three children had been attending another local church that started out being very loving and welcoming, but when it came time to become members, they were not permitted to join because they were gay. They were stunned! Though the church appeared welcoming, full participation was not an option for them.

One day, the couple came to me to ask if I thought they would be welcomed at our church, so I went over to talk to them about it.

"I'm not going to lie," I said to them. "It is going to be risky coming here but I can help you navigate the church so that it is less risky for you, if you want to come."

I told the women, "I am the pastor of the church and I welcome you. More importantly, Jesus welcomes you here. Don't let anyone else give you crap. You are welcome here."

The couple came to the church and I invited them to join our small group. Before they joined, I prepared the group to welcome our new members. There was some resistance at first by some of the members of our group. The turning point came when a woman, who was usually quiet as a mouse, sent a long email to the group expressing her support. She shared that when she heard about the couple wanting to come, she was a little uncomfortable at first and didn't think it was going to be good for the group. Then, the Lord really changed her heart and she felt that we should absolutely welcome them. Everyone was shocked at how this quiet woman was inspired to speak up and it encouraged the rest of the group to think differently. One family did leave the group, but the rest welcomed this family with open arms.

The new couple and their family have been a wonderful addition to the group. They are both therapists and add a new dimension that has been very helpful in many ways. But mostly, they are a dear family that God has used to open and grow our hearts for others.

A year after they joined our group, through tears of joy, one of the wives expressed that because they were so welcomed by our small group, she experienced God's love for the very first time. She said that she always thought that God didn't love her because she was gay, but now she knew He did. That was a very sweet moment for everyone. There was not a dry eye in the room.

It is interesting how I was so uneducated about the LGBTQ community when one of my brothers was gay. His sexual orientation was simply something that our family never really talked about. Though it was not a big surprise, I found out he was gay shortly after my son was born. I was thirty-one years old at the time and my brother thirty-six. Two of his close friends had recently died of AIDS. In concern for his health and well-being, I decided to just ask him about his sexuality.

"Hey, I know this is none of my business but are you gay?"

He said, "Yes, I figured that you knew that. I am your single brother living in San Francisco."

"Well, have you ever told Mom and Dad?" I asked.

"Yes, I told them years ago," he replied.

"What did they think?" I asked.

"Well, they just thought if I met a nice girl that I wouldn't be gay anymore," he answered.

Knowing he had lived with one of my brothers for a while, I asked if he knew about my brother being gay.

"Oh sure, he knew."

I went on to ask, "Well, I know that your friends just passed away. Are you healthy? Have you been tested?"

"Yes, I have been tested. I don't live a very *active* life in that way. I am careful and cautious. I am fine," he answered.

"Good, I was concerned about your wellbeing," I responded.

"I appreciate that," he said.

That was the end of the conversation about my brother being gay. It didn't change the nature of our relationship. I actually think we were closer because of having such an intimate conversation. And, my brother being gay continued to not be a topic of discussion in our family, not even between brothers.

As my brother got older, he battled depression that he medicated with alcohol. My brothers and I organized an intervention and we got him into rehab. This was transformative for him and the last years of his life were probably the happiest.

We discovered, during his time in rehab, that my brother had esophageal cancer. My brothers and I really grew close as we cared for him. He died a year later.

I believe that my brother really regretted not being in a long-term relationship and never having children. He just didn't feel that he had the freedom socially or even in our family to do that. That was a real loss. I wish we could have accepted and loved him in such a way that he would have been able to have that experience.

Through my role as a pastor I have come to see clearly that the church has often been very hurtful to people who are considered "on the fringes of society." Though I am not directly responsible, I have, on several poignant occasions, as a representative of the Church, asked people for forgiveness for the pain that has been inflicted on them simply because they didn't fit the mold of the typical church-goer. Many times, tears of relief flowed. It is amazing how healing it can be when confession and repentance are expressed.

I have learned, over the years, that experiencing pain and difficulty expands our ability to feel compassion and empathy. A major source of growth took place when my wife and I discovered that we were unable to have children biologically. That was a real loss that opened my heart up to experiencing compassion in a new way. Personally, we did have the joy of raising two sons through adoption. I love these young men more than life itself and am so fortunate to be their dad.

When our older son turned sixteen, the wheels on the cart of his life began to come off and he really began to struggle. We did all we could to help him, but he pulled away. It was a very painful time for our family. He had significant addiction issues and experienced a lot of challenges that were self-inflicted. Then, he chose to be completely alienated from us for a time. This was the most brutally painful experience of our lives and it changed us. Today, we are so very thankful that our relationship has been restored.

Four years ago, I left my position at the church and started a company that provides in-home nursing care for the elderly and others who are vulnerable. An individual plan of care is created for each client so that they are able to thrive in the homes they love. Rather than moving to an assisted living community or nursing home, our amazing Caregivers provide everything someone might need to stay in their home. End of life care is also provided in partnership with hospice. Caregivers are carefully matched with clients so that the experience is the very best for everyone involved; the Caregiver is loved and blessed by serving and the client is loved and blessed by the person serving them.

People sometimes ask if I miss being a pastor. I truly don't, for a variety of reasons. I don't have any interest in "teaching" anyone anymore or trying to convince people of something. I prefer to take the posture of a learner and simply love the people God puts in my path. When invited, I do enjoy mentoring people in business or ministry or in life in some way, but more as a friend or guide than a pastor or teacher. I simply want to encourage people on their journeys and help them know how much they are loved.

If I were planting a church today, which I am not, it would be affirming of gay marriage. I believe to my core that God's love is higher, longer, deeper, and wider than we can ever fully grasp. He longs for every person to experience that love through each other. Maybe I'd be "wrong" in affirming gay marriage, but I would prefer to err on the side of love and grace. In truth, I think it is impossible to *err* on the side of love. Jesus was castigated by the religious conservatives of His day for loving those that were believed to be unlovable. I would be honored to be treated the same way.

I have had a lot of doctrinal teaching poured into me through the years from Catholic school and throughout my life as an evangelical. I have come to believe that God has a higher value than doctrinal compliance.

Jesus said that all of the law and all of the teaching of the prophets are summed up with, "Love the Lord your God with all your heart and with all your soul and with all your mind...and Love your neighbor as yourself." Matt 22:37-39.

Above all else, God's will is to bring unity and harmony among people. Ephesians 1:9-10 says, "He (God) made known to us the mystery of His will according to his good pleasure, which he purposed in Christ, to be put into effect when the times reach their fulfillment – to bring *unity* to all things in heaven and on earth under Christ."

My greatest hope is that the world would become a place where all are welcomed, all are loved, and all reflect the spirit of God. I pray that I might be an ambassador of love, grace, and acceptance toward that end, even if I am a piece of work.

Isaiah is a husband and a father to grown children and commits much of his time to loving and caring for his family, and an occasional round of poorly played golf.

He volunteers on the board of an organization that mentors young men from father absent homes. He supports them with fundraising and encouragement.

Embracing the Journey

When Greg and Lynn discovered that their son was gay, God took them on a transformative journey of faith that changed their hearts forever.

They had never interacted with anyone from the LGBTQ community before and found themselves without resources or support to respond to their new life.

"At first, we tried to 'fix' him, to no avail. Even in the earliest days of our journey, we clung to two absolutes: we would love God, and we would love our son."

In August 2015, their experience led them to establish, "Embracing the Journey", a non-profit organization created to build bridges between LGBTQ individuals, their families, and the church.

The Story of Greg and Lynn

Life is an amazing journey with many twists and turns. It can be long, and sometimes painful but each experience helps to form us into the people that we are today. It is an evolution of sorts. Each new experience causes us to examine what is true, and can be an opportunity for us to change and grow.

We have found this to be true about our view of the LGBTQ community, though our heart did not develop overnight. It evolved. Each step on our journey contributed to what we believe today.

Lynn

God put a sense of justice in my heart very long ago. As a young child in elementary school, I remember seeing my brother picked on by the other students as we rode home from school on the bus. They were so unkind to him, calling him hurtful names. I tried to come to his defense but they would pick on me too, but it was nothing like they did to him. That experience did something inside of me. It made me want to defend anyone that was being hurt. I chose to become their friend.

The Catholic church became a needed refuge for me growing up. It was the only place where I experienced peace and I really needed it. My homelife was not so peaceful. Dad was an alcoholic and my mom had mental health issues. Being with God made me feel safe and I always remember loving Him.

On Sundays, our family appeared normal. We would attend church and then afterwards go out for a pancake breakfast. After my parents separated when I was sixteen, I continued to go to church on my own. I was so enamored with God that I thought I wanted to be a nun…until I met Greg in junior high.

Our family moved half way through the school year when I was in junior high making it necessary to change schools. I remember feeling so sad because I really wasn't leaving any close friends behind. I wouldn't even be missed.

I was surprised when everyone at the new school wanted to be my friend. I was instantly popular but I quickly learned that that wasn't necessarily a good thing. I observed how the popular group mistreated some of the other students. They picked on the other students and I didn't like that. I was nice to the students in the popular group but I made the decision to not closely associate with them. Suddenly, I was no longer as popular but that was okay with me.

I needed to find friends that had similar values and weren't in the same group and I did and they were really great friends.

Greg

I grew up in a very loving home. My parents were wonderful and really cared deeply about our family. They were good people and taught our family right from wrong.

We lived much of my childhood in a big city in the Midwest. When I was going into junior high, my parents moved our family to the suburbs and I started going to the same school as Lynn.

I found the students at the school not quite as friendly as Lynn did. They would pick on me unmercifully and one even pushed me down a flight of stairs one day. It was traumatic but instead of becoming bitter, I began to develop a compassionate heart for the students that found themselves in the same position. I never realized that until much later.

Life got a lot better for me when I began dating. My first date was on my 16th birthday, the very same day I got my driver's license… go figure. I dated a number of girls and unfortunately, was very promiscuous. I regret that to this day.

One sunny afternoon, I ran into Lynn after school. From the first day I saw her, earlier in Junior High, Lynne rocked my world. She, however, didn't know I existed previously. This particular afternoon, we actually spoke. I was sitting on my motorcycle at an intersection in our neighborhood and Lynn was in her car. We greeted each other and began talking.

Lynn said to me, "We should get together sometime." I immediately asked her out on a date for that evening. I was not going to let the opportunity escape me. She agreed and that was the beginning of our life together.

Lynn was like no one I had ever dated. I was completely infatuated with her. It was as though we were kindred spirits from the very beginning. A year later, I realized that I could never imagine my life without her, so I asked her to marry me. She was just 17 years old at the time and I was 19. Less than a year later, we were married. I remain completely infatuated with her to this day.

I really didn't have much of a faith background growing up. Our family only went to church a few times a year. My life changed dramatically when I came to know Jesus later in life. I was twenty-seven years old.

Lynn

After we got married, we didn't attend church very much until I became pregnant with our second child. It was then that I realized how much I had missed church and wanted that for our family. Greg wasn't interested in going so I started to go to church on my own. I was eight months pregnant at the time. Greg would drop me off at the church, run errands, then pick me up when church was over. It worked for us.

Greg

When we lost our first child to a miscarriage, I was heartbroken and I began to consider if there really was a God? It was the first time in my life that I ever questioned if God existed. If God did exist, He must have died or fallen asleep because He was not present in my current situation. If He was in control, He never would have let bad things happen.

It was at that point, I started living my life as if there was no God. That was not a good thing. Though I wasn't raised in church, my parents had taught me the difference between right and wrong. If there was no God, then all of that went out the window.

It was during that same time that numerous people began speaking into our lives about Jesus. My brother and his wife, in particular, invested pretty heavily in us. They could see that we were struggling and would drive 150 miles to our house just for the afternoon to spend time with us. Sharing the gospel was a large part of our time together. I wasn't very receptive at first. I thought I was a good guy and was not buying the "We are all sinners" thing.

Over that three-year period, Lynn and I started to listen to Dr. Charles Stanley's messages. They were inspiring and we really enjoyed them, so I shared some of what we listened to with my brother and his wife.

We had many conversations with my brother about what we were learning and finally, he asked about our faith.

While Lynn and I were on the phone with him one day, he asked, "Hey, I just need to know, you guys are acting like you are Christians. Have you ever accepted Christ as your Savior?"

When we answered "No," he asked, "Well, what's stopping you?"

Over time, my study of the bible made me realize that I actually was a sinner. I had broken many of the Ten Commandments physically, and those I didn't break physically I certainly broke in spirit. My brother's question really made me think.

I knew I needed a Savior but was concerned about how much I would need to change, so I said to him, "You Christians don't look like you have any fun! I like to drink and smoke and tell off-color jokes."

"Listen," he said. "If you have stuff in your life that God doesn't want there, He'll point it out to you."

"You mean to say that all I need to do is confess my sins, attempt to follow Christ and I will go to heaven?" I said. It all sounded too easy.

"Yes, it's not meant to be complicated," he said.

Lynn and I prayed with my brother that night and our lives were immediately turned upside down. Much like the apostle Paul, I went from persecuting Christians to where I was on fire to share the good news with everyone I met. Believing in Jesus was the way to eternal life, I proclaimed.

Lynn

I remember going to bed that night, thinking about all of the repetitious prayers I had prayed through the years; Hail Marys' and the Lord's Prayer. What Greg's brother had shared with us was different.

Greg said to me that night, "If we are going to be Christians, we should probably go to church."

I responded, "Well, that sounds like a good idea."

We wanted God to make His plan for us really clear so, we started praying about where we should go to church. The following week, we had a knock at the door. One of our neighbors was canvassing the neighborhood about something.

During the course of the conversation he said, "If you are ever looking for a church, we have a good one for you."

We knew the answer was clearly from God. The next Sunday, we found ourselves in church. We were a little fearful about being separated from our kids, sending them to Sunday school while we were in the service, but we did it.

We learned to really love the church. Overtime, we became close friends with the pastor and his wife. We remain friends with them to this day, despite our geographic distance.

Neither one of us had an idea of what it looked like to raise a family up in the church so we contacted an organization that we thought could help us; *Focus on the Family*. We studied hard and believed every word they taught us.

It was from *Focus on the Family* that we developed our negative beliefs about the LGBTQ community. Early on, James Dobson, suggested several reasons that one might have a gay child; a dad who was absent from the home or a mom who was overbearing. In either case, if you had a gay child, it was your fault.

Another message Focus on the Family presented was the "gay agenda." "Gays just want to destroy the family and family values," he said.

We bought into all of it until we discovered that our son was gay.

Greg

I used to meet with a close pastor friend every Friday for lunch. One day, here shared with me that he was brokenhearted because he discovered that his youngest son was using the family computer to access pornography. I remember thinking after our conversation that I should probably pay closer attention to what our son was watching on his computer so I did. I, too, discovered that our son was accessing pornography but I was shocked to find that it was gay porn.

When we confronted our seventeen-year-old son about our discovery, it didn't go well. He admitted that he was gay. At the time, Lynn and I believed homosexuality was a choice and we were concerned that his bad decision was going to mess up his life. He would be at risk for disease, hate crimes and unimaginable things and we were terrified.

The first thing we shared with our son was how his decision to be gay would affect us. Suddenly, everything became about Lynn and me. Our reputation was at stake and would be tarnished. He was interfering with the dreams that we had for our family. Between that and the fact that he was hiding it from us, we grounded him.

I told him, "We are not grounding you because you are gay. We're grounding you because you lied to us. You made us believe that you were straight, and you weren't."

Looking back, we understand that he didn't tell us about being gay because we were not a safe place for him. We reinforced that by our actions.

Though we told him we loved him and nothing would ever change that, we also said, "We need to get you fixed."

Our response to our son coming out caused him much pain We were anything but Christ-like. The love we expressed to him was conditional. It was based largely on our fear and our pride, but at the time, we didn't see it.

We had been Christians for twenty years at this point and thought we had the answers for everything. The world was black and white. God's word was black and white and there was no in between.

Our relationship with our kids had always been good. Our house was the place where all of their friends would hang-out. We loved their friends and would often take them on vacation with our family.

When this happened, Lynn became very proficient at using the bible as a weapon. Not only was it used on our son, it was used on his friends, as well. We learned later that our son had another set of friends that we had never met. If he ever decided to bring them by, we would use the bible to plead our case.

It didn't take long before it became painfully obvious that we had pushed our son and his friends away from us and God. There was nothing attractive about our version of Christ. We had totally lost our voice to influence them in anyway and we were responsible for it.

In our efforts to raise our level of awareness about the LGBTQ community, we went to the bookstore to see what had been written about this topic. We found absolutely nothing.

At the same time, we turned our energies toward studying the bible to see what God had to say about our situation. We looked at four aspects: Who did Jesus say He was? Who did he hang out with? How did He treat people? And, what did He have to say? Our study revealed that if Jesus was south, we were north. We had gotten it all wrong and we needed to rectify the situation.

We started with a conversation with our son, apologizing for our behavior. We told him that we wanted to love him well. Understandably, he was very cautious of our gesture, and held us at a distance for a while. We had dramatically changed course. Eventually, our son began to see the authenticity of our words.

When our son became more comfortable and began to trust us again, he started bringing his friends around. We became very focused on loving unconditionally. We didn't try to change them, we just wanted to love them as they were.

People often think that if you are attempting to reconcile your beliefs around LGBTQ matters, the bible no longer applies. What we have found is just the opposite. It's not in spite of the bible, but because of the bible that we are to respond to one another in love: Love God, our neighbor and our children.

Lynn

When the disciples asked Jesus, "What is the greatest commandment?"

Jesus replied with this, "Love the Lord your God with all your heart and with all your soul and with all your mind. This is the first and greatest commandment. And the second is like it, Love your neighbor as yourself. All the Law and the Prophets hang on these two commandments." Matthew 22:36-40.

Jesus' inclusivity and unconditional love can be very attractive. As parents, all we needed to do was reflect that in our lives. As a result, we became attractive to our son's friends and they wanted to spend more time with us.

Greg

As we continued to study the bible and to develop new relationships with our son's friends, we began to realize that nearly none of what we had heard about the LGBTQ community from the church was true. We knew our son and had met his friends. They were kind young men, and many were believers. This was inconsistent with what we were hearing from Christian leaders and it didn't sit well with us.

Our hearts began to change, and after our move to Atlanta, Georgia. Lynn and I began volunteering with a secular ministry in the city called *Lost N' Found.* The ministry was for LGBTQ individuals who were homeless. In our city, there are 950 LGBTQ homeless kids on the streets every night. Lost N' Found helps them with personal hygiene items, showers and secures shelter for the night.

We would gather with the kids, share a meal and listen to them share their stories of why they were on the streets. The majority of the kids had been kicked out of their homes. Our hearts were captured. It gave us a desire to really make a difference in the lives of the LGBTQ community and their families.

Lynn

It didn't take long for us to become a resource in our church. Parents of LGBTQ kids needed help and came to us for advice. It started with one couple then grew to several groups across the city. They wanted to understand how to reconcile the teachings of the church with their reality. They wanted to love their kids well. This was the beginning of our ministry, *Embracing the Journey.*

The church can have the harshest response to the LGBTQ community. It has been heartbreaking for us to watch this group of marginalized people be harmed. When people are being hurt in the name of God, that is just wrong and we were called to respond to it. It is because of the bible that we started to open up this discussion with churches.

Many churches have not even been willing to have conversations about the LGBTQ community because they believe that same-sex attraction is a sin. When speaking to pastors, we recognize that there are two ways of thinking about the LGBTQ community in the church. Many believe that living a gay lifestyle is sinful and the solution is living a celibate life. Then, you are acceptable to the church. Though you will be included in the church community. you may be limited in your opportunities to serve.

Our ministry creates a venue for pastors to enter into a discussion with us about God's heart for all people. We do this by exploring scripture and challenge pastors to reconcile what it looks like to love the whole church as God intended. It has been exciting to see how more and more churches are willing to enter into complex discussions such as this.

Greg and I have had a very colorful life, especially before we became Christians in our twenties. Right after I came to know Christ, I started praying that God would begin to eliminate some of the bad habits we had established through the years. I thought I knew which ones should be eliminated in Greg's life first and when God's order was different than I thought it should be, I was disappointed. God kindly reminded me that I was "not the Holy Spirit." It was not my job to convict anyone, much less my husband. I've learned that if there is something in your life that needs to be changed, God will help you do it.

This has been very helpful as I respond to the negative comments that I hear about LGBTQ individuals from conservative Christians.

My response is more of a question. "Are we going to trust God to speak into the lives of others or are we going to take that role of the Holy Spirit on ourselves?"

I just keep remembering the two commandments that Jesus gave about loving God and loving your neighbor.

Greg

Lynn and I have listened to story after story of those who came out as gay. Young people who prayed for years for God to take away their desire for the same sex.

"God, I don't want to be like this," they say.

When you hear someone's story, it changes everything. It became personal for us and we went into action.

As we look back over our son's life, it was obvious there were a lot of signs suggesting Greg, Jr. was gay. When he was three years old, we noticed that he liked to do things that most girls did; play house, with dolls, and putting on plays. I remember watching our son run around the corner of our house with a bunch of kids. All of the little boys were running wildly while our son was running very delicately with his hands by his side. It was painfully obvious that something was different about him.

We inquired about Greg Jr. while in a session with our Christian marriage counselor and she suggested that we have a family observation.

The conclusion from the observation was, "He will be fine. Peer pressure will straighten him out. He has loving, caring heterosexual Christian parents. He is going to be just fine." And life went on.

Those tendencies became more apparent as our son grew older. He was so different than our nephews. Our nephews and nieces were always rough and tumble kids. When we went to my parents' cabin in the woods together, our nephews and nieces would run off into the woods with our daughter on adventures. Our son would rather be in the cabin with his grandmother painting and drawing art.

Lynn

Even in the Christian elementary school our children attended, our son began to experience persecution. The other kids noticed he was different. Riding the bus was difficult because his schoolmates would tease him and call him *gay* and *queer.*

It didn't take long for our son began to have nightmares, waking up screaming and crying. Lynn and I would take turns going into his room to ask him what was the matter and to comfort him.

He would say, "I don't want to grow up. I don't want to grow up. I don't want to grow up."

We would assure him that he didn't need to grow up yet he was only eight. He really didn't need to worry about it now either. When he was older, he would love being a grown up. There would be cars to drive and many other great things he would be able to do.

Night after night, he repeated the same scenario. This went on for months.

It wasn't until a few years ago, when we were writing our book, that our son told us why he didn't want to grow up when he was younger. He explained that the kids on the bus were calling him gay and he asked some of the older kids what that meant. When they told him, he knew that he didn't want to grow up to be gay.

Our son never shared that with us before because he was aware of the messages we gave about the gay community.

Our response to television shows that had gay people was, "Turn that off, it's disgusting!"

He did not want to be that. It breaks our hearts to think of the pain that we caused him by our reaction.

Greg

It's an interesting phenomenon that when LGBTQ sons and daughters come out of the closet, 99% of the time, parents go into the closet. There are several reasons for this. In most cases, their child has been processing their sexuality for years. Parents are forced to process the news all at once. They are in shock and experience great loss. The hopes and dreams they have for their child have been shattered; grandchildren. They feel like they may have failed as parents.

Pride is a huge issue for many parents. *What will my family and friends think? What about the neighbors and people at work? Will they think less of me? Will they shun my child? What about my church? Will I still be able to serve there? How are they going to treat my family?* Life does not look the same and the unknown is before them.

No one wants their child to struggle under the weight of persecution. Most parents want the best for their children, for them to live a joy-filled life without any hardship. many Christian parents attempt to protect their son or daughter by taking on the responsibility of the Holy Spirit. They bombard their child with scripture taken out of context in an attempt to change their mind, believing that being gay is a choice. Lynn and I understand this very well.

Lynn

Often, many parents become fearful. But fear can paralyze us and take us down a very dark road.

The church teaches that fear is not from God and He doesn't want us to live that way. *Perfect love* is what *casts out fear* and the giving and receiving of perfect love brings hope and healing to relationships.

What we have found in our ministry is that when parents are able to get past the fear and love their children unconditionally, their relationship grows, and everyone grows closer to God. It is amazing to watch this happen.

Greg

As we have loved our kids and their friends unconditionally, we have seen God move in the life of our family. It took a couple years for my son's friends to come back around but when they did, they trusted us. They began coming to us for advice in their relationships with their parents. Some had been kicked out of their homes and needed a place to stay. Several asked for us to be their "Adoptive parents." Today, there are numerous kids (age 18-42), spread across the country that refer to us as "Mc Mom and Mc Dad." We stepped in when parents rejected their kids. That never would have happened had God not changed our hearts.

Lynn

When the church loves conditionally, it has the power to push away a few generations of people. Those people in their 20s and 30s will not tolerate hypocrisy and will leave the church, possibly avoiding church altogether.

When LGBTQ individuals hear the church say, "Being gay is a sin," they hear, "I am sin."

This causes wounding to happen in the name of God, giving people a distorted view of our loving God.

It is clear that the church needs to begin to rethink their view of the LGBTQ community. Being gay is an identity not a behavior. People don't choose to be gay any more than others choose to be straight.

Greg

God is writing each of our stories and only He knows what is best for us. Sanctification is a life-long process and when we try to take on the role of the Holy Spirit, we alienate people from us and from God. But Lynn and I had to learn this.

Lynn

Soon after I became a Christian, I learned that as we are obedient to God, He changes us and desires for us to respond to Him according to what He has taught us for His glory. I experienced this in a very profound way through my interaction with a homeless woman. I saw her outside of the grocery store pushing a cart with all of her belongings. I had seen her many times before, but this time, I felt called to respond. I watched as she went into the store, leaving her cart outside. As she entered the store, she stopped to check the pay phone for spare change. I thought to myself, *Oh, she needs money.* I clearly felt like God wanted me to do something for her so stopped and prayed. I knew my husband kept a small new testament bible in the glovebox of the car so I opened it and began reading. Immediately, I came to the verse that said, "If anyone has material possessions and sees a brother or sister in need but has no pity on them, how can the love of God be in that person?" John 3:17. Reluctantly, I took $20 from my wallet and proceeded toward the woman. As I approached her, I introduced myself. She did the same telling me her name was Sheila.

I said, "I know you don't know me but I have seen you around and wondered if you needed anything. A ride? Or something else?"

The woman came out with an expletive word and smiled, replying, "I know I look poor because I'm missing teeth, but I'm ok I'm living with my daughter."

I said, "Okay, well it was nice meeting you." And as I was walking away, I felt like I was supposed to give her the $20. I turned around and said to her, "I know you don't need anything but I wanted to give this to you. It really isn't from me it is from God."

Her response surprised me, "No, no, I don't want money. I am fine."

When I got back to my car, I was really angry at God. "Really, God? I felt like you wanted me to help this woman and yet, she didn't respond the way that I wanted her to."

I felt God say, "Listen, you aren't responsible for how she responds but you are responsible for how you respond to what I call you to do."

That was an early lesson in our ministry to parents. We realized that we were responsible for what God was calling us to do in *Embracing the Journey.* We were to build bridges between parents and their LGBTQ kids, and the church. We are not responsible for how people will respond to the message. We need to do what God calls us to and let Him do the rest.

Greg

Many of the stories we hear on a daily basis are not unlike our son's story. Most LGBTQ people do not want to disappoint their parents, so they live in the closet for a very long time. If people from the LGBTQ community were raised in the church, they do not want to position themselves to be judged. They have spent years and years praying for God to change them. Most people in the church have no idea about what people from the LGBTQ community have gone through because they have never asked them to share their story.

Lynn

As far as our own family is concerned, we hope that our grandchildren will grow up with hearts that are open and accepting. Presently, they are aware that their uncle is married to another man. Our eleven-year-old grandson understands much more than our six-year-old grandson and three-year-old granddaughter. The children attended the wedding and are old enough to remember it. Our daughter did carefully prepare them for the union. She explained that when two people are in love, they choose to get married. The challenge is that our daughter and her husband are very conservative and have also communicated that anything other than a man and a woman is sinful.

"It is not God's way," she said.

Our daughter and her husband don't always put a lot of emphasis on that and usually try to focus on the love of family. We feel fortunate in that. We have seen, too often, how families can be divided because of the inability to accept the situation and love their family members despite their personal beliefs.

Lynn

Unfortunately, it is not unusual to have some friendships change when someone comes out of the closet. When we first became Christians, we started going to a church and became "Christianized." We went to church every Sunday, learned the Christian lingo, everyone was smiling and everything was "great, great, great." You would never question what was taught. So when we first shared our son was gay, some of our friends had a hard time even having a conversation with us about it. It was almost like they intentionally avoided it.

Greg

We knew people loved us but I think many were so brokenhearted about our son that they didn't know how to enter into a conversation. The majority of our friends were quiet and said nothing. The silence can be more painful than the direct discussion.

Martin Luther King, Jr. summed it up really well for me with, "In the end, we will remember not the words of our enemies, but the silence of our friends."

In the beginning, we took the silence very personally. Their silence felt like rejection, but we came to realize it wasn't rejection, in most cases, they just didn't know what to say. We need people in our lives that are willing to walk with us even when they have no answers. It would have been an amazing gift to have someone come alongside of our son to encourage him.

Greg

When Lynn and I were really diving deep into the gospels, looking at Jesus, something became very obvious to both of us. In most stories in the bible, Jesus was consistently misunderstood and He was totally okay with that. At some point, I became indifferent with persecution and strapped a bullseye on my chest. I am okay with being misunderstood.

Most of the parents that have heard about their son or daughter being LGBTQ and reach out to us, are in a complete free-fall. They are hemorrhaging with grief. We do a great deal of triage. One of the things parents have trouble with is being misunderstood. Many of their Christian friends have communicated that if you love your gay child, you are condoning their behavior. The parents are already feeling guilt, fear and shame, so they have to learn to handle the expectations of their Christian friends.

Parents also question how a good and perfect God would create someone the bible calls an abomination. There are a half dozen things in the bible that God considers abominations; pride, lying lips, murder, wicked schemes, feet that are swift to mischief, and causing dissention. Everybody that walks the face of the earth will at some time be an abomination but we don't see that. Instead, people want to focus on my child's "issues" rather than their own.

Andy Stanley has a quote in his book, *Irresistible,* "People who were nothing like Him liked Him. And Jesus liked people who were nothing like Him." What is it about Jesus that people were attracted?

Most Christians today spend their time with people who are just like they are; believe what they do, look and dress like they do, and talk the same lingo. Jesus did not do that.

We live in this tension between the real and the ideal. There are so many parents who believe that if they attend their gay son or daughter's wedding, they are somehow condoning their lifestyle. They are concerned more about their child not living up to what they believe is the ideal marriage, than their son or daughter. But we live in the world of reality not the ideal. We respond with love.

Isolation can be a real problem for parents of LGBTQ. Many parents think they are an anomaly and do not come out right away. They have no one they can talk to about this and have no idea that statistics show about 5% of the population is LGBTQ. When we looked around our church, we realized that 20% of the people are either gay themselves or have someone in their lives that is.

Lynn

For whatever reason, God has trusted us with a gay son. We are thankful for that. He has taught us so much about what love looks like.

Greg

God is intentional, He knows every hair on our heads. He knew us before we were born and knit every cell together with love.

Lynn

When I get to heaven, I would rather have God say to me that I loved too much than I loved too little. I will choose love every time.

People might look at me and say, "Lynn, part of love is telling the truth." I no longer believe that. I trust God to reveal His truth.

Our ministry is not about changing people's theology or making them affirming. We desire to encourage parents and their children in their relationship with God and with each other. God does the rest.

We need to be patient with the church as they try to seek God's truth. We cannot expect them to change overnight. But we do need to have the conversation about LGBTQ individuals and what love looks like.

I hope and dream that the LGBTQ community can feel included in church the same way that we feel included. We want them to have space to be able to wrestle with their questions; spirituality, sexuality, or anything else. We want them to be able to participate and use the gifts God has given them, and to share their faith with others. There are so many young people in the church that need to hear a word of encouragement from an LGBTQ Christian. They need to know there is hope.

Greg

And, everyone needs to experience love. One of my favorite quotes is from Tim Keller:

"To be loved but not known is comforting but superficial. To be known and not loved is our greatest fear. But to be fully known and truly loved is, well, a lot like being loved by God. It is what we need more than anything. It liberates us from pretense, humbles us out of our self-righteousness, and fortifies us for any difficulty life can throw at us."

Timothy Keller, The Meaning of Marriage: Facing the Complexities of Commitment with the Wisdom of God

Lynn

The hope that I have for parents of LGBTQ sons and daughters is that they remember that we have a good God. He is loving, not cruel. God uses our experiences to grow and encourage us in our walk. I want them to know that life has not ended because your child is gay, life is just beginning. God is going to reveal things that you never would have realized without going through what you have. Hope is right around the corner.

When I think about our grandchildren, I hope they will love all people well. I am hopeful that they will see their uncles for who they are, love them and never judge. Because God has allowed them to have gay uncles, I hope that they will understand the depth of God's love and learn whatever God has for them in that experience.

Greg

I thank God for His continuous protection over our family and pray that He would continue to expand the love that we are currently experiencing today. May we move forward together in our ministry to love the LGBTQ community well.

Greg and Lynn believe that it is through the hearing and telling of stories that attitudes about people are changed. May their efforts change the church and bring God's kingdom of love forth for all people.

The Story of Emily

Emily is a licensed counselor working with college students at a large University in the Northeast. Her clients present with different mental health issues, ranging from general anxiety about being in school to a history of trauma and abuse. Several of her students are in the process of reconciling their sexuality. Being raised in a conservative Christian home, Emily had views about people from the LGBTQ community that changed dramatically when she heard their stories. She is now able to better affirm and encourage all people, bringing hope and healing to their lives.

I was nine months old when my identical twin sister and I left our home in the Northeast to accompany our parents to a small country in Asia. Our parents moved with the intention of encouraging and empowering the people there. My dad brought new agricultural techniques in organic farming, and my mom taught English. Their efforts have made it possible for the Asian communities to better support their families.

My twin sister and I have always been best friends. I believe that our unique experience of growing up overseas, contributed greatly to that. She is the one who knows me the best. Many people do not understand the filter with which we look at life, but we understand each other.

Education in Asia was an interesting and sometimes challenging experience for us. My sister and I went to a local school outside of our neighborhood for preschool and kindergarten. It was essential for us to become bilingual. We spoke the native Asian language in school and with our friends, and English at home with our parents. Overall, I have good memories of our time there and am thankful for the experience.

But, when we were in first grade, my parents made the decision to withdrawal us from the local school. The teachers in the local school used shame-based consequences to correct student behavior and it was harsh. I have memories of disobedient students being told to stand in the front of the room with tape over their mouths during the lesson because they had been talking. We were required to be perfect in every way in school. I was told that I got a "C" on a coloring assignment because my coloring was imperfect. This was in preschool and kindergarten.

Most of my childhood memories in Asia include me being aware that I was different, "other" and white. The attention I got from being so was very embarrassing. At school, my sister and I were the only Americans, and the only white children. I remember being so embarrassed one day when our class had to try on Christmas outfits for the concert at school. The teacher had the entire class strip down to their underwear. All of the children just stared at my sister and me…the white ones. Although this was a humiliating experience, having every other child have to do the same kind of normalized the situation for me.

I do not have any specific memories of playing with children at school but we really looked forward to coming home after school to play with my neighborhood friends. We played with friends in our home and outside. When neighbors came over, we played with blocks, Legos, and restaurant. We especially enjoyed riding bikes on our street. One of our favorite activities was to pretend to sell candy in front of our house. Some of my friends wanted to learn English and would come for English club where we would read books together.

After we were withdrawn from the local school, my parents felt that the best option for us was to be homeschooled. Our mom homeschooled us from first through eighth grades. These were very difficult years. I did not enjoy being homeschooled at all. My mom was not a trained educator so when I was identified as having dyslexia at age nine, which explained a lot, it did not make life easier. Not only did I struggle with reading, writing and math, but the learning disability colored my view of myself. I felt less than. My mom did the best she could but it was a challenge for all of us.

Being identical twins, my sister and I were constantly compared, from our abilities to our disabilities; academic and athletic achievements. This happens with siblings in general, but when you add identical twins to the mix, it adds another layer of comparison. My sister is brilliant, having a propensity for languages. She easily speaks four languages at various levels. She never really struggled academically so it was painful to be compared to her in that way. My academic challenges would, at times, cause my mom to have periods of frustration, tears and yelling. That did not help. Again, she did the best she could, but this was not the best learning environment for me.

My dad's profession made it necessary for him to travel all the time. He was gone from our family four to five days out of the week. This was difficult for our family. I remember feeling very sad while he was gone.

We were close to my dad but when he was home, he used that time to catch up on doing things around the house and having time with my mom. My sister and I really didn't have much quality time with him. I missed that.

For the last few years of middle school, three other international kids joined our little class of two. Although it was nice to learn with other peers, the level of pressure and comparison heightened for me. Now, I was not only compared to my sister, but four other kids my age. I was so embarrassed by my learning disability that I hated myself. I wanted to erase my disability from my record because it had not been kept confidential.

My sister and I did have extracurricular activities outside of school. We were both involved in gymnastics, music and dance. My sister played the violin and I played the flute. We really enjoyed that time. It got us out of the house and with other people.

Deep friendships were really hard to maintain. In my parents' line of work, people would come and go. Often, just as you were making friends, they would move away, forcing us to make new friends. This was even more difficult in middle school being home schooled.

My sister and I did have several national friends from our neighborhood when we were young, but as we got older, everyone went their separate ways. Maybe because of the social awkwardness of being an adolescent? I guess our lives were different as we got older; different schools and interests. I'm not really sure why that happened.

Our high school experience was at the international school from ninth grade through twelfth. High school was awesome. I made many close friendships, most of which were from the country where we were living. I enjoyed everything about my new community.

The academic comparison continued to plague me throughout my high school years but now I was learning with other people who were not my sister. I love my sister so much, but she was perfect at everything and that made it very difficult for me. The friends I made at school excelled and struggled with different things. That made things a little easier. It was during high school that I learned it was okay to excel at English, but not at math. I loved most of my teachers and began to realize that I did love learning after all.

The social benefits of being in a class with more than five people was the best part. It was so nice to finally have friends who were not coming over to my house to be homeschooled but to just spend time together as friends. In high school, my self-esteem started to climb and I went from hating myself to being proud of what I had accomplished. I had very few negative memories of high school and absolutely loved being there.

Now my mom would say that we were really good kids. We had many rules growing up There were things that were acceptable and things that were not. We worked very hard to never break those rules. Some of those were based on our religious beliefs. We were required to be in communication with our parents about what we were doing and where we were going at all times. There was no question as to what was morally right and acceptable in our household.

Though we are identical twins, we also have many differences. We were both stubborn and rebellious, but my sister was far more stubborn than me, and I far more rebellious. During high school, the stubbornness and rebellion came out. It was normal for most adolescents, but not for us.

One time, my sister and I decided to skip school with a few of our friends, to visit a city four hours away. We had done this before but this particular time our mom found out. Mom was a teacher at our high school. In passing, one of my teachers asked my mom if my sister and I were sick.

My mom said, "No, why?"

My teacher then informed my mom that we were not in school. Things went quickly downhill from there. We were in big trouble. Mom texted and called us several times. Because the city was so far away, we did not get home until late that night. My dad waited up for us and we went to bed immediately. We knew we were going to "get it" the next day.

The worst part of this experience was that we chose to skip one of our last days of school. I don't know what we were thinking. We had made plans to spend time with friends leading up to graduation and the consequence was that we were unable to be with our friends.

Punishments were always very severe. Discipline was not just, "You aren't being an obedient child" but it was taken to the level of "You are a sinner." Shame and guilt were a heavy burden to carry.

That is how I grew up, conceptualizing what was acceptable under the guise of sin and morality. It was not until a few years ago that I began to realize that sin is between you and God. Sin is not for others to put upon you.

We did have some wonderful memories growing up. Trips to the beach with our close family friends was a highlight every January. We spent a week with the same group of people every year.

These vacations were always perfect. We would wake up to an amazing buffet breakfast every morning with the view of the ocean. After breakfast, we would go to the beach to build sand castles and boogie board in the ocean. We would swim in the pool after the beach. Marco Polo was always a favorite game. The restaurants were amazing and many nights included a trip to get the best ice cream. There were also so many shops and I would usually use some spending money to buy a new beach wrap every year. I usually let my mom do the haggling because she was really good at it. We would end most nights staying up late playing games.

That tradition continued for as long as I lived in Asia, seventeen years. When I look back at family photos, there are pictures of me as a toddler on the beach all the way up to the last vacation in high school. Many hotel staff personnel knew my family by name because some of them had held my sister and I as babies.

We moved back to the U.S. after my sister and I graduated from high school. The plan was that our whole family would be together for a year then my parents would return to Asia. But, a dangerous car accident during that year made it impossible for my mom to return and my dad commuted back and forth for months at a time. We saw even less of him than we did before. It was very difficult. Eventually, my mom joined him and we see them twice a year now.

The adjustment to a new culture was wrought with challenges. I had lived most of my life in Asia until going to college. I didn't realize how unique my experience was until then. In the U.S., I didn't know what was "acceptable" and what wasn't. It was uncharted territory.

I remember being discouraged with the college I had chosen to attend but I went anyway. My mom really did not want me to go there. She had another one in mind that she believed was more suitable. I had struggled so much in school in the past. And though I really wanted to obey my parents and make them proud of me, the college I chose had the major I wanted so I made the choice to go there. It was not as prestigious as the other school but it was perfect for me.

College was initially very difficult for me. I may have looked Caucasian, but on the inside, I was all Asian. Navigating the differences between the Asian culture and the American culture was difficult. I had left all of my friends that knew and loved me and I was forced to make new friends of people who really didn't understand me at all. It was humorous to see how many students had no idea about the geographical location or culture of the place from which I had just moved. My life to this point had been far different than the other college students.

I found that my experiences living abroad made me a little more mature than the typical college student which made it very challenging. The college culture that I was in was very focused on sex, money, partying and drugs. I had never been exposed to any of that. Those were not the values that my friends had reflected in Asia. I couldn't attribute it to my Christian upbringing because many of my friends in Asia were from other religious backgrounds.

So for the first year of college, I searched for those people whose values were consistent with mine. Thankfully, I did find them. There was a Christian group that met weekly on campus, and there, I began to form lasting friendships which have remained to this day.

I am so thankful that I decided to go to the college I did because I met the man who became my husband there. His parents are from the Caribbean and their culture is very much a part of their daily life. Though he was born in the United States, my husband clearly reflects his upbringing. Believing I was culturally savvy with the international community, I learned very quickly that I knew very little about the differences between African Americans and Caribbean Americans. I had never spent much time with either people group. This added another cross-cultural experience to my life.

Dating my husband brought racism before me for the very first time. We are like night and day. He is black and I am blond hair and blue eyed so we did not go unnoticed. It was then that I began to understand the privilege that comes from having white skin. I never realized that until I started to observe what my darker skinned friends were experiencing.

There were so many experiences that revealed my white privilege. I did not have to worry about money in college because I knew I could lean on my parents, unlike my darker skinned friends. My parents were able to take out loans for my education. My black, first generation, college friends were not afforded the same. While my parents signed me up for the best meal plan, helped me pay for books, and buy items for my dorm, I had black friends who came to college with very little. I was guaranteed a job on campus, but I knew of some minority students who had to resort to selling drugs to feed themselves, pay for school, and survive. One black student was jailed for being in possession of a small amount of weed. His family was not notified and he was jailed for days. At the time, I questioned why someone would not go to jail for possessing drugs. After learning more about mass incarceration of people who are black, I began to recognize that the manner in which that student was treated, was a grievous act of racism. Having worked in Student Affairs in two universities, I have seen the disparities in treatment among races. A white student arrested for the same crime would usually walk away with a simple warning.

My husband and I did a long-distance relationship after we graduated from college for a few years. He went back to his home town the followed the lead of his friends to move to another state to work in sales. While he was working in sales, I was pursuing a graduate degree in Counseling. He worked twelve-hour days and I was a full-time graduate student, working three jobs. We saw very little of one another.

The graduate school I chose allowed me to have a concentration in trauma. It was more expensive than other schools and despite my mom's attempts to discourage me from enrolling, I did it anyway.

Graduate school required much effort but working in addition to that created a very demanding schedule. Looking back, I have no idea when I even slept.

Managing three jobs was a challenge in itself. I was a behavioral therapist, working seven hours a week. I worked a full-time job as a Graduate Resident Director, on call day and night to meet the needs of students across campus. Then, my third job was approximately 40 hours a week where I worked as a sexual assault counselor in the crisis center. In this position, one day a week, I would be on call for 24 hours to meet clients at emergency rooms, police stations, or just to be a listening ear. I had many roles from advocating for them as they completed an emergency sexual assault forensic exam at the hospital, helping to file police reports and advocating for them as they navigated the court system. In addition, I led a counseling group. There were never enough hours in the day. Many times, I did multiple jobs and school work at the same time.

Although we barely had time for ourselves, my husband and I were intentional about staying connected and would try to text, call, or Skype daily. We visited one another each month for a weekend, alternating who would travel. Eventually, he moved to the same city where I was living my second year of grad school. We began to see how our short distant relationship was going to work. We soon became engaged and got married.

I was drawn to my husband because of his Caribbean culture. I felt more understood by him then I did by my American friends. Though he was born in the U.S., his parents were acutely aware of what it was like to come from a country that was unlike the U.S. They too had to adjust to the culture. They knew what it was like to be different. I may have looked American but I was far from it.

Coming from different cultures can be a very interesting experience but there have been times that our cultures clash. Adjustment to being married can be really difficult but when your come from different cultures and are living in a third culture it can be a real challenge. Most of the time we celebrate our differences.

Fortunately, my sister came to the U.S. when I did so we have been able to support each other through the transition and throughout life. My sister has always been the person who has kept me grounded and moving forward. I hope I have done the same for her. We struggle with similar issues and understand each other well. When she was in an abusive marriage which ended in divorce, I was able to be there for her in ways that others could not. She is resilient and that has been an encouragement to me to persevere through whatever the obstacles come before me.

That is probably why I chose the field of study that I did, Social Work. I know what it looks like to struggle and I also know what it looks like for others to come alongside to support you. I have had to reach deep into my core beliefs to discern what is true for me, then trust in that truth. So, I use what I have learned personally to help others. It is a privilege to listen and encourage people as they rise up from insurmountable circumstances.

I have been in the U.S. for ten years now and am still finding myself transitioning and surprised by some of the culture I experience. I question why I am feeling uncomfortable in different situations at times and remember, I am not from this country. I was raised in Asia.

I am thankful to have had the experience of growing up in Asia. I never realized how special that it was until much later. Living in another culture, a developing country, where I was the minority, was really extraordinary. I was exposed to many different people that practiced different religions, giving me a view of them that was unlike what I saw in the U.S.

After 9-11, there was a stigma attached to Muslim people in general. I had grown up with many Muslims and found that the people that I had known and loved were being characterized in ways that was inaccurate. It was hurtful. It was our Muslim friends that came to our family to tell us that they loved us and were going to protect us from harm.

I felt safer in Asia than I have ever felt in the U.S. There are micro-aggressions that I have experienced here just for my being a female. In Asia, women are perceived to be "less than" men. Even with this being the case, I was never sexually assaulted in Asia. I cannot even tell you how many times my body was violated by men while being in the U.S. I have found men to be aggressive, entitled, and disrespectful of women here. I have a fear of men in the U.S. that I never had in Asia.

It's very clear how God has been working in my story. Through my experiences, He has given me a heart for people that I may not have developed otherwise. The reason I am a counselor today is because of how He used my parents to model love to others in Asia. I remember at age seven going to the store to get food to make packets to distribute to those who were in need on the streets. We had an English library in our house and my parents were always inviting people over for English classes and conversation. Their focus was always on loving and caring for other people. I knew from a very early age that I wanted to do the same. I just didn't know how. All of these experiences helped to build compassion in me.

I originally went to college to study Criminal Justice to work for child protective services but when I realized I was able to do a double major, I added Psychology to my study and loved it. This was so helpful to preparing me for what I believed was my calling; to help homeless children. I had witnessed many homeless children on the streets in Asia. These innocents were drawn into sex trafficking and experienced much abuse. I wanted to help protect them so my long-term goal is to go back to Asia to rescue and empower homeless children. I have contacted an organization in Asia whose focus is helping children who are being sex-trafficked, with the hope of supporting them in some way.

My husband and I have both been very excited about pursuing this goal. We went for a visit back to my country to explore possibilities. The purpose of the visit was primarily to see if my husband could tolerate living there long term. We also wanted to see if the agency we wanted to work with was a good fit. We fell absolutely in love with the agency. I enjoyed every moment of our two weeks there. Although I was unable to visit my Asian family or return to my home city, being back in the country felt like home.

When my husband and I visited Asia, we had just passed our first-year wedding anniversary. We were, and still are learning about each other and about marriage in general. The reality is our marriage is young. We are not ready to move overseas yet but it is still something we are holding before us as a possibility.

The last three years have been rewarding and challenging as we have learned about ourselves and how to be married. My heart still longs to be back in my home country, and I'm trusting that if that is part of God's plan us, He will make it happen.

My concept of America, while living in Asia, was that it was the land of the free and the home of the brave, and everyone had all that they needed. People didn't struggle. I discovered much later that I really didn't understand the culture or the history of America at all. Whenever we visited America, we stayed with family and friends so my sister and I were very sheltered from learning about the country. We never really encountered anyone who was in need or struggling. Even after moving to the U.S., my college was in a very white country town. I was surrounded by privileged people who looked like me.

When I went to graduate school, I lived in a large city and began to understand that what I believed about the U.S. was only partially true. I began to see economic and other disparities to which I had never been exposed. Through internships and other jobs, I have worked with many different people who are struggling with mental health, finances, and other things, at no fault of their own. Having not had those struggles myself, this was very foreign to me. I have grown much more compassionate as I have watched other people in their struggles.

I have witnessed persecution on many levels, as well. While in college, people didn't understand why I cared about Muslims, refugees, and the world in general. When I would try to have conversations around these topics with my friends, they didn't understand me. I was usually the odd-man out. No one understood why we would open our borders to refugees or care about homeless. Most of my friends had never even been out of the country or around people that were not like them. They didn't understand and they didn't care to.

The concept of social isolation became very real when my husband and I started dating. I am very fair-skinned and he is very dark. Whenever we would go out in public, people always stared and they continue to do so. We have gone to restaurants and not been served. I have had people ask me why I am with a black guy. My husband has been stopped and frisked for no reason. He has been followed around stores because they are afraid he might steal from them. I have experienced aggression and trauma just because I am married to a man who is black.

Even in my own family we have seen racism. When I was dating my husband, my grandfather told me to stay away from black people.

Though this has been very painful to experience, I believe that it has made me into a more compassionate counselor who is sensitive to these issues.

Persecution is everywhere, even within the Christian church. There are so many rules. Having grown up in that environment, I have witnessed members of my own family and friend group who look down on people who are struggling. It was heartbreaking when a friend of mine got pregnant and in desperation had an abortion. My family's reaction was appalling.

They responded with, "Oh my gosh, how could she do that? She is such a sinner."

The response I was looking for was, "Yes, that is tragic and very sad."

They failed to recognize her difficult position and had expectations for her that were unrealistic. She did not have the same options that anyone in my family would have had. Their reaction caused me to develop even more compassion for people who were struggling.

I have also witnessed judgement directed toward single mothers who have chosen to keep their babies. Some are just trying to raise their children well. They work hard and try to stay sane and yet they too are judged.

It's hard for me to see situations such as these because it is not reflective of the Jesus that I know. Jesus never looks down on people. He tells us to care for widows and orphans and yet, some Christians look down upon anyone who is not living up to their standards. People are often judged for circumstances for which they are not responsible.

My relationship with God is very personal for me. When people try to tell me how to interpret my experiences with Him, it can cause me to question God's voice in my life. I can also second guess my choices and wonder if I've missed opportunities in the past. That is not always helpful.

I have also been extremely sheltered throughout my life and that has not served me well. There is so much to understand about people. From Jesus I have learned that He positioned Himself among those that were in need, isolated and rejected by society. I hope that as I continue to grow as a person and as a professional that I will step out of my comfort zone to engage with people who are different from me. I consider how Jesus willingly went into unsafe places and challenged the religious leaders in support of those who were marginalized by society. He was often questioned about his interactions with people but He chose to love all people, that is how I desire to live my life.

My husband and I are currently members of an open and affirming Presbyterian Church. It is a "come as you are" church environment, so reflective of Jesus' heart. All people are welcome there. This does not just happen automatically. Churches need to be intentional about welcoming and seeking out people of diversity.

God has continued to grow my heart for all people. When I arrived at the university, employed as a counselor, I was placed in the dorm for the *Living Learning Community for Gender and Sexuality.* I had no idea that was where I would be placed until I arrived. Initially, I was shocked by the experiences of the students that I was expected to counsel. I had had experience with students with autism and spectrum disorders, and those with anxiety, depression and trauma, but I had very little experience with anyone from the LGBTQ community. I felt very uncomfortable and had never really allowed myself to explore anything about sexuality. To be perfectly honest, I had never explored my own sexuality. I just *assumed.* I was raised believing that because I was a girl, I was to marry a boy. No questions asked. It was during this time that I finally asked myself the question. After much thought, I discovered that I do like men and identify as female.

After I learned of my dorm placement, I informed my director that I had very limited experience with gender and sexuality and I would need more education in this area.

He responded with, "Okay, so go get it."

And, that's what I have been trying to do ever since.

In the beginning, I was in denial believing that I would never have anyone on my case load that had gender and sexuality concerns. That was very closed-minded of me. What I found was that many of the people I counsel are questioning, they have concerns about their sexuality and are struggling in different ways. Not only were many experiencing the stress of being away at school, many were also experiencing persecution from their family and friends about their sexual identity. For most, their safe place was school, away from family and friends.

I realize, now, that it is a privilege to support those who are struggling with their identity. I am very honest about my limited experience but the students appreciate that I am learning. I try to never say anything that might offend and encourage the students to tell me if I do so I can learn how to better respond.

In the past, I was very unsure about sexual identity issues. I didn't understand what was okay and what was not because my Christian upbringing had labeled anyone outside of the norm a sinner. It was during this time as a counselor that I became intentional about revisiting my conservative Christian roots and I began to shed some of the beliefs that were inconsistent with the love of Jesus. I read a lot of scripture, read a lot of books and asked people that I respected to help me understand the LGBTQ community. I learned what is consistent with what I believe about people and God and what is not. The people that give advice that reflects a hate-filled response, I totally disregard. Many Christians have built a case against the LGBTQ community based on misinterpreted scripture. I am thankful to those who have given me a new perspective that reflects love.

Working at the *Living Learning Community for Gender and Sexuality* has been a wonderful opportunity of growth for me. I never had anyone in my life that was openly gay before or even questioning. It is the hearing of their stories that has given me a deeper understanding. I have learned so much and am seeing differently now. I couldn't be more thankful for the privilege of serving people in such a way.

Currently, Emily and her husband are doing all that they can to serve the people that are brought before them in the U.S. Emily is still working as a counselor at the university, and her husband is a patient care technician in an area hospital, with hopes of going to nursing school. They look forward to the serving opportunities that God has for them in the future.

I See You

By Carol Marchant Gibbs

The sweetest words that we can hear...
I see you.
I hear your words.
I know your struggles.
I feel your pain.

The most encouraging words...
I see your heart.
You are forgiven.
You belong.
There is hope.

The most powerful...
I know you.
You have purpose.
I will go with you.
You are loved.

I see you!

Chapter 6
Perceptions About the Homeless

"Just Look at Her"

My husband and I always loved learning about and exploring new places. We had heard wonderful things about the fine city of Seattle so, five years ago, we took a few days and went to see for ourselves. What we found was that Seattle is indeed a great city. It was a coffee lovers paradise! And, yes, we are coffee enthusiasts. There was not a street corner without a coffee shop of some kind. It was awesome!

But like any city, Seattle also has its challenges. I remember being shaken by the large number of homeless people there. It was an overwhelming sight and I struggled with knowing what to do with my feelings toward this heartbreaking scene. I noticed that the young people seemed to gather together in small communities which was encouraging, but the older homeless wandered alone on the streets muttering to themselves. I prayed as we walked that God would show me how to respond.

After walking a while, we ducked into a shopping mall to sit in the atrium, to read and sip delicious coffee. My mind wandered to a book I had been reading earlier, *Life Together in Christ*, by Ruth Haley Barton. There, she explained about the power of listening to others. Too often in our culture, it is believed that adding our "two cents" to someone else's story might possibly be an encouragement to them. The book explained that interjecting one's own experiences into someone else's story could possibly have an adverse-effect, causing the person to feel diminished. I was surprised by this and began to really think about how this might affect my future interactions with others.

As I sat and thought about this very powerful message, an older homeless woman carrying several bags came and sat near me. She took out her newspaper and began to comment on the articles as if she was broadcasting the news to everyone around her. It was a little unnerving at first. No one was paying any attention…but me. She just kept talking very loudly about things that did not make sense, mentioning Mao Tse Tung and Winston Churchill quite a bit during her discourse. It was very unsettling and I did not know what to do. Do I respond or do I pretend that I am not hearing her like everyone else? It just did not feel right to ignore her, so, I prayed.

Then, I heard God speak, "Just look at her."

It wasn't an audible voice but a voice spoken to my heart. I found myself thinking – *Lord, I have attempted to avoid her gaze in hope that she would stop***.** This was a place of vulnerability to which I was very reluctant to travel.

And God repeated… "Just look at her."

So, I did…right in the eyes. Her gaze was fleeting. She looked around as if there was a veil covering her eyes, but she often looked in my direction as if she knew I was watching.

As she continued to talk about things that made absolutely no sense, I smiled and nodded my head as if I understood her, praying the entire time, *Oh, Lord, when will she stop?* Then, after about ten minutes of talking, she stopped as abruptly as she started. I was totally undone. I signaled my husband to walk with me so we could debrief this experience, asking for his response to what just occurred. He had no idea what I was talking about. At first, I thought he was joking with me. I wept when I realized that this moment was just for me. It was God's response to my prayer. *Help me to know how to respond.*

I will probably never see that woman again, but God was doing something that day as I listened to her discourse. What she shared certainly did not make sense to me but the love of God was being expressed to her without my uttering a word.

"Just look at her."

Homelessness

The U.S. Department of Housing and Urban Development (HUD) is the federal agency that oversees national policy and programs related to housing needs and fair housing laws, which includes homelessness.

According to HUD, a person is homeless if they "lack a fixed, regular, and adequate nighttime residence."

To determine the number of homeless in this country, one night a year, an estimate of the homeless population is taken by counting the people staying in shelters, transitional housing, parks and cars. According to the last count, as of December 2022, there are approximately 582,500 individuals that are homeless.

Because the reasons for homelessness are numerous and are in response to one's life circumstances, individual needs must be addressed in order to provide life changing support.

The following organization, Open Table, originally started to address the homeless, has been instrumental in helping people to rise above their various circumstances and thrive.

Open Table

Open Table is a 501 (C)(3) whose vision is for each person to experience and be a reflection of a life living for each other. Their mission is to develop models and training that bring community relationships, networks, and their resources into partnership with organizations working to empower people to live into the lives they envision for themselves and their families. Open Table believes everyone in our human family can have a better life when the response to people with complex needs moves from transactions to transformations. When people have access to supportive relationships and social networks, they thrive. When they don't, their human potential collapses. Open Table's partners include organizations in business, education, faith communities, government, healthcare, and community-based social services agencies. Theopentable.org

Invisible Enemy

By Carol Marchant Gibbs

It is present in the lives of *others* every day.

Unseen by the human eye but its sting is felt deep in the heart.

It hides under a shroud of empty words;
deceptively projecting good.

It waits in watch for the *unknowns* to confirm the *truth* and judges much.

Destroying lives in its path, it relentlessly searches for another victim.

It has the power to extinguish large groups of people.

It is evil.

Prejudice.

Chapter 7
Living with HIV-AIDS

HopeSprings

HopeSprings is an organization that was established to address the health and general needs of people living with HIV-AIDS. By raising awareness, it has been able to awaken individuals, faith communities, and community groups, to help them understand that HIV is an epidemic that needs a response.

Human Immunodeficiency Virus, HIV, is a virus that attacks the cells in the body that help to fight infection, causing a person to be more vulnerable to serious infections and diseases. HIV is contracted when one individual comes in contact with the bodily fluids of another person who is infected with HIV.

There is no cure for HIV but treatment is possible and can help an infected person to live a long healthy life. Early detection is one's best defense. Testing sites have been established all over the country for anyone who is at risk. When the virus has been identified, antiretroviral drugs can help to prevent its advancement. In fact, when identifying HIV early and getting people into treatment, it can help them live long healthy lives and prevent further spread. With the help of antiretroviral therapy, individuals are able to get to an undetectable viral load where the virus can no longer be detected in the bloodstream. Recent studies have proven that when someone is undetectable, it is impossible to spread the virus to someone else. This is often called *U=U, Undetectable=Un-transmittable*. If left untreated, HIV will progress to AIDS, causing one's immunity to be severely compromised. Without treatment, people with AIDS typically live only about 3 years.

But, HIV-AIDS is not *just* a health issue. It is also a social justice issue to which many have not responded positively. The stigma associated with HIV-AIDS has been the cause of much pain. Poverty-related health disparities increase the likelihood of contracting HIV significantly, while also posing barriers to life-altering healthcare.

Historically, the church has led the way in neglecting to recognize or support the community of people impacted by HIV-AIDS. The church has done wrong, causing harm to many people. It is through the building of relationships between the church and the HIV community that healing begins to occur. Through hope and the *collective act of repentance* the church is able to reverse the stigma associated with HIV-AIDS. The social environment can dramatically affect the outcome of healing.

The focus of *HopeSprings* has been to encourage, train, and draw upon the capacity of the church to bring change. The church has great power and potential to bring hope and healing, and can alter the course of people's lives.

Community awareness is crucial. *HopeSprings* encourages churches to understand their responsibility to their neighborhoods, to be aware of the communities that surround them, and to develop relationships. There has often been a huge disconnect between communities of faith and the lives of their neighbors.

Posture is really important, as well. There is power in being present with others, in listening to their stories. Presence can be really difficult for many people so *HopeSprings* provides avenues for people to engage.

Poverty is one of the leading indicators for new HIV infections. Many people in the HIV community are more vulnerable to falling prey to those who would seek to take advantage of them, and they find themselves in poor financial circumstances. *HopeSprings* tries to offer as much wholistic support as possible.

HIV is not discriminatory but does disproportionately affect people of color and sexual and gender minorities. One out of every two gay black men will have HIV sometime in his life. For us to be faithful to do this work well, as we intersect it with the faith community, it is necessary to train people about sexual orientation and gender identity. This conversation is not easy in the church. It is either neglected or becomes and outright debate so *HopeSprings* has tried to create space for dialog, with the hope that it increases understanding and accurate knowledge about the LGBTQ community served.

Partnership is key. Many organizations have generously offered medical care and churches have helped with testing. At a single day event, *HopeSprings* can test over 1000 people. Larger organizations have partnered with

HopeSprings to do city-wide testing, encouraging a broader population to be aware of their status.

Live well tables provide support to individuals who are ready to take the next step to embracing a new life. A group of people commit their time and resources to assist the person in identifying their goals. Education, employment, financial, family, and spirituality are some of the areas focused upon. Each person volunteering on the *table* partners with the individual to accomplish one of their goals. Together they carry one another. When guidance and available resources are provided, lasting change is made possible. A new life emerges.

Financial literacy training has also been offered for those who are interested. It's not just about sound financial decisions or building a budget. A dollar for dollar savings matching program is available as an incentive to all of those individuals who have completed the course. *HopeSprings* will match up to $500. This can be a great opportunity for them to pay down their debt or have money for a security deposit on a place to live. They are given tools and some financial assistance. The idea of *pulling yourself up by your bootstraps* is great in theory but not always productive. Sometimes people just need a little boost to get them started.

We all have had times in our lives when we have needed help. Most people have family, friends and the church to lend support. People living in poverty do not have the same kind of resources. Much of the time, everyone is in the same situation. Live well tables help them to rise above their circumstances and have hope for a better future.

The Story of Ryan

Ryan is an ally to many, and he wears several hats in expression of that. He is a leader, teacher and a shepherd. Ryan understands his calling to be a pastor and when you spend time with him you experience first-hand his pastor's heart. He is a very gentle man who listens well and thinks deeply before uttering a word. As a leader and teacher, Ryan strives to help people identify God's movement in their lives, and learn how to partner with and respond to God.

Ryan currently works for a nonprofit that helps congregations to promote healthy community engagement, particularly concerning some of the more marginalized.

I believe that God has a special heart for those who have been marginalized. My partnership with God is a transformational experience that equips me to respond to those who are disenfranchised. I strive to be a better lover of God, of others and of myself, and to help others realize their responsibility to do the same. I am in a constant state of learning and as new opportunities come my way, my calling takes on new aspects.

It can be frustrating when faced with those who are critical of the community that I serve. I try to honor the uninformed by sharing and listening. But I feel a sense of responsibility to lovingly shepherd people to a deeper understanding of the facts about HIV. I name the words spoken that were untrue, and then what words were harmful and why.

I continuously find myself in conversations such as this. I guess I don't feel threatened by them because my life was nothing like the community I serve. I was born into white privilege and have been changed by my work. A young black man living with HIV could possibly walk away from the conversations I have had feeling hurt. It is my hope that by my enduring these difficult conversations, I can educate others so that less and less people are harmed. I hope that my heart for the community inspires others to care.

I was born and raised in the south in a very loving home. My dad is a Baptist pastor, and my mom is a nurse and the daughter of a Baptist pastor. Faith has always been integrated into my life. My dad was very invested in his ministry. The lines between home and work in church were always blurred. He was involved in helping to start several churches, one of which involved meeting in people's homes, schools, and even a country club. He would plant a church and stay with them for a while, around ten years, then move on to plant another. We often met in homes. One of my earliest memories was of sitting on a trampoline in someone's backyard during a Sunday service.

I am close to my sister who is two and a half years younger. We have always had a typical brother-sister relationship. As her older brother, I would tease and antagonize her unmercifully. But in our adult life, we have become a lot closer, having helped each other through really challenging times.

My dad was an athlete. He played basketball in college and after until his knees wouldn't let him anymore, so sports found their way into my childhood. Though I was really lacking in aptitude., I managed to get awards when I played. *The most improved player trophy*, which I understood to mean that I was a pretty terrible player but was less terrible by the end of the season. My mom told me that I was always the biggest encourager from the dugout. For me, sports was about the social connection. I was never very good or competitive for that matter.

I was very successful in school, loving to read and study. Music was a big part of my life, playing violin for a few years until middle school. In middle school, I had a teacher that was more about the discipline than the enjoyment so I decided that I really didn't enjoy playing anymore and stopped. I discovered the guitar at that time. I would play for hours in my room. I loved it. This followed me to high school, where I played in several bands. Then later on, I played in both church and non-church settings.

My parents' professions impressed a sense of service in our family. Life was about caring for other people. In my adult life, I find it very natural for me to visit someone in the hospital or spend time with them in a crisis. When I was young, I accompanied my dad on hospital visits so it really feels comfortable doing that now. My mom worked at a nursing home for a while so visiting her at work also prepared me for the future. The patients would love when I would come and sing hymns for them. It was ingrained in my family life to care for others.

I wasn't really sure what I wanted to do when I grew up. I knew that I loved to read, study and play music. People often asked if I was going into the *family business.* I'd just laugh and politely respond with *no*. My dad worked eighty hours a week and I really didn't want to do that. He has committed much of the later part of his life to world missions, so he travels all over training church planters in a Muslim context. I didn't want to do that either.

I went to a primarily white church growing up. The demographics were most of the reason and churches were and still are pretty segregated by race. There was one black family that fared well in our church. They seemed like they were accustomed to being in majority spaces and appeared very comfortable, staying for a long time. But the racial dynamics of the south often demanded that the church be segregated. There were white churches and black churches, much more visibly discriminatory.

Over the years, our area became much more diverse. By the time I got to high school, it had become totally integrated. The new businesses and technology jobs brought many new people to the area, which helped with increasing the diversity. Our church really grew during that time with the influx of people.

Though I had a generally positive experience with church, I witnessed the ugly white underbelly at times and saw the injustice. Many of my friends elected to stop going to church when they were old enough to drive, and I understood why. I didn't have language for it at the time but when I got older, I began to understand more fully their decision. The legalism and lack of diversity turned many away. The intensity of the "purity culture" to young teenagers was also very instrumental in pushing people out of the church.

We had a new youth pastor when I was completing my senior year of high school. His wife worked for the crisis pregnancy center. After I graduated, I would return to help lead music and serve as a young leader. I was shocked by the new programming. For eight weeks straight, as part of the outreach, they had programs all about being *pure.*

One of the weeks, a woman came into the group to do health-like classes saying, "These are all the things that will happen to you if you have sex."

She used fear-based tactics with horrible graphic images. It was so heavy handed and manipulative. All of the teenagers were blown away and requested to talk about another topic. My relationship with this youth pastor was quickly being destroyed by his judgement.

He coached me on bringing kids to the group.

He would say, "You are a cool guy, and play cool music, all the girls like you so you can really use that to bring people here."

He used my giftedness and the fact that people knew me to draw kids to the group. I really became disillusioned at that point.

I remember the youth pastor inviting me to go to a conference in Nashville. I was eighteen at the time and was interested in a college there so I went.

When the programming was finished for the night, he gave me $100.

"Have fun! Just make sure you are back before I wake up in the morning," he said to me.

My first thought was that this shouldn't be ok but, I decided that I was eighteen and in Nashville and I went out. So, I stayed out late, hung out with friends at a music showcase and really had fun. I remember coming home that night thinking that this isn't right. The youth pastor didn't last very long at the church after that.

That was the start of my seeing the ugly underbelly of the church. The culture that the leader created caused some damage and I saw many of my friends hurt by it and very disillusioned about the church. We found out later that the youth pastor had been lying about many things that really didn't matter but he lied anyway. The trust that had previously been cultivated in adult leaders was really destroyed by this for me and many.

After graduation, I took a year and went to a state school on the Hope scholarship, tuition free. I lived at home until my parents sold the house and moved out of the area to work for another church, half-way through my second semester. I moved in with a family from the church to finish out the school year.

I loved music so when my friends invited me to play in the band they had just formed, it was an easy decision. They needed a guitarist, and I needed a place to live, so I moved in with them. Playing guitar was an amazing opportunity. The band moved around a bit and it was really fun for a while. I attempted to do college distance learning for a year without much success. My dad called it *a year of waste.* But I disagreed. I was playing music, working two jobs and attempting to go to college. I learned a lot that year.

It was in that environment that I started to have a sense of calling. The church I was attending at the time talked about being a church for the *unchurched* or *de-churched.* It was for people who had been hurt by the church and needed hope and healing. When I heard the story of the church while going through their membership class, it really appealed to me.

After a year of playing with the band, I decided to go back to school and entered a Bible college, majoring in Biblical Studies with an emphasis in Urban Missions. The school was very close to where my parents had moved, so I landed up moving back in with them.

A young woman, I had been dating while in the band, followed me after I quit the band and went back to school. She decided to go to school, as well. We dated off and on throughout college. Then, summer before my senior year, we got married.

Life was good. I was married, loved my program and was very drawn to doing work in the city. I was hoping to continue this work later.

After graduation, I reconnected with a wonderful youth pastor that I had been very close to while growing up. This was not the same youth pastor that was let go for being irresponsible! He mentioned that he was moving north to start a new church and wanted me to join him. I had finished all of my course work but just needed to complete an internship. I expressed my interest for serving in the city and he agreed to it. A few days after I finished my classes, my wife and I packed up and moved north.

I started my internship with the church and worked part-time in a bank to help pay the bills. A year and a half later, I came on staff with the church. This was my first full-time ministry position. It involved being a worship leader and an administrator. I was able to use my musical gifting and grow in how to be pastoral.

A month into the job, my wife sat me down and told me that she was leaving me. Sure, we had our differences, but I thought we were addressing them in a healthy way. I was in total shock. We had been married two years at that point.

Divorce was very stigmatized in the church community where I grew up so not only was I broken hearted, I was also embarrassed. When someone got divorced, there was always blame to go around. I found that the way the church offered support to me, was probably the best I have ever experienced. Not everyone in the church was that way, however. Some of my close friends responded very poorly.

When we separated, my wife made plans to stay with a friend but I really didn't want to stay in our home so I spent our first night apart in my office. The next night, I called my longtime friend who was also working at the church with me, and told him I had something going on and wanted to know if I could stay with him. He agreed and was very respectful of my desire not to talk about my situation. I stayed with him for a few days and eventually shared with him my loss.

However, one of my challenges was that Sunday was coming and it was my responsibility to lead worship in two services. How was I going to do that when my heart was breaking apart? I asked my friend what I should do about leading worship, he turned the question around.

"What do you think you need to do?" He said.

I wasn't sure whether I should do it or not but I decided to go forward and do it. It was the only thing that I had control over in my life, at that moment.

Somehow, I made it through, feeling sick to my stomach and crying in the bathroom in between the two services.

I shared with my pastor about my separation and asked if I could come over to his house to hang out. I spent the rest of the day there, crying and talking.

Then…I needed to tell my parents. I had waited to tell them because I was too embarrassed and ashamed. I felt like I had failed them and everyone else for that matter. They responded with deep grief and concern for me but they also responded with deep love. I took a couple weeks to be with them, to grieve, process, and figure out how to move forward. I'm so grateful for how my family loved me through such a painful and shocking time.

I always struggle in sharing the story of our separation because I have my part to tell but so does my ex-wife. I wasn't perfect but I also didn't decide to leave our marriage. I hope we have both been able to heal and grow from this experience.

There was one person in particular that was very hurtful in response to my situation. We had spent a great deal of time together, playing music and sharing about our married lives. A few weeks after my separation, I decided to tell him.

He sat me down and said, "Ryan, you may think this is not your fault but it is. You really need to search and understand the things that you might have done to make her do this. You need to get your act together and go reclaim your wife."

I was shocked by his response. I believed I had done everything I could possibly do but his words brought forth the doubts I struggled with when she left. I had been beating my head against the wall trying to determine what I did to encourage her to leave. His words really stung. I was thankful for my response.

I told him that, "It really hurt to have you say this. I don't think that everything you said is true. My wife is not in coat check. I can't just reclaim her. She's a person. That's not how this works."

His response to me caused a division in our relationship for a long time. Eventually, we reconciled our friendship. He confessed to me that his reaction to my separation was more of a response to his relationship with his wife. He needed to do some things in his relationship with her that had been neglected. I suspected that was true but the pain I was experiencing at the time prevented me from even inquiring.

During the time after my separation, I kept a list of the words that people offered me. Some were difficult and some very encouraging. I was super angry and keeping a list was my way of maintaining power over the situation.

As a leader in the church, I questioned whether I could be effective as I navigated through this challenge, so I went to talk to the pastor about it.

"Is my job on the line here? Do I need to step down? Is it disqualifying for me to be in the midst of a divorce and be a leader in the church? I don't know what is going to happen next."

His words really were a source of encouragement. "Well, we don't know what is going to happen next but here is what we do know. We are committed to you…and we are committed to her."

The same resources that were made available to me were also made available to my wife. She just didn't take them up on that. I had counseling for a year and didn't have to pay for it.

It was very difficult going through such a life experience having people know nothing about it. I did tell a few people but it was exhausting telling them one at a time. I really needed people to know what was happening so, a few weeks after my conversation with the pastor, we had a time in the service to share.

The pastor stood before the congregation and said, "This is what Ryan is going through right now."

He explained my situation and the support that the church was providing, adding that these same resources were being offered to my wife.

"We are a community of family and are committed to walking through these things together. We don't know what it is going to mean. For those of you that know and love Ryan, would you please come forward to lay hands on him and pray."

Despite the situation, this was one of the top ten experiences of my life. I felt extremely loved and that was just the beginning of the encouragement that I received. This was the church at one of its finest moments!

I had a pastor leader that really cared about me. He had known me since I was in fifth grade. That made all the difference. It was personal.

Not everyone agreed with the pastor's support or responded well to me. Some left the church because they didn't approve of how it was handled. Many thought I should no longer be in leadership if not permanently, for a season.

The pastor and I talked about my taking a little time away but it was my choice. What is good for me? What is good for the church? What did I need? The church did give me some extended paid time to process this with my family. The church really took care of me.

This was the first time in my life I had ever experienced anything really difficult. I grew up having a pretty charmed life. I had been witness to many people that abandoned their faith when something such as this happened in their lives. That didn't happen to me. It really wasn't an option, but I could surely be angry at God and I was intensely angry. I believed that I had been honoring Him with my life, even marrying the woman that I did. At this point, I felt like the bottom had dropped out of my life. God had let me down.

I really didn't have language around being angry with God so I went seeking the words to express that. As a worship leader and preacher, I searched for resources to help me and found rest in the practice of praying Morning Prayer, in the Book of Common Prayer, and the Psalms. I needed to be in a place where I could receive from God. The more liturgical tradition was where I most connected with the church. Anywhere I could go and take communion and they would let me, I would go. I needed to be fed so when I was off on Sundays and during the week, I would go to other churches.

I was raised in a church tradition that reflected, "We sing from our heart and we pray from our heart, offering spontaneous prayers to God."

We didn't do rote things. Worship was a very emotionally packed experience. It was an outpouring of your heart. When the Spirit was moving, it looked and felt like something amazing.

My job of leading worship every Sunday began to feel exhausting and disingenuous. When you are going through an experience that causes you to be angry at God, confused, or disillusioned, it is a challenge to pretend so, I needed to learn how to worship differently. Worship began to evolve to reflecting what I was feeling and experiencing with God at that moment.

The Book of Common Prayer helped me with that, as did the Psalms. As I read the Psalms, I could find myself all over the pages.

"God, where are you? Have you forgotten about me? Have you forgotten about your promises? These people are whispering about me." I had never connected with the Psalms like that before.

For the first time, I understood what it was like to be hurt, to be misunderstood, and to be powerless. *My bones were groaning* and I was *rolling in my bed.* The Psalms were describing depression and I felt like there was *no health within me.*

I found comfort in the traditional words and the sacraments. I allowed myself to receive from God. Instead of taking communion, I was receiving communion. This was a very powerful experience for me.

It just so happened that it was the Lenten season. Lent is a time to repent for sin in preparation for Easter. As a church community, were going to learn how to lament. We needed to step into that space of loss together. All of the *hallelujahs* were removed from every song. I even wrote some songs of lament during that time as well.

This caused a little conflict with the pastor. It was really sad worship.

"Ryan, can't we move on?" He asked.

I replied, "No, I need for us as a church to know how to do this."

I knew what it was like to show up and sing joyful songs. It was Lent, a time to reflect on our very deepest selves. Psalm 137 says, *How can we sing the Lord's song in a foreign land, Babylon?* I wasn't in exile but I certainly could resonate with those feelings. Don't tell me to sing happy songs when I am mourning. I really felt like God was doing a work in me in that place.

It was during this time that I was introduced to Henry Nouwen's book, The Wounded Healer. It gave me a sense of hope but it also named what I was experiencing. It helped me to understand why I was connecting with some people and not others. Some people could relate to me in that place. Others had either never hurt as I did, or were afraid to look inward with me. This entire experience allowed me to embrace what it meant to be human and has had a profound effect on how I do ministry now.

I cannot say that I am glad that this happened because I am not. But there have been parts of it that have been redemptive. For that, I am very grateful.

I was ordained in 2012 and stayed at my church for four more years.

My divorce was final a year after the separation. Months after we separated, I met the woman who later became my wife. She was a friend of a friend. I was totally surprised by this new person in my life and felt that I needed to submit this to my church community, so I went to talk to my pastor for guidance. It would have been easy to receive her as a gift from God but I wanted to be sure. She was an amazing woman and has been an icon of God's grace to me since we met. It was important to me to see that I was worth being cared for…that someone as amazing as she wanted to be with me. It was encouraging that I was being healed and I would have a future. We were married a year and a half later and have been married seven years now.

My wife is a wonderful encourager and lover of people. She is a speech therapist that works with students with special needs.

All of these experiences have come together to make me a more sensitive pastor. I have experienced rejection, anxiety about how others will respond to my situation. *How will my church receive me? Will they embrace me or not? What are people thinking about me?*

I have seen how the church can surround you during a crisis and provide love and support. Our church community is not a perfect one, we've made mistakes, but our desire is to really love people well. I have experienced it firsthand.

When our church really began to grow, we developed neighborhood churches to meet the need of the people. I started serving in a local congregation where God continued to show me what love looks like.

I met a young man, John, there who started to attend our church with his roommate, Philip. John wanted connection and immediately started serving in the church. The church needed some renovation so he would come to help with demolition. After we worked, we would go out to lunch. This allowed time to get to know one another. Our conversation about running led to our running together on Friday mornings. As we ran together, a close relationship developed.

One morning, John told me something he thought that I "needed to know" about him.

"Ryan, it is important for you to know that I've experienced same sex attraction over the course of my life and I have been in relationships and then not been. I have been running away from it," he explained.

As I listened to John share more about himself, I realized that he had a lot happen in his life for a young man. After he shared, I thanked him for sharing all of that with me, for trusting me.

"I felt like it was important for you to know," he replied.

John also shared that Philip was not really his roommate but his partner…off and on.

His roommate had shared with me about being gay. "It's who I am and I am ok with that."

Philip told me that he wanted to serve in other ways in the church.

He wanted to sing. "I want to sing. Is that a problem?"

I knew why he asked that question and because our church had no *expressed* policy about the LGBTQ serving in the church. I told him he was very welcome to serve.

Both John and Philip became very active in the church. We became church family and did things together. I invited them to visit a home group that my wife and I led and they both started to attend.

Overtime, my friends started dating again. When they became serious, John came to me to share that he had resolved that fact that he is gay.

"This is who I am," he explained.

I told him that I was "glad that he was able to resolve that. What do you think that means for you?"

"Well," he said, "I think it means that I need to start telling people."

"If that is what you need to do. How can I help?" I asked him.

John had been serving in so many areas of our church but where he was really amazing was in the children's ministry. He was one of the most extraordinary volunteers I had ever seen in my life. He revamped all of our safety and security procedures, higher accountability for everyone. He had a lot of experience with emergency response and brought that to his work with us at the church. We were better for it.

Then, one day, John expressed his concerns about being in a leadership position such as this.

When I asked him what he was afraid of and he replied, "I am afraid that when I start doing this of how people will respond because I am gay. I work with people's kids."

I wasn't concerned because I knew him but it was important for him to share that with me.

I told him that I truly believed that "No kid is safer than when they are with you. But this is your news to share and I am not going to manage how you do that. For me, your being gay does not change your ability to serve in this capacity."

When the news got out that John was gay, there was much whispering about it. Very little of it got back to me. There was one couple that came to me to say that they were very concerned about his leadership.

"We have an unrepentant homosexual leading our kid's ministry," they said.

I replied to them, "Ok, help me understand why this makes you concerned for the safety of your child?" They had no answer.

"I'm sorry you feel that way. It is my decision about who is in positions of leadership. I've heard your concern. I believe this would be very hurtful to him but if you are really that concerned, you should have the courage to tell John. If you are choosing to remove your child from the children's ministry, you should tell him why. Know this, he has my full support," I said with conviction.

I have no idea whether they talked to John about it or not but the couple did remove their child from the ministry.

A few months later, John came to me and told me that he felt like he needed to come out because his relationship had become serious and they were considering getting married. Shortly after that, they got engaged and he made the decision to step down from leadership.

"I can't continue serving in this position. I can't deal with parents making decisions to remove their children from the ministry because they disagree with the LGBTQ. I feel like I am causing problems," he said.

I responded with, "I would really hate for you to stop but you have to do what's best for you."

John left the church a short time later.

When John and Philip asked me to officiate their wedding, I became aware of the church policy on officiating same-sex weddings. It was more defined and clear than I was led to believe. The policy, which was not made available publicly, was that pastors at the church were not permitted to officiate same-sex weddings. I had been in my own process of discernment around whether I would officiate a wedding, and was willing to do so. My church's policy did not allow me, and I was told that this policy document was not to be shared with others.

With tears, I had to go to my friends to tell them the result. I was in a situation where I could attend the wedding, but could not officiate. My dear friends were so supportive of me and very upset that they had put me in a position to jeopardize my job.

They so deeply cared about me. "This is causing you so much distress and we hate that. We don't want to cause problems for you. We just thought that this would be a joyful way for you to celebrate with us." I was able to make a referral to a colleague who was able to perform the ceremony.

My relationship with my friends continued to grow because we were able to talk honestly with one another. I am thankful for this exceptional friendship.

For various reasons, I chose to no longer be on staff at that church.

There are a few things I have learned and would do differently knowing what I do now. Churches need to be honest and have clear policies established. When policies are kept internally within the church leadership and not disclosed to the public, people are misled and can get hurt. I am not comfortable with that. I do not think that church leadership does it intentionally but they justify their actions because they believe that they are protecting the church. They don't realize the impact of what withholding information does. It is not loving others.

It would have been helpful to John and Philp to know what the policies were in the church. They had invested their lives there. They had served and had given financially and that was all welcomed. They should not have been blind-sided with the policies that were against their lifestyle afterwards.

The loving thing to do would have been to be clear about the church's position and how leadership came to that decision, not avoid the conversation altogether. I would have much more respect for churches that took this approach.

But I know what it is like to not be able to see and understand the LGBTQ. I was once in that same position. Education is really important to understanding. Hearing a person's story is critical.

The majority of churches today hold the belief that marriage is intended for one man one woman, which alienates the LGBTQ community. People from the LGBTQ community are permitted to attend many churches but many also believe that people from the LGBTQ community should live a celibate lifestyle. They require a life of singleness but the church offers no ideas on how to best do that. There is no language around that singleness.

Marriage is always considered the end all and be all in churches. This can be difficult for straight single people as well. The church needs to be more sensitive to all people in this area.

In the latter part of my ministry at the church, women in church leadership became an issue. There was much division as a result, and many people left the church.

My wife and I were invited to John and Philip's wedding and had planned to attend but could not because we had a foster child placed in our home at the just prior to the ceremony. After the wedding, they came to our house with wine and the gift they had given to their guests who attended. We had our own small reception together.

Looking back, I realize that I had not been prepared to love my gay friends well. I wish I would have known the church policy so they were protected from the hurt. I could have been a better shepherd to my brothers in Christ. I could have loved and supported them better.

Our friendship continues to grow. I have learned as much from them as they from me. I lament over my belief that I failed them. In my many attempts to apologize, they have always responded to me with love.

They have told me to *stop worrying* about what I didn't know.

"We have no doubt in our minds that you love and care for us," they say. They have loved me well.

I have not experienced much discrimination personally but because I am a pastor and an ally that supports people living with HIV AIDS, I have had my theological ideas called into question.

Recently, some pastors have shared with my colleagues that they "are not sure where Ryan is theologically. We don't know what box to put him in."

They give a warning, "Be careful around him."

I find it very hurtful when people that really know me respond in such a way. They could have actually called me on the phone and asked.

"Where do you stand on this issue?" But they don't.

Then, there are others who have affirmed my efforts.

I have learned many lessons in my life. The one that stands out above all the others is that everyone wants to be known and loved.

I heard this message from a gay man who was quoting from a book about marriage written by a more conservative author, Timothy Keller.

"To be loved but not known is comforting but superficial. To be known and not loved is our greatest fear. But to be fully known and truly loved is, well, a lot like being loved by God. It is what we need more than anything." Timothy Keller and Kathy Keller, *The Meaning of Marriage* (London: Hodder & Stoughton, 2013

I am learning, that saying *I love you* to someone is a very serious thing. It must be built on a foundation of knowing someone. That doesn't happen quickly or easily. Not everyone gets that opportunity. I'll never forget when my friend came out to me.

He said, "I want you to know me."

There was a level of trust built and that allowed me to receive his words. It was such a beautiful gift and gave me the opportunity to better love him.

Human beings are not very adept at knowing one another, nor are we very self-aware.

I had a close friend who, for a year, was a discipleship coach for me. It was one of the most transformational experiences of my life. He was able to give me a new framework for understanding life. We were an encouragement to one another sharing axioms that spoke into the moments of life.

One of the most powerful axioms was, *God is always present and at work.* Even when the world seems like it is falling apart, God is working behind the scenes. It is up to us to discern and discover His plans.

Another axiom is, *God only meets us where we really are.* That is the only place He desires to meet us. His focus is not on where we think we should be to the extent that I am able to be in the present with God, I am able to do that with people, meet them where they really are.

I believe that this is one of the greatest challenges as western Christians. If we don't know and love ourselves, we will find it difficult to know and love others. I have found this to be true for me. But I couldn't learn how to do that on my own. I needed other people's help and encouragement. I didn't have a clear picture of myself.

Encouragement is one of the gifts that comes out of a healthy marriage or a deep friendship. We need loving people to speak into our lives, to help us process our hopes and dreams, discouragement and fears. We need to be ready to listen to and receive what they have to say. We are called to learn from and help each other process life experiences.

When someone comes to you to share that they are experiencing same sex attraction, or they are HIV positive, or their marriage has ended, it is not an invitation to make a pronouncement to them or to try to fix it. It is an invitation to sit in their life circumstances with them and help them identify how God is present in it all. We may not see God's purposes for a while either so we must patiently wait with them. I have had the privilege of people faithfully walking with me through some very difficult moments. I know how the power of God can be displayed in those moments and I desire to encourage others to have that same realization when encountering adversity.

My journey ahead is unknown but I have just completed my Seminary degree and am currently in an internship in the Episcopal Church discerning my next step. My greatest hope is to see the church and the people of the church well-connected to their communities in ways that make a tangible difference in lives of others. I desire to create spaces where we can learn how to approach relationships in ways that are absent of judgement because that is where we encounter God. I am hopeful that I am going to help generate more hope and healing in the world.

I am about to become a father for the first time. Raising a child in this current world climate is very frightening for me but I am trusting that God will be present in all of my life experiences. My prayer is that my children will encounter the world that I imagine could be…a place of hope and healing.

May we all learn to how to better love God, others, and ourselves. The greatest commandment is not just a good idea. Love looks like something. We love God by living out our worship in our relationships.

I use to wonder if my being a white man attempting to bring diversity would be an effective way to bring change. I have discovered that I do have a voice to which people listen and I can be instrumental in encouraging others to exercise their voices as well.

A few years ago, I was invited to a meeting with a very diverse group of worship leaders. People from several countries and races were present. My friend Joseph, whom I had met at a multi-ethnic worship leader conference seven years prior was also there. Whenever I am invited to speak at such a meeting, I find myself apologizing for being the white man in the room. I looked like a hipster dude, dressed in jeans and a plaid shirt. What did I know about diversity?

My apologies for being white happened several times until one day, my friend Joseph stopped me in my tracks with his words.

He put his hand on my shoulder and said, “Listen man, I need to tell you two things. First of all, when I first saw you, I already liked you because you reminded me of all my neighbors in my home town. Especially, because of that plaid flannel. Second, you need to stop apologizing for who God made you to be.”

I responded with, “I’m sorry.”

He said, "No, don't apologize. You don't have to be here. There are plenty of worship spaces that are set up for you but you chose to be here with us because it matters to you."

"Yes, it does really matter to me. I don't want to be in those other spaces," I said.

"You have a heart for this but people look at you and don't expect that. People look at me and expect me to have a heart for this because I am black. I will probably be invited to speak about diversity and racial reconciliation because of who they assume I am. But you are going to be able to speak in places that I will probably never be invited to go. You will be heard by people who would not listen to me," he said.

"But it shouldn't be that way," I responded.

"But it is, which is why we are here today," Joseph said.

This life-changing conversation has stayed with me ever since. We all have a voice. Who we are is intentional and necessary to God's work. Privilege and power can be used to the glory of God for the benefit of others.

So, we press on to do the work we are called to do. Take a chance and just show up. God will reveal to you how He desires for you to serve.

Ryan's deepest desire is to connect the church to the community bringing change to the church's response to all people. He seeks answers to the questions; What is causing disunity between the church and the community? What is preventing diversity in the church? He longs to be a voice that draws attention to those who have important words to share. Ryan hopes to continue his work by becoming the pastor of a church that ministers to an entire community, not just a segment of it.

The Story of Evelyn

Evelyn discovered that she had HIV-AIDS after being married for three years. She was unaware that her husband had an addiction and had been sharing needles with people that were infected with HIV. After he died, she sank into a deep depression, turned to alcohol and became homeless for a year. Then, HopeSprings came along to rescue her from the streets. They gave her hope and put her on a path to recovery. Her gratitude has compelled her to dedicate her life to being an encouragement to others who have found themselves in a similar situation.

I first met Derek, the former director of HopeSprings, at a support group that encouraged people living with HIV-AIDS to embrace a healthier lifestyle. Derek had a heart for those affected by the disease and provided much support to the group through his kind words.

After being in the group for a season, I was invited to be involved in another group that was designed specifically for me. With the support of my new friends, I spent the next two years discovering and creating a life of my choosing. They empowered me and helped me to take charge of my life, providing opportunities that I never had been afforded. They asked me what I most wanted for my life and helped me to achieve those goals and much more. It was through *Open Table* that my life was changed forever.

I grew up in a family of seven children in a large city in the northeast, raised by my mother and stepfather. I did not meet my biological father until I was five years old. Then, I saw him again when I was thirty-two.

Because I was the oldest child, my mother and stepfather learned about parenting by practicing on me. I was the "learning one." It was easier for the children that followed me. My siblings were born after my mother and stepfather were married.

My stepfather was very strict. When the street lights came on, I was required to be in our house. I was never allowed to go to parties or even friends' houses but my home was always open to my friends.

Despite my stepfather's strictness, we had a good relationship. He had his ways but he also had deep family values. Every Sunday was family day and he would take us out to dinner after church. We loved going to Kentucky Fried Chicken. Afterwards, my parents would take us to the amusement park or to the drive-in movie. We had fun together. Time with family was of prime importance.

My stepfather also knew the value of the dollar. Brand name clothing or anything like that was forbidden because it was exorbitantly expensive.

He would say, "All that you are doing is paying to wear someone's name on you. It is better to wear something that is cheaper that will hold up. This way, you will have extra money in your pocket."

At the time, my siblings and I thought my stepfather was being mean, having so many requirements but he instilled many deep values in us for which we are thankful.

I was never very close to my siblings growing up but I always loved them. I was the big sister, the protector and caretaker of all.

My mother was my best friend. She was a very strong person who loved life. She was raised in a time when parents never talked about sex. As a consequence, she landed up giving birth to me when she was sixteen years old.

"You can get pregnant from watermelon seeds," they told her.

Because of her experience, Mother was intentional about the things she taught, always very straightforward with the facts. She didn't want us to make the same mistakes that she did so there was constant communication between us. My siblings and I were permitted to ask her anything and she always told us the truth. She knew that if we listened to our friends, we wouldn't get an accurate story.

I was baptized in the Baptist Church. My grandparents had their own church in the mid-west and we attended it for the years we lived in that area. We were in church all the time and that made me resentful. I really didn't like going after a while, so when I was fourteen years old, I stopped. It was at that time, that my parents had started letting my siblings and I make some of our own decisions and that was one of them. We decided not to go to church.

My parents encouraged us to explore all religions to determine what we wanted so that is what I did. I started visiting several types of churches to find a place where I fit; Episcopal, Baptist, Lutheran. I looked at all of them. It was then that I began to see how judgmental many of the churches were and I didn't like it. People were judged because of the way they dressed, by what they did, or by their lifestyle and the people of the church gossiped about it. So, I stopped going to church altogether. I didn't need to go to a church to praise God. I could do that right in my own house and there, I didn't have to worry about people judging me.

When I was in eighth grade, my family moved to a large city ninety minutes north of our old home in the northeast.

It was during this time of life, I became very interested in law. In junior high, I thought about law enforcement or something of that nature. When I attended high school, I wanted to be an FBI agent. Realizing that I would have to become a police officer first, I never pursued that line of work. Being a police officer really didn't appeal to me. I also thought about becoming a lawyer. This focus continued until I was a senior. For some reason, I began to lose interest in school and my grades dropped. I don't know whether I was just tired of the academics or what. I had done some college courses already with a university not too far from where we were living.

When I was close to my high school graduation, the university extended an invitation for me to come there if I chose to go to college. It made sense. I already had some credits there.

But instead of going to college, I enlisted in the Marine Corps. That was quickly precluded when I discovered that I was pregnant with my first daughter. I was almost twenty-one years old.

My next two children were born out of an abusive relationship. My boyfriend was very controlling and I had very little self-esteem at the time so I stayed in the relationship for eleven years. He never wanted me to be around my mother or to have any friends. Eventually, I had enough of his abuse and moved out of town with the children. The morning that we left, I sent the children to school, went to pick up my check at work, and met my mother at my house. My boyfriend had no idea that I was leaving. I left everything behind, got my children from school, and we boarded a train to go south.

That was not the end of our relationship, however. My brother told my boyfriend where I was living and he came to see me. We stayed together another four years until it finally ended.

I met my husband while I was trying to reconcile with my boyfriend. They worked together. My husband would always joke with me that he was getting married.

I would laugh and say, "Can I come to the wedding?"

He would say, "Yea, you're going to be there."

When my financial situation changed dramatically because of an accident. I had fallen on city property when I was pregnant and received money as a result. When my boyfriend started to spend the money I had gotten in the settlement, I decided that I had enough of him and I kicked him out.

I tried to make ends meet by working odd jobs to help support my family. My first job was with the Department of Recreation. That lasted for two years. Then I worked at the Department of Social Services.

I continued to work as my family grew. I had learned from my parents' mistakes and tried to do differently with my own children.

I began dating my old boyfriend's colleague who told me I was going to be invited to his wedding. He was right. I was the bride.

We had only been married three years when my husband became very sick and was hospitalized. The doctor who was caring for him was my sister-in-law's boss. He had offered his services because my husband didn't have health insurance.

The hospital completed a battery of tests and when the results were available, my husband's family members along with the doctor came to our house to share the results. Every eye was looking at me.

"What's going on?" I asked.

The doctor spoke up and said, "You need to go in and get tested. Your husband has AIDS."

I had no idea my husband was a drug user and had been sharing needles with those who were infected.

In shock, I immediately went to get tested at a clinic near my home. The doctor that was caring for my husband told me that he was going to walk with me through my disease and he has. It has been thirty-two years since I was diagnosed.

Family and friends reacted to the news differently. My children were three, nine, eleven and thirteen years old at the time and really didn't totally understand the possible impact on their lives. They were fine. Most of my family was very supportive. The diagnosis brought my sister and I closer. My step-father did refuse to talk to me for a while but that didn't last very long. I had a really good friend for twenty years and when she found out I was HIV positive, she wouldn't speak to me. Most people were kind and caring.

My husband died shortly thereafter. The day before he died, he explained to me why he never told me about his addiction and where he had been using. He believed I would leave him if I knew about him and despite his problem, he loved me.

I moved back north to take care of my aging mother because she had taken ill. Because I wanted to get my own place to live, it was recommended that I enter a program called COMA. From COMA, I got into a program called *Teach*. They paid you to take a twelve-week course about HIV so that you can learn how to better care for and advocate for yourself. It opened my mind and eyes up to many new things. From there, I joined *AFKA* which is an activist group that advocates for people with HIV. I began to advocate for those who were unaware of possible services available to them.

I began my advocacy for those with HIV-AIDS by speaking to government agencies about housing for those in need. Housing is an issue for people living with HIV and if they have a place to live, they are more apt to take medication and stay healthy. When you live on the streets, it is much more difficult to keep up with your medication. You are thinking about other things like, *Where is my next meal coming from? Where will you sleep that night?* So, I began to advocate for people needing housing.

I was well aware of homelessness. I had lived on the street for a year after my husband died in 2006. I could have moved in with my kids but I didn't. I chose to hang out with friends in "abandominiums." We fixed up an abandon building to look like a house. I was drinking a lot at the time to numb the pain of my loss and of knowing I had HIV. I should have been seeing a therapist to help me grapple with my pain. I didn't, and continued to sink into despair.

I have learned that anyone who gets a diagnosis of HIV needs to have help to deal with their illness, not only with the medications but with the emotional aspects, as well. There was so much shame associated with HIV thirty years ago. When people would find out about your diagnosis, there was a good chance that you would be shunned, so I did my best to keep it hidden. The medication was brutal back then. The treatments were so severe that some died from it. I would take my medication but I would be sick as a dog. It was supposed to keep me alive.

I was invited by HopeSprings to be the recipient of services provided by *Open Table*. Open Table is a 501-3C designed to support people through some of life's greatest challenges. A table of eight to ten people committed their time and resources to surrounding me to support me as I identified life goals and take the steps necessary to accomplish them. They helped me get my own place to live and I have been there for two years. I also wanted to go back to school for education in drug addiction. This played an important part in what I did for my job. HopeSprings helped me through the application process and I was accepted. I just needed to get through the pandemic for it to be completed.

I also had a goal to see my son who is in prison. He was incarcerated for attempted murder eight years ago. When the man died five years later, it became a murder charge. We are still working on that goal to visit him. It has been through relationship, encouragement and guidance, my life was changed. This was a wonderful experience for me and I have made some lifelong friends.

My children are grown now; one is deceased, one is incarcerated and two are at home with me. My daughter is forty-two. My son who died, would have been forty. The son that is incarcerated is thirty-eight, and my youngest son is thirty-two.

I was living about an hour away from my grown children when my oldest son died. I received a call from my youngest son. He was with his brother when he was shot in an attempted robbery. He was twenty-three years old. It was tragic for our family.

I no longer practice the faith that my parents did. Faith for me today involves believing in a higher power, something that is stronger than me. I don't really practice a certain religion.

I try to stay connected to my extended family and we had a delightful family reunion about six years ago. We came from all over and gathered at a campground to spend the weekend catching up on life. Everyone was there; siblings, spouses, children and grandchildren. Some fished, while others swam. We had campfires and roasted marshmallows at night. The older members of the family sat in a big circle being entertained by the sharing of life stories. These were things we didn't usually do and it was great fun.

My mother was a beautiful person. She instilled in me the importance of valuing others.

She would say "If someone comes to you and tells you they are hungry, you feed them. It doesn't hurt you to share."

That really stuck with me.

"When you've got a little bit of something and your neighbor has a little bit of something, together that makes a big something," she'd say.

I took that to heart and have done that. One neighbor might have meat, another potatoes, we'd pull our resources and make a whole meal.

"You never know how God is going to come see you," she'd say.

Even now, if I am walking down the street and see someone digging in a trashcan, I give them food. If I have lunches to share, I offer them. Sometimes, I go home and bring them back a plate of food. I would rather give the food to people than throw it away.

I realize that people can really be a challenge. When I was around those struggling with addiction, they would tell you anything to get money out of you. They'd say their children were hungry or make up some excuse. I'd find out later that that wasn't the case.

I have learned that once I give you something, what you do with it isn't my concern anymore. I can't hold myself responsible for what they do with what has been given. When I give, I give it from my heart.

My mother taught me that when you help someone, it also helps you. Not in a monetary way but in an emotional and spiritual way.

I have been the recipient of the generosity of others. I remember when I was homeless, restaurants would offer me the leftover food from that day. It meant more than I can express.

For the last six years, I have been a community health worker for those suffering with HIV-AIDS. Prior to that, I volunteered, doing testing and counseling. The hospital found that there were so many people returning who were not staying on their medication that they decided to hire me full time to teach others how to live healthier lives. I love what I do. If I can help one person get on their medication, stay on it, and have hope to press on, I have done my job. I don't allow them to use others as an excuse to be unsuccessful in life. I have been there and done that. They are encouraged when they know that they can care for themselves. It's empowering.

I have learned four important lessons in life. First, it is important to treat people the way you want to be treated. The second is you can't take things at face value. There is always more to the story. Third, you must stay open minded. Life is always changing. Fourth, never be judgmental. You have no idea what someone has been through in their life.

HIV-AIDS does not discriminate. I have met people from all walks of life; screenwriters, ballet dancers, transgender, gays, doctors, lawyers, and professors. Often, when people get diagnosed, they lose sight of what they are doing in life. Some go forward and live healthy lives, others never come back and are lost. I have found that it is what you do with what you learn and you must be willing to fight for what you want.

One of the questions that I ask my clients is "What are your plans when you leave here?"

We try to establish short-, medium and long-term goals. I work with them to try to meet them. I will do whatever I can to help them reach their goals. Life doesn't have to end after a diagnosis. For me, it was a beginning. It made me take care of myself.

I really want to make a difference with my life. I want to encourage my grandchildren to work hard. If there is something they want to do, go for it. I want them to care about and strive to give back to this world. As far as my job is concerned, I hope I can keep doing it for as long as possible.

People are people. We are not all the same nor do we think the same. We must be open to embracing our differences. We can learn from one another. That is a beautiful thing.

Today, Evelyn serves as a community health worker at one of the largest hospitals in the country, University of Maryland. Her team of three, a nurse and a social worker, work with people who are newly diagnosed with HIV-AIDS and with those who are out of care, eliminating the barriers that prevent them from being in a consistent treatment program. HopeSprings supports her by helping the people in her care attain birth certificates and other identifications, by providing Thanksgiving baskets and Christmas gifts, as well as counseling, training and recreational activities.

Evelyn adores her family, children and six grandchildren. They have always been there for her and watch over her with loving care.

I Choose

By Carol Marchant Gibbs

It would be all too easy for me to be overwhelmed with the challenges of this life…

but I choose to:

Receive each new day as a gift.

Cherish every person along the way.

Believe I am loved.

Trust that God has my back.

And Love like it matters for all eternity.

Chapter 8
Escaping Sex Trafficking

Araminta Freedom Initiative

Sarah is the Director of Church & Community Engagement for Araminta Freedom Initiative. Araminta's vision is to alleviate the sex trafficking and the exploitation of minors in vulnerable communities in the inner city. They accomplish this by awakening, equipping, and mobilizing the Church and community through education, prevention strategies, and restorative survivor services. Their focus is survivor centered, and they work to restore, redeem and bring justice for all.

The Story of Sarah

The experiences I have had with Araminta have been transformative for me personally and I hope will directly affect our culture and society as a whole. My efforts move in two streams. I interact with those individuals who have been sex trafficked, providing a restorative response by connecting them to the faith and broader community. Our hope is that community awareness, training, and the offering of opportunities to serve those who have been victims, will help to prevent future injustices.

Study is the second stream. I feel compelled to understand God's heart for those individuals who have been exploited, His interaction with them, and our responsibility in response. So, I am currently attending Seminary, studying sacred texts in both the Old and New Testament with a doctorate in ministry as my goal.

But, the formation of my heart for others began long ago.

I grew up in the mid-west, the youngest of ten children. We were born over a fifteen-year range; girl, four boys and five girls. Because I was the youngest, my life was built around my sisters. In our family, the boys were viewed as rebellious, while my sisters were all academic achievers. My brothers were always a challenge to my parents. All of my brothers struggled in school, except for one. They had learning disabilities that were unidentified so they were viewed as poor students with behavioral problems. Their educational issues went unaddressed. One of my brothers served in Viet Nam and went on to college. All of my sisters went to college and to post graduate school.

Faith was a very important distinction in our area of the mid-west. The east-side was predominantly Jewish and the west-side was Catholic/ Protestant. We grew up in a Catholic community and lived in a Golf country club scene. Country clubs were also divided according to faith and those divisions exist even today.

Our community was composed of other very large families. Four of those families had a youngest child living with a disability. At the time, people were encouraged to institutionalize children with disabilities, even children with autism, though it wasn't called as such, and those with Down Syndrome. One day, the parents with children living with disabilities and their friends gathered together to discuss the matter, deciding that they were not going to do what was recommended. Together, they formed a political and restorative response in the disabilities community called HELP.

I grew up watching my parents fight for the rights of the most vulnerable, specifically people with disabilities. We went to town hall meetings to get Day Homes established for children, a school for the disabled. We found out forty years later that we were one of the first in the country to establish HELP. HELP was responsible for some Federal laws in support of people living with disabilities. They had a mighty impact.

My parents instilled in me a sense of justice for all. I was raised to care for those most vulnerable. I remember my parents' response at the town hall meetings when people made disparaging remarks about the disabilities community. They became irate in defense of their friends and wanted justice for their friend's children. They were the children with whom I was growing up. There was a tremendous misunderstanding about the disabilities community at the time.

My parents had great hearts but they were not perfect. There was some racism occurring in our home. It was mostly toward the Jewish community. Antisemitism was mostly reflected from my dad.

As a young child, who was a deep thinker, I recognized a conflicting message in my home early on. It was confusing to hear my parents care deeply for some people and hear inconsistent comments for other people. We went to church every Sunday, but would pull out of church after the service and yell at the drivers. I was very aware of the inconsistencies.

My mom and maternal grandfather were significant people in my life growing up. My mom created a home where you wanted to be and would invite others to visit. Mom was incredibly fun. I cooked with her most days, and love to cook to this day because of my time with her. As much as I enjoyed my friends, I never missed a family meal.

My grandfather and my grandmother had a farm about eighty miles from our family home. It was an idyllic place. There was love and peace there. My grandfather was a very tender man, far more emotionally tender than my dad. I loved his strong farmer hands, climbing into his lap and everything else about him. We would take walks to the chicken coop where we named every chicken. My siblings and I talk about the farm as if it was utopia. It was special and remains in the family to this day. Every two years, we have a reunion with family and friends at the old farmhouse.

I learned so much from my grandfather. When I was an early teen, my grandmother started to have some dementia. I watched him for fifteen years following as he cared for her, even when she didn't recognize him. He loved and honored her. I learned a lot from that.

I was involved in a variety of activities growing up. I liked playing sports, though I really didn't excel at them. I enjoyed solitary sports; swimming and running. I remember roller skating ten miles all by myself.

I wasn't lonely. I was very independent. Growing up in a family of ten children, solitary activities allowed me time to recharge. Now, I understand what an introvert I am.

I also enjoyed stories, narratives and film. I went to movies and plays mostly by myself. Sometimes I would drag some friends along. My mom loved art so we frequented museums. I would go to them alone at times.

I shared a room with the older sister right above me. We would laugh and have all those sister memories but we were really not very close. We were different people. She was a highly academic achiever. From a very early age, she strived for perfection. Her identity was wrapped up in it all. She was a gymnast, a fine artist, a writer and had 52 trophies in our bedroom. I had one trophy for the "most improved bowler." It was difficult to measure up to that so I grew up not realizing my true potential. I was not her level so I believed that I wasn't very smart. It didn't help that teachers would often compare me to her. It took me a very long time to know that I could take advanced studies. Where I didn't go to Harvard like my sister, I had a capacity to learn and loved it. It took many years for me to figure that out. Despite my sister's achievements, my parents never made a tremendous deal over it so I in no way felt *less than* her. But, the difference between my sister and me was real. I wasn't an achieving academic, and she was.

I am not sure my identity was wrapped up in seeking independence. It's more that I was energized by my times of solitude. My academic identity was stifled as a result of internal and some external comparison from teachers with my sister.

Mom was always a "farm to table" type of cook. My siblings and I really found humor in the way she would be an advocate for butter, against the use of margarine. This was thirty years before the studies were done. So, we grew up in a family where we would go to markets, then home to cook the meal. My friends weren't doing that. Their parents were feeding them macaroni and cheese. I thought that was a phenomenon. Orange macaroni and cheese?

I loved my family. Some of my happiest memories were around the table at mealtime. The preparation and the meal itself were an event with so many children. We would laugh and share stories of the activities of the day. Even today, mealtimes remain some of my favorite memories with family.

Though we all loved each other and had fun together, I wasn't very close to any of my siblings. I was a loner for the most part. My mom worked very hard to keep us close, however. In addition to mealtime, we were a big game playing family because of her efforts and I have fond memories of that time.

It was difficult growing up with a dad who did not communicate emotionally. This took quite a toll on all of us but was most difficult for my brothers. It resulted in the lives of my brothers as drug use and their inability to relate to others. For the female side of my family, we experienced the unhealthy parts of striving and achieving. It defined us. There was a cloud of sadness about that.

Importance was placed on appearances. My parents would entertain often and I can remember the family spending the entire day working to prepare for that. It was hard work and didn't always go very smoothly. When the guests arrived, we appeared like the Von Trap family. This was not always how we felt but there was pressure to appear as such. My parents took great pride in showing off their *idyllic* family. I remember thinking at a young age that we were not who we appeared to be. We were okay but there was also a deep ache and wanting there. My dad wasn't emotional and it really affected us but no one knew. I didn't figure it out until adulthood.

When you grow up in a family with ten children, you learn to be very strategic in your interaction. You need to fight to be part of the conversation and learn early on that being a good communicator is critical, otherwise, no one will listen to you. If you have something to say, you have to be quick about it. It's funny how each of my siblings has a different perception of our upbringing. Some will vilify with my mother and some my father. I tried to do neither one.

Our Catholic upbringing had a profound effect on us. My grandmother, on the farm, was incredibly spiritual. She was president of a Catholic league in her community and went to Rome to experience the influence of the Pope.

She also had a 3D Jesus in her farm house that literally bled on the wall. When it bled on the wall, she left it that way. It became a folklore in our family. We'd take photos of it and the photos wouldn't come out. The priest even came one day to test the legitimacy of the blood agreeing that it was actually blood. My grandmother loved this and it gave her great comfort. My grandfather was not really impressed, but this phenomenon became famous in the community surrounding our family farm.

Since I was a little girl, I have had many spiritual questions and ponderings. The Catholic school I attended did not appreciate how inquisitive I was. When I was in seventh grade, I told the priest there about the bleeding Jesus on my grandmother's wall, asking many questions. The priest made it very clear that neither he nor the school staff liked all my questions. One day, he came to inform my parents about it. As I sat quietly on the stairs, I heard the priest tell my parents that he and the school staff believed that I had some kind of a demonic influence because of all my questions. My parents were mortified by the priest and kicked him out of the house. It was a fortifying moment for me to see my parents come to my defense.

The mid-west was not very diverse. Out of 3,500 students in my high school, there were only six African American students by the time I graduated. I remember signing up to participate in an exchange program with a predominantly all African American High school. I was the only one from my school that did. There was clearly something stirring in me. I was not afraid to put myself in a position where there are people different than me. There was nothing noble in me doing that. I just thought it would be a good experience. When I was at the school for a few of weeks, I found that I really liked being around people who are different than me. In the beginning, it wasn't easy. It was a cross-cultural experience and it made me nervous but we were all high school students. I could feel something changing in me and that was good. I really grew from that experience.

I also was involved in a program to *adopt* an inner-city child for a few weeks in the summer. I was determined to help someone so I committed to doing it. My parents agreed provided that I was willing to take sole responsibility. I wanted my young friend to have a wonderful experience so I took him to every amusement park, every pool, every lake and to Sea World. We just chummed around for a few weeks. When, I think back, I wonder what was that like for him? Here we were a rich white family with a large house in the country and he was a young African American child who lived in a small place in the city. I realize that it was very reflective of the prejudice at the time. My heart was in the right place because I really wanted to help. For years following that summer, my family stayed connected to their family. Then, we lost touch.

My parents were always supportive of me so whenever I expressed a desire to learn about and serve others, they encouraged me to go forth and do so. I think that this was one of the few times that I could see the tender side of my dad's heart. He was proud of me and he told me that. I think he believed that he could not do what I was doing but he was pleased that I could.

I tried to reconcile the inconsistencies of the antisemitism that I saw in my home and how I heard one was supposed to love others from church. I was aware of the darkness that people could harbor in their hearts from what I had seen in my family and in my own heart. This began a quest to understand faith more fully. I certainly wasn't having my questions answered by the Catholic Church so I looked elsewhere and began to find a deeper faith.

I dated a guy through high school and off and on in college, becoming very close to his family. When his older brother returned from college, everyone noticed he was different. He had had a spiritual conversion experience. His family thought he was weird but there was something about him that drew me to him. I could feel it. *He's not weird*, I thought. Whatever he had, I wanted. I had never had that experience before.

So, when I went off to college, I looked for a Christian organization that would have the same profound effect on me. I didn't know what I was looking for, I just knew I wanted the same spiritual experience. I was way too cool on the outside to ask anyone, so I just looked for it. Eventually, I discovered Campus Crusade for Christ. I attended a night where the organization shared a slide show about faith. They passed around cards to people in attendance to see if they had any questions. I wrote on a card, "I cannot wait to talk to you because I have so many questions. Please call me." Shortly thereafter, a woman called me and came by my dorm room to talk. She shared a track with me, saying that I was already a Christian. I was so eager to learn more about God, to know Christ. This was the beginning of my journey.

I was a Psychology major in college but the most formative class for me was the one on the Holocaust. The class was called *The Psychology of Prejudice.* One of the things we did in class was to watch all of the live footage from the Holocaust, six hours of black and white recordings. To study antisemitism, after growing up in an antisemitic home, intermingled with my new developing faith was a very powerful experience for me. I was passionate about seeking God. I began to understand more fully who He is and His love for me.

The college I attended in southern Ohio was barely diverse. I was drawn to people different than me. I could learn from them and I liked that. I had a close friend from my sorority that was Jewish, Judy. Another dear friend was African America, Maxine. My college had so few African American students that they had to form a committee, *The Minorities Students Affairs Council*, with the purpose of attracting a more diverse group of students. The council included all eight black students from the school and me. There was obvious discrimination back then.

Maxine and I would venture out and visit one another's churches. When she came to my church, she would find it very subdued, to the boring point. When I visited her church, everyone would hug me and we'd dance and experience freedom in our bodies during worship. I'd never experienced anything like it. It was great. Her church was fun. We really began to understand each other's lives and it was good for both of us.

I believe that much of my openness to people different than me was due to my mom. Although it was a very prejudice time in history, our door was wide open. My mom was always receiving of others from all ethnicities and races. This, I think, she got from her dad. My grandfather had a pond on his property where people would pay a nickel to come to fish. My grandfather had a sign that informed African Americans that they were also welcome to fish there. This was radically inclusive at the time. Community was built at that pond.

In my twenties, I began to have a confessional awareness. There is something about the cross of Christ, Christ shaped living and theology that both speaks to the darkness of the human heart but also to the responsibility that we have to care for others. For me, it began with the disabilities community I was exposed to when young.

My faith continues to grow and remains with me today. I probably have seen every film and play related to the Holocaust and read constantly about it. There were so many people that made a difference at that time and I am driven to learn about their experience. There were also many who committed vile acts but were awake enough to be conflicted and there were those who awoke during this nightmare to seek redemption for themselves and for their neighbors. All of this speaks to me.

Through the years, I have recognized that I have a high capacity to be around evil; scary movies, books, situations. It is an inner strength that allows me to learn about difficult things and not be negatively affected. I look for the potential for restoration for those who suffer, the redemption at the end of the story. If there isn't any, then I imagine it. I believe that I was created that way.

All of these experiences have helped to form who I am today and have led me to serve in the way I do at *Araminta Freedom Initiative.*

But despite my efforts, at times, I have been misunderstood because of the work that I do to eradicate sexual exploitation.

"Oh, bless your heart," I would hear or "How do you do something so hard? How are you around that kind of evil?"

I don't say it but I think, "How are you not?"

I am drawn to love and support others and provide hope and healing for their future. To not respond to atrocities is to deny reality. As human beings, we have a responsibility to care.

People who are aware of sexual exploitation appreciative that I am willing to talk about this serious issue and receive me warmly.

Most people are very appreciative of my efforts but sometimes those who are being served question my motives and commitment. *Does she really care? Am I a project?* These are very fair questions. It is a healthy caution. Overtime, I have developed some long-standing relationship with survivors and value them deeply.

The response that we are to have to the most horrific evils and darkness in our culture, from churches is very clear in scripture. We are called to gain an understanding of God's heart and care for all people, and be an example of how we are to interact with the most vulnerable people in our communities.

It is my hope that the actual conversation about sexual exploitation can get back into the church. We are exploiters and we have been exploited and we have a responsibility to make that conversation happen. I hope that we do the right thing; to care for one another within the church and for those outside. There is a power in the church and that power can be used for good in the mutually transformative gift of being with "the other"; anyone with whom we share differences: racial, gender, political, socio-economic, etc.

The restorative community around a survivor is vital.

Recently, I heard a survivor say, "I don't know what I would do without my community. That's my family."

The community has been faithful to surround her for years. I hope to see many more examples of this; families surrounding people.

Sarah continues to serve with Araminta Freedom Initiative helping to provide training to educate and prevent sexual exploitation in communities. She, also, sits on advisory boards for many survivors to offer support and resources to secure a better future.

Araminta Freedom Initiative: restore, redeem, with justice for all.

The Story of Becca

Becca's life was filled with friends, family and love but things changed when her dad lost his job. Stressed out, her parents spiraled into alcohol, drugs and violence. A home full of love transformed into a very scary place.

The nightmare started one evening when my dad offered me to his drug dealer in exchange for the drugs he could not afford. I begged them to stop but they wouldn't and they returned again and again.

At school, my favorite art teacher noticed a change in me and asked what was wrong so I shared about what my life had been.

When I returned home from school, a social worker was waiting with my brother. Because no foster home would take both of us, I was sent to a group home. I missed my family and had trouble connecting with my new art teacher, therapist and even the other kids at the home.

Then one day, I met an older boy. He bought me nice things and made me feel special. He told me that we were in love, and that we could be a family. I wanted that so much that I believed him. He convinced me to run away with him. I did and found out later that I was not his only girlfriend. But the other girls in the home warmly welcomed me, sharing their expensive clothing.

He told me that in order to stay with him, I needed to contribute to the family by working like the other girls. He kept all the money we made and it still was not enough.

His love slowly turned to threats and violence. I was forced to sell myself in the back room over and over again.

Then one night, instead of a customer waiting for me, there was an FBI agent waiting. I felt all alone, scared and wondered how I ended up in that moment. The agent told me that I was safe with her. There were people that wanted to help me but I didn't believe her at first. Why would I? That had never been true before.

What I came to find out later was that my new art teacher had been trained by *Araminta Freedom Initiative* to recognize the signs of child trafficking. When I disappeared, my teacher filed a report and got the FBI involved. The agent handed me a backpack of clothes that had been donated by *Araminta.* That simple gesture was the first genuine kindness I had experienced in a long time.

The FBI agent took me to a shelter, where a mentor trained by *Araminta* visited me. She didn't ask about my boyfriend or the motels, she asked what I liked to do. No one had ever asked me that before. We spent the entire day discussing my art and when she left, I never thought I would see her again, just like everyone else.

The next week, the mentor returned and she kept coming back. Sometimes she helped me with my schoolwork, other times we just talked. She even helped me design a portfolio for art school applications.

I met other girls with similar stories at special events hosted by *Araminta* and we encouraged each other. At the end of the night, we each received a prom dress, thanks to donations from community members.

After earning a scholarship to an art school, I graduated with honors. Among the cheering audience are my *Araminta* friends and mentor.

I was broken and not knowing who I could trust but not anymore. I am Becca and I am a survivor. Because of *Araminta,* my future is bright and it's all my own. *Araminta* has shown me what real healing, relationships and restoration look like. *Araminta* has become my community, my family and my friends.

Becca is free now but there are others who are not. Every day young people continue to be exploited across the country and you can help them. Support Araminta and become a part of another survivor's restorative community.

Conclusion

Stories change lives. I hope that these stories have not only made you more aware of the challenges associated with each of the groups represented here but you have been given a new vision for the importance of empowerment.

Radical Resilience does not happen in isolation. Radical Resilience happens when people partner to encourage and empower one another to greatness. Whether you are one who has available resources to empower or one who is in need of support, we all receive when this partnership occurs. We need other people to help us achieve our fullest potential.

There is an Ancient African proverb that says, "If you want to get somewhere fast, go alone. If you want to go the distance, go together."

Sure, we can get to a destination by racing through life alone but will we actually arrive at the right destination? Will we accomplish all that we were created for during the process? Will we have formed all of the necessary relationships along the way? When we arrive, will we be prepared for what we will encounter?

Radical Resilience is a superpower that can only happen when lives are joined for the same purpose...to create legacies of hope and bring radical change to our world.

Resources

Books

Bales, K. (2012) *Disposable People: New Slavery in the Global Economy.*

Bales, K. and Soodalter, R. (2009) *The Slave Next Door: Human Trafficking and Slavery in America Today.*

Belge, K., Bieschke, M. and Robinson, C. (2011) *Queer: The Ultimate LGBTQ Guide for Teens.*

Bigner, J. and Wetchler J. (2012) *Handbook for LGBT-Affirmative Couple and Family Therapy.*

Blumenfield, W. J. (ed.) (1992) *Homophobia: How We All Pay the Price,* Boston: Beacon Press.

Brill, S. and Pepper, R. (2008) *The Transgender Child.*

Coles, G. (2017) *Single Gay Christian: A Personal Journey of Faith and Sexual Identity*, IVP Books.

Ehrensaft, D. (2011) *Gender Born, Gender Made: Raising Healthy Gender-Nonconforming Children.*

Fakhrid-Deen, T. and COLAGE (2010) *Let's Get This Straight: The Ultimate Handbook for Youth with LGBTQ Parents.*

Finkelstein, A. (2017) *After Silence, A History of AIDS through Its Images.*

France, D. (2016) *How to Survive a Plague, The Inside Story of How Citizens and Science Tamed AIDS.*

Gibbs, C. M. (2018) *Who Do You Say I Am? Personal Life Stories Told by the LGBTQ Community.*

Hepburn, S. and Simon, R. (2013) *Human Trafficking Around the World: Hidden in Plain Sight.*

Krieger, I. (2011) *Helping Your Transgender Teen: A Guide for Parents.*

Lee, J. (2013) *Torn: Rescuing the Gospel from the Gays-vs-Christians Debate,* Jericho Books.

Levithan, D. and Merrell, B. (2006) *The Full Spectrum.*

Lloyd, R. (2012) *Girls Like Us: Fighting for a World Where Girls Are Not for Sale: A Memoir*.

Mallon, G. (2010) *LGBTQ Youth Issues: Practical Guide for Youth Workers Serving Lesbian, Gay, Bisexual, Transgender and Questioning Youth*.

Miceli, M. (2005) *Standing Out, Standing Together: The Social and Political Impact of Gay-Straight Alliances*.

Miner, Rev. J. and Connoley, Rev. J. T. (2002) *The Children Are Free. Reexamining the Biblical Evidence on Same-Sex Relationships*, LifeJourney Press.

Riggle, E. D. B. and Rostosky, S. (2011) *A Positive View for LGBTQ: Embracing Identity and Cultivating Well-Being,* Rwoman Littlefield.

Websites and Phone Numbers

Araminta Freedom Initiative

https://www.aramintafreedom.org/

(888) 373-7888

Araminta Freedom Initiative reduces the threat of child sex trafficking—the buying and selling of minors for the purpose of sexual exploitation—and restores the mind, body, and spirit of those who have survived the trauma of modern slavery.

Asylee Women Enterprise

kkriss@asyleewomen.org

(443) 850-0627

Asylee Women Enterprise journeys with asylum seekers and other forced migrants as they navigate the immigration legal process, begin to heal from past trauma and rebuild their lives.

Athletes Serving Athletes

https://asa.run/

P.O. 4222

Lutherville, Maryland 21093

We elevate the quality of life for individual with limited mobility by empowering them to train for and participate in mainstream running events.

Center for Action and Contemplation
https://cac.org/contact-us/
1705 Five Points Road SW
Albuquerque, New Mexico 87105
The Center for Action and Contemplation (CAC) is an educational nonprofit introducing seekers to the contemplative Christian path of transformation.

Epilepsy Foundation
https://www.epilepsy.com
(800) 332-1000
3540 Crain Highway, Suite 675
Bowie, Maryland 20716
The mission of the Epilepsy Foundation is to lead the fight to overcome the challenges of living with epilepsy and to accelerate therapies to stop seizures, find cures, and save lives.

GLBT National Resource Hotline
1-888-THE-GLNH (1-888-843-4564)
Confidential peer counseling and information on local resources. Open Monday through.

The Jacques Initiative
Call or text 443-386-1746
http://www.jacques.ihv.org/about/contact-us/
University of Maryland School of Medicine, The JACQUES Journey Center
880 Park Ave. Suite 300Baltimore MD 21201
The JACQUES Initiative, a program of the Institute of Human Virology at the University of Maryland School of Medicine, is an outreach program that changes lives, engages communities, and supports health systems affected by HIV and Hepatitis C.

Just the Facts: Primer Booklet on Sexual Orientation
http://www.apa.org/pi/lgbt/resources/just-the-facts.pdf
An information booklet designed for principals, educators, and school personnel on sexual orientation and youth. This booklet was created in response to the recent rise in sexual orientation conversion therapy and those beliefs being wanted to be shared in school settings.

National AIDS Information Line
1-800-CDC-INFO
For HIV and AIDS information-24 Hours a Day, Seven days a week

National Runaway Switchboard
1-800-RUNAWAY (1-800-786-2929)
The National Runaway Switchboard is a toll-free crises line operated by Chicago's Metro-Help. It operates twenty-four hours a day, year-long, and is designed to serve the needs of youth and their families. The phone lines are staffed by trained volunteers who use crisis intervention and active listening techniques to help callers identify their problems, explore options, and develop a plan of action. Their services are secular (non-religious), nonjudgmental, and non-directive. Volunteers try to give callers factual information and confront irrational perceptions and solutions. They also offer message-relays (communication between runaways and parents without disclosing location of runaway) and referrals to over 8,000 social service agencies nationwide.

National Suicide Prevention Lifeline
1-800-273-TALK (8255) English 1-888-628-9454 Spanish
http://www.suicidepreventionlifeline.org/
Crisis hotline and online chat available

Our Daughters & Sons/Nuestras Hijas y Nuestros Hijos
Questions & Answers for Parents of Gay, Lesbian & Bisexual People
http://www.pflag.org/fileadmin/user_upload/Publications/Daughters_Sons.pdf (English)
http://www.pflag.org/fileadmin/user_upload/Publications/Nuestras_hijas.pdf (Spanish)

Q Christian Fellowship
https://www.qchristian.org/contact
(888) 203-7798
P.O. Box 21267
Denver, Colorado 80221
Q Christian Fellowship is cultivating radical belonging for LGBTQ+ Christians and allies.

Resource Guide to Coming Out

http://www.hrc.org/resources/entry/resource-guide-to-coming-out

A PDF electronic guide to assist in the process in coming out as a LGBTQ individual. It offers advice and guidance while acknowledging the real emotions and difficulties one experiences while coming out.

STD Info Line

1-800-227-8922

For STI Information

Monday-Friday, 8:00am-11:00pm Eastern Time

Teenline

www.teenlineonline.org

(310) 855-HOPE (4673) or (800) TLC-TEEN (852-8336) (toll-free in California only) *Helpline that offers teen to teen support and guidance. Open 6pm to 10pm Pacific Time, every night. Texting also offered.*

The Trevor Project, Inc.

thetrevorproject.org. 2017

1-866-4-U-TREVOR (1-866-488-7386)

The Trevor Project is focused on crisis intervention and suicide prevention to LGBTQ youth.

Provides several services including a helpline-The Trevor Lifeline, chat/communication services – Ask Trevor and Trevor Chat and supports a social networking site for LGBTQ youth and supporters. Also, is involved in public policy advocacy and research. The Trevor Project is not just a suicide hotline; they can help with all kinds of issues.

The Gay Christian Network

gaychristian.net. 2017

Youth-Focused Hotline

1-800-246-PRIDE (1-800-246-7743) www.glnh.org/talkline

Milton Keynes UK
Ingram Content Group UK Ltd.
UKHW022227301123
433577UK00009B/611